FLASHMAPS

NEW YORK

Editorial Updater
Martha Schulman

Cartographic Updater
Mappi

Proofr
Susar

Editor
Robe

Cove
Chie Usnio

Creative Director
Fabrizio La Rocca

Cartographer
David Lindroth

Designer
Tigist Getachew

Cartographic Contributors
Edward Faherty
Sheila Levin
Page Lindroth
Eric Rudolph

Fodor's   www.fodors.com

Fodor's Travel Publications
New York, Toronto, London, Sydney, Auckland

Contents

Special Sales

Fodor's Travel Publications are available at special discounts for bulk purchases for sales promotions or premiums. Special editions, including personalized covers, excerpts of existing guides, and corporate imprints, can be created in large quantities for special needs. For more information, contact your local bookseller or write to Special Markets/Premium Sales, 1745 Broadway, MD 6-2, New York, NY 10019, or e-mail specialmarkets@randomhouse.com.

ISBN 978-1-4000-0764-6   **ISSN 1527-4853**

PRINTED IN CHINA 10 9 8 7 6 5 4 3 2 1

Area Codes: Manhattan (212, 646, 917); Bronx, Brooklyn, Queens, Staten Island (718, 347); Nassau/Suffolk (516); Northern NJ (201, 973). All (212) unless otherwise noted.

EMERGENCIES

AAA Emergency Road Service
☎ 800/222-4357

Ambulance, Fire, Police ☎ 911

American Red Cross ☎ 877/723-2767
www.nyredcross.org

Animal Bites ☎ 311

Animal Medical Center ☎ 838-8101

Arson Hotline ☎ 800/FIRE-TIP

Child Abuse ☎ 800/342-3720

Crime Victim Hotline ☎ 577-7777

Domestic Violence Hotline
☎ 800/621-4673

Drug Abuse ☎ 800/395-3400

Lesbian and Gay Anti-Violence Project ☎ 714-1141

Mental Health Crisis Hotline/LifeNet
☎ 800/543-3638

Poison Control ☎ 800/222-1222

Rape Hotline ☎ 800/656-4673

Runaway Hotline
☎ 800/RUNAWAY

Sexual Assualt Reports
☎ 267-7273

Suicide Prevention/Samaritans
☎ 673-3000

SERVICES

AAA ☎ 757-2000
www.aaa.com

ACLU/NY ☎ 607-3300
www.aclu.org

AIDS Hotline (CDC)
☎ 800/CDC-INFO
www.cdc.gov

AIDS Hotline (NY)
☎ 800/825-5448

Alcoholics Anonymous ☎ 647-1680
www.aa.org

Amex Lost Travelers Checks
☎ 800/221-7282

ASPCA ☎ 876-7700
www.aspca.org

Better Business Bureau ☎ 533-6200
www.newyork.bbb.org

Big Apple Greeters ☎ 669-8159
www.bigapplegreeters.org

Convention & Visitor's Bureau
☎ 484-1222; 800/692-8474
www.nycvisit.com

Dept of Aging ☎ 311

Dept of Motor Vehicles ☎ 645-5550
www.nydmv.state.ny.us

Employmen Law Project Hotline
☎ 888/218-6974

Housing Authority ☎ 306-3000

Human Resources Administration Infoline ☎ 877/472-8411

Immigration Information Line
☎ 800/375-5283
www.uscis.gov

Legal Aid Society: Immigration Law Unit Hotline ☎ 577-3456
www.legal-aid.org

Lesbian & Gay Community Service Center ☎ 620-7310
www.gaycenter.org

Mayor's Office for People With Disabilities ☎ 788-2830

Medicare ☎ 800/MED-ICAR
www.medicare.gov

NY City Information ☎ 311
www.nyc.gov

NY Public Library Telephone Reference Service ☎ 930-0830
www.nypl.org

Overeaters Anonymous ☎ 206-8621
www.overeatersanonymous.org

Passport Information
www.travel.state.gov

Planned Parenthood
☎ 800/230-PLAN
www.plannedparenthood.org/nyc

Social Security ☎ 800/772-1213

Taxi Complaints www.nyc.gov

Towaways ☎ 311

24-Hour Locksmith ☎ 247-6747

UN Information ☎ 963-1234
www.un.org

US Customs ☎ 877/CBP-5511
www.cbp.gov

US Post Office ☎ 800/ASK-USPS
www.usps.com

WALKING TOURS

Adventure on a Shoestring
☎ 265-2663

Big Onion Walking Tours ☎ 439-1090
www.bigonion.com

Central Park Bike Tours ☎ 541-8759
www.centralparklaketour.com

Dr. Phil's NY Talks and Walks
☎ 888/377-4455
www.newyorktalksandwalks.com

Enthusiastic Gourmet ☎ 646/209-4724
www.enthusiasticgourmet.com

Joyce Gold History Tours ☎ 242-5762
www.nyctours.com

Municipal Art Society ☎ 439-1049
www.mas.org

Nosh Walks ☎ 222-2243
www.noshwalks.com

NYC Discovery Walking Tours
☎ 465-3331

SITE TOURS

Central Park ☎ 360-2726
www.centralpark.org

Lincoln Center ☎ 875-5350
www.lincolncenter.org

Madison Square Garden ☎ 465-5800
www.thegarden.com

Radio City ☎ 247-4777 www.radiocity.com

Rockefeller Center Tour ☎ 664-3700
www.rockefellercenter.com

UN Tours ☎ 963-8687
www.un.org

Yankee Stadium Tours
☎ 718/579-4531
www.yankees.com

BUS TOURS

Gray Line ☎ 800/669-0051
www.newyorksightseeing.com

Harlem Spirituals ☎ 391-0900
www.harlemspirituals.com

BOAT TOURS

Circle Line/Seaport Liberty Cruises
☎ 563-3200
www.circleline42.com

NY Waterway ☎ 800/53-FERRY

Spirit Cruises of NY ☎ 866/399-8439
www.spiritcruises.com

WaterTaxi ☎ 742-1969
www.nywatertaxi.com

World Yacht Cruises ☎ 630-8100
www.worldyacht.com

HELICOPTER TOURS

Helicopter Flight Services ☎ 355-0801
www.heliny.com

NY Helicopter Tours ☎ 361-6060
www.newyorkhelicopter.com

PARKS AND RECREATION

Bronx Zoo ☎ 718/367-1010
www.bronxzoo.com

Brooklyn Botanic Garden
☎ 718/623-7200
www.bbg.org

Central Park Boat Rental
☎ 517-2233

Central Park Conservancy
☎ 310-6600
www.centralparknyc.org

Central Park Tennis Center
☎ 360-8133; 280-0205

Central Park Zoo ☎ 439-6500
www.nyzoosandaquarium.org

Downtown Boathouse
☎ 646/613-0375
www.downtownboathouse.org

Ellis Island ☎ 363-3200
www.nps.gov/elis

Empire Skate Club ☎ 774-1774
www.empireskate.org

Five Borough Bicycle Club
☎ 932-2300 www.5bbc.org

Governor's Island
☎ 514-8296 www.govisland.com

Hudson River Park ☎ 627-2020
www.hudsonriver.org

NY Botanic Garden
☎ 718/817-8700 www.nybg.og

NY Cycle Club ☎ 828-5711
www.nycc.org

NY Horticultural Society
☎ 757-0915
www.hsny.org

NY Road Runners ☎ 860-2280;
423-2249 (NYC Marathon Hotline)
www.nyrrc.org

Parks Events ☎ 888/NY-PARKS
www.nycgovparks.org

Prospect Park ☎ 718/965-8999
www.prospectpark.org

Riverside Park 96th St Tennis Center
☎ 978-0277

Shorewalkers ☎ 330-7686
www.shorewalkers.org

Transportation Alternatives
☎ 629-8080
www.transalt.org

SPECTATOR SPORTS

Aqueduct & Belmont Race Tracks
☎ 718/641-4700
www.nyra.com

Brooklyn Cyclones
☎ 718/449-8497
www.brooklyncyclones.com

Continental Arena
☎ 201/935-3900
www.meadowlands.com

Madison Square Garden ☎ 465-6741
www.thegarden.com

Meadowlands Box Office
☎ 201/935-3900
www.meadowlands.com

Meadowlands Race Track
☎ 201/THEBIGM

Nassau Coliseum ☎ 516/794-9303
www.nassaucoliseum.com

NJ Devils ☎ 201/935-6050
www.newjerseydevils.com

NJ Nets ☎ 201/935-8888
www.njnets.com

NY Giants ☎ 201/935-8111
www.giants.com

NY Islanders ☎ 516/501-6700
www.newyorkislanders.com

NY Jets ☎ 516/560-8200
www.newyorkjets.com

NY Knicks ☎ 465-5867
www.nyknicks.com

NY Liberty ☎ 877/WNBA-TIX
www.nyliberty.com

NY Mets ☎ 718/507-8499
www.mets.com

NY Rangers ☎ 465-6000
www.rangers.nhl.com

NY Yankees ☎ 718/293-6000
www.yankees.com

Shea Stadium ☎ 718/507-6387

Staten Island Yankees
☎ 718/720-9265
www.si.yanks.com

US Open Tennis ☎ 718/760-6200
www.usopen.org

Yonkers Raceway
☎ 914/968-4200
www.yonkersraceway.com

TRANSPORTATION

Access-a-Ride ☎ 877/337-201
www.mta.info

Airport Travel Info
☎ 800/AIR-RIDE

Airtrain JFK ☎ 877/535-2478

Airtrain Newark ☎ 888/397-4636
www.panynj.gov/airtrainnewark

Alll MTA phone numbers www.mta.info.

Amtrak ☎ 800/872-7245
www.amtrak.com

Bus & Subway Accessibility
☎ 718/596-8585 www.mta.info

Bus & Subway Customer Service
☎ 718/330-3322 www.mta.info

Bus & Subway Information
☎ 718/330-1234 www.mta.info

**Bus & Subway Metro Card
Information** ☎ 638-7622
www.mta.info

Bus & Subway Service Status
☎ 718/243-7777 www.mta.info

Coach-USA ☎ 877/894-9155
www.coachusa.com

Ellis Island/Statue of Liberty Ferry
☎ 877/523-9849
www.statuecruises.com

EZ Pass Information ☎ 800/333-8655
www.e-zpassny.com

Fire Island Ferries
☎ 631/665-3600
www.fireislandferries.com

Greyhound Bus Lines
☎ 800/231-2222
www.greyhound.com

JFK Airport ☎ 718/244-4444
www.panynj.gov

La Guardia Airport
☎ 718/533-3400
www.panynj.gov

Long Island Railroad (LIRR)
☎ 718/217-5477
www.mta.info

Manhattan Cruise Terminal
☎ 246-5451

Martz Trailways
☎ 800/233-8604
www.martztrailways.com

Metro-North ☎ 532-4900;
800/METRO-INFO
www.mta.info

NJ Transit ☎ 973/762-5100
www.njtransit.com

MAP **vii**

NY Airport Service
☎ 718/875-8200
www.nyairportservice.com

NY Waterway Ferries
☎ 800/53-FERRY
www.nywaterway.com

Newark Airport ☎ 973/961-6000
www.panynj.gov

Olympia Airport Express
☎ 877/894-9155

PATH ☎ 800/234-7284
www.panynj.gov/path

Peter Pan Bonanza
☎ 888/751-8000
www.peterpanbus.com

Peter Pan Trailways ☎ 800/343-9999
www.peterpanbus.com

Port Authority Bus Information
☎ 564-8484

Roosevelt Island Tram
☎ 832-4543 www.rioc.com

SeaStreak Ferry ☎ 800/262-8743
www.seastreak.com

Short Line ☎ 800/631-8405; 311
www.shortlinebus.com

Staten Island Ferry
☎ 718/815-2628
www.siferry.com

SuperShuttle ☎ BLUE-VAN
www.supershuttle.com

Trailways ☎ 800/858-8555
www.trailways.com

**Triborough Bridge and Tunnel
Authority** ☎ 360-3000 www.mta.info

Vermont Transit ☎ 800/552-8737
www.vermonttransit.com

Water Taxi ☎ 742-1969
www.nywatertaxi.com

ENTERTAINMENT

Big Apple Circus ☎ 268-2500
www.theshow.bigapplecircus.org

Brooklyn Academy of Music
☎ 718/636-4100
www.bam.org

Carnegie Hall ☎ 247-7800
www.carnegiehall.org

Central Park Summerstage
☎ 360-2777
www.summerstage.org

City Center City Tix ☎ 581-1212
www.citycenter.org

Fandango
☎ 800/FANDANGO
www.fandango.com

Guggenheim Museum
☎ 423-3500
www.guggenheim.org

Historic House Museums ☎ 360-8282

Lincoln Center ☎ 546-2656
www.lincolncenter.org

Metropolitan Museum
☎ 535-7710
www.metmuseum.org

Movie Phone ☎ 777-FILM
movies.aol.com

Museum of Modern Art
☎ 708-9400
www.moma.org

Radio City Music Hall ☎ 247-4777
www.radiocity.com

Reduced Price Theatre Tickets (TKTS)
☎ 539-8500
www.tdf.org

**Shakespeare in the Park/Delacorte
Theater** www.publictheater.org

Telecharge ☎ 239-6200
www.telecharge.com

Theater Mania ☎ 212/352-3101
www.theatermania.com

Ticket Central ☎ 279-4200
(off and off-off Broadway)
www.ticketcentral.com

Ticketmaster ☎ 307-7171
www.ticketmaster.com

Whitney Museum ☎ 570-3676
www.whitney.org

MAP 1

New York City

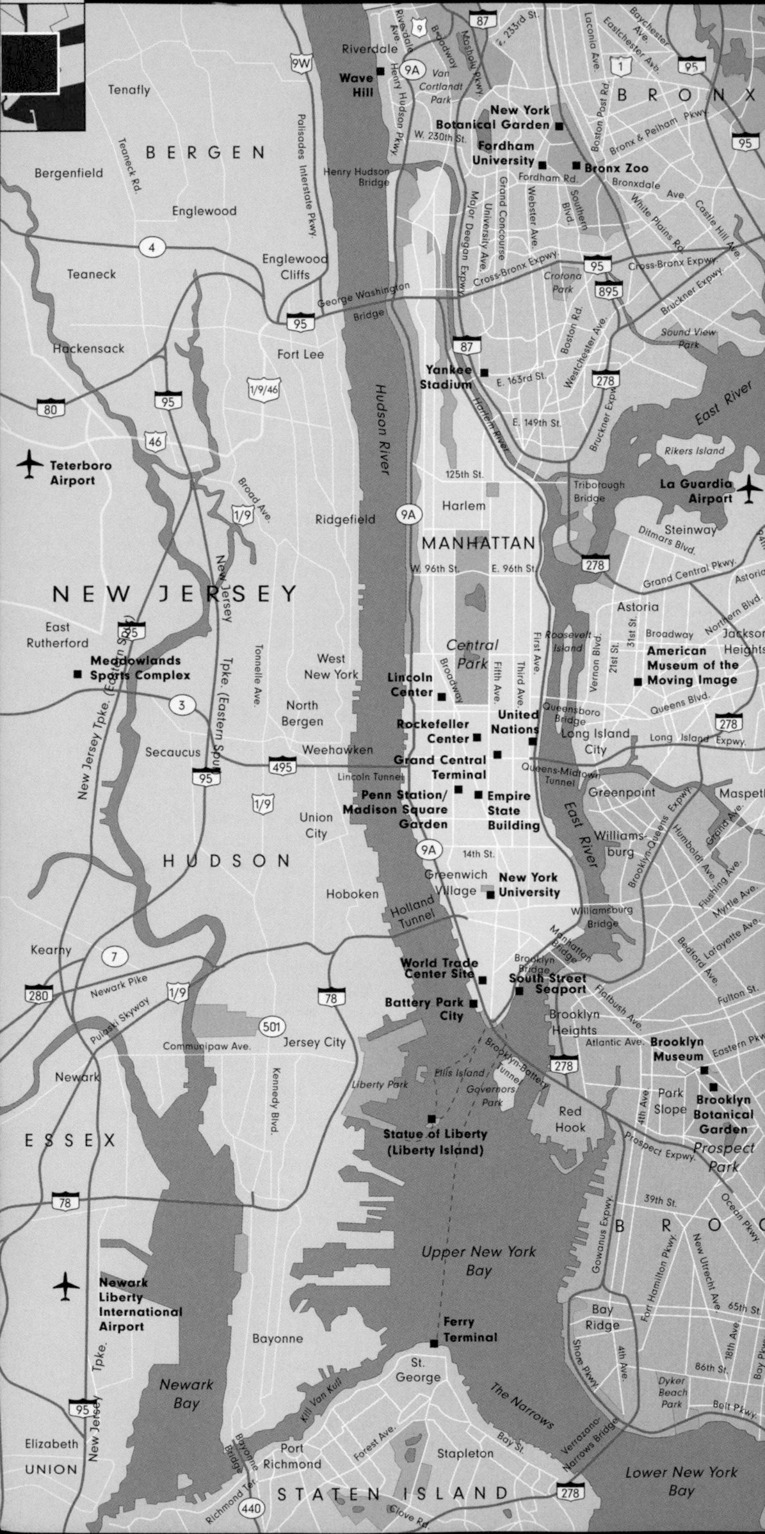

BERGEN

Tenafly

Bergenfield

Englewood

Teaneck

Hackensack

9W

Riverdale

Wave Hill ■

Henry Hudson Pkwy

Van Cortlandt Park

W. 230th St.

New York Botanical Garden ■

Fordham University ■

Bronx Zoo ■

BRONX

1

95

Bronxdale

Fordham Rd.

Webster Ave.

Southern Blvd.

95

Cross-Bronx Expwy.

Englewood Cliffs

George Washington Bridge

1/9/46

Fort Lee

4

95

Teterboro Airport

80

46

1/9

Ridgefield

Crotona Park

895

278

Bruckner Expwy.

E. 163rd St.

Yankee Stadium ■

87

E. 149th St.

Harlem River

Sound View Park

East River

Rikers Island

La Guardia Airport

NEW JERSEY

East Rutherford

Meadowlands Sports Complex ■

3

95

Secaucus

495

1/9

Union City

HUDSON

Hudson River

125th St.

9A

Harlem

MANHATTAN

W. 96th St. E. 96th St.

Central Park

West New York

North Bergen

Weehawken

Lincoln Tunnel

Lincoln Center ■

Rockefeller Center ■

Grand Central Terminal ■

United Nations ■

Fifth Ave.

Triborough Bridge

Steinway

Ditmars Blvd.

278

Grand Central Pkwy.

Astoria

American Museum of the Moving Image ■

Queens Blvd.

278

Long Island Expwy.

Queensboro Bridge

Long Island City

Greenpoint

Maspeth

Roosevelt Island

Penn Station/ Madison Square Garden ■

Empire State Building ■

Queens-Midtown Tunnel

East River

Williamsburg

Brooklyn-Queens Expwy.

Hoboken

9A

14th St.

Greenwich Village

New York University ■

Holland Tunnel

Williamsburg Bridge

Manhattan Bridge

Kearny

7

Newark Pike

280

1/9

Pulaski Skyway

501

78

Communipaw Ave.

Jersey City

World Trade Center Site ■

Battery Park City ■

South Street Seaport ■

Brooklyn Bridge

Brooklyn Heights

Atlantic Ave.

278

Flatbush Ave.

Fulton St.

Brooklyn Museum ■

Newark

ESSEX

78

Liberty Park

Ellis Island

Governors Island

Brooklyn-Battery Tunnel

Red Hook

Park Slope

Brooklyn Botanical Garden ■

Prospect Park

BRON

Statue of Liberty (Liberty Island)

Upper New York Bay

Gowanus Expwy.

39th St.

Newark Liberty International Airport

Bayonne

Newark Bay

St. George

Ferry Terminal ■

Bay Ridge

Fort Hamilton Pkwy.

4th Ave.

65th St.

86th St.

Dyker Beach Park

Belt Pkwy.

Elizabeth

UNION

95

Port Richmond

Bayonne Bridge

440

Stapleton

Clove Rd.

STATEN ISLAND

The Narrows

Verrazano Bridge

278

Lower New York Bay

MAP 1

Orchard Beach

Long Island Sound

Hart Island

City Island Ave.
City Island

Manhasset Bay

Port Washington

Kings Point

Great Neck

Eastchester Bay

25A

Northern Pkwy.

495

Throgs Neck Expwy.

295

Throgs Neck Bridge

Little Neck Bay

Great Neck Estates

Bronx-Whitestone Bridge

NASSAU

Cross Island Pkwy.

College Point

678

Whitestone Expwy.

Francis Lewis Blvd.

150th St.

Clearview Expwy.

Bell Blvd.

Auburndale

295

Northern Blvd.

25A

Flushing Bay

Northern Blvd.

Flushing

Utopia Pkwy.

Main St.

Kissena Park

Shea Stadium

USTA National Tennis Center

Flushing Meadows-Corona Park

678

Grand Central Pkwy.

25A

Roosevelt Ave.

Junction Blvd.

495

Queens Blvd.

Forest Hills

Elliot Ave.

Metropolitan Ave.

Bayside

Little Neck Pkwy.

Crocheron Park

495

Little Neck

North New Hyde Park

Throgs Neck

25B

25

Alley Park

73rd Ave.

Union Tpke.

Floral Park

Belmont Park

24

Long Island Expwy.

Cunningham Park

Queens Village

84th St.

Jewel Ave.

Queens College

St. John's University

25

Jamaica Ave.

Hillside Ave.

Francis Lewis Blvd.

Springfield Blvd.

Cross Island Pkwy.

Southern State Pkwy.

Grand Central Pkwy.

QUEENS

St. Albans

Van Wyck Expwy.

Jamaica

Sutphin Blvd.

Guy Brewer Blvd.

Farmers Blvd.

Springfield Gardens

Southern State Pkwy.

27

Valley Stream

Forest Park

Myrtle Ave.

Lefferts Blvd.

Atlantic Ave.

Liberty Ave.

Linden Blvd.

Rockaway Blvd.

Brookville Park

Ridgewood

Jackie Robinson Parkway

Jamaica Ave.

Woodhaven

Ozone Park

South Ozone Park

Aqueduct Racetrack

Rockaway Blvd.

Bushwick

Bushwick Ave.

Broadway

Conduit Blvd.

27

678

John F. Kennedy International Airport

East New York

Linden Blvd.

Pennsylvania Ave.

Cross Bay Blvd.

Rockaway Pkwy.

Kings Hwy.

Flatlands Ave.

Utica Ave.

27

Canarsie

Belt Pkwy.

Remsen Ave.

Flatbush Ave.

Wildlife Refuge (Gateway National Recreation Area)

Jamaica Bay

Beach Channel Dr.

Cross Bay Veterans Bridge

Rockaway Fwy.

Linden Blvd.

Ocean Ave.

Brooklyn College

BROOKLYN

Flatbush Ave.

Floyd Bennett Field (Gateway Natl. Rec. Area)

Flatbush Ave.

Brooklyn Marine Park

Marine Pkwy. Bridge

Beach Channel Dr.

Kings Hwy.

Ave. U

Stillwell Ave.

Belt Pkwy.

Bensonhurst

Manhattan Beach

Rockaway Point Blvd.

Jacob Riis Park (Gateway National Recreation Area)

Surf Ave.

Coney Island

Brighton Beach

New York Aquarium

Rockaway Inlet

ATLANTIC OCEAN

N

0   2 miles

0   3 km

MAP 2

Manhattan Post Offices

MAP 2

Listed Alphabetically

Ansonia, 21.
178 Columbus Ave ☎ 362-1697

Audubon, 4.
511 W 165th St ☎ 800/ASK-USPS

Bryant, 26.
23 W 43rd St ☎ 279-5960

Canal Street, 45. 350 Canal St
☎ 966-9573

Cathedral, 14.
215 W 104th St ☎ 800/ASK-USPS

Cherokee, 19. 1483 York Ave
☎ 517-8361

Chinatown, 48. 6 Doyers St
☎ 349-8264

Church Street, 52. 90 Church St
☎ 330-5313

College Station, 7.
217 W 140th St ☎ 283-7096

Colonial Park, 5. 99 Macombs Pl
☎ 368-1294

Columbia University, 12.
534 W 112th St ☎ 864-7813

Columbus Circle, 22. 27 W 60th St
☎ 265-8748

Cooper, 39. 93 Fourth Ave
☎ 254-1390

Dag Hammarskjold, 28.
884 Second Ave ☎ 800/ASK-USPS

Federal Plaza, 51.
26 Federal Pl ☎ 608-2420

Fort George, 2. 4558 Broadway
☎ 942-5266

Fort Washington, 1. 556 W 158th St
☎ 923-1763

Franklin D Roosevelt, 23.
909 Third Ave ☎ 330-5508

Gracie, 17.
229 E 85th St ☎ 800/ASK-USPS

Grand Central Station, 29.
450 Lexington Ave ☎ 800/ASK-USPS

Greely Square, 33. 39 W 31st St
☎ 279-5474

Hamilton Grange, 6. 521 W 146th St
☎ 281-1538

Hellgate, 13.
153 E 110th St ☎ 860-1896

James A Farley (Main), 31.
421 Eighth Ave ☎ 800/ASK-USPS

Knickerbocker, 47. 128 E Broadway
☎ 608-3598

Lenox Hill, 20. 217 E 70th St
☎ 879-4403

Lincolnton, 8. 2266 Fifth Ave
☎ 281-3281

London Terrace, 35.
234 Tenth Ave ☎ 255-1394

Madison Square, 34.
149 E 23rd St ☎ 673-3771

Manhattanville, 9.
365 W 125th St ☎ 662-1540

Midtown, 30. 223 W 38th St
☎ 819-9604

Morningside, 11. 232 W 116th St
☎ 800/ASK-USPS

Murray Hill Finance, 32.
115 E 34th St ☎ 679-9127

Old Chelsea, 37. 217 W 18th St
☎ 800/ASK-USPS

Park West, 15. 700 Columbus Ave
☎ 866-1981

Patchin, 40. 70 W 10th St ☎ 777-6819

Peck Slip, 49. 1 Peck Slip
☎ 964-1056

Peter Stuyvesant, 38.
432 E 14th St ☎ 677-2165

Pitt, 46. 185 Clinton St ☎ 254-6159

Planetarium, 18.
127 W 83rd St ☎ 873-5698

Port Authority, 36. 76 Ninth Ave
☎ 645-0351

Prince Street, 44.
124 Greene St ☎ 226-7869

Radio City, 24. 322 W 52nd St
☎ 265-3677

Rockefeller Center, 25.
610 Fifth Ave ☎ 265-8024

Times Square, 27. 340 W 42nd St
☎ 502-0420

Tompkins Square, 42.
244 E 3rd St ☎ 673-6415

Triborough, 10. 167 E 124th St
☎ 534-0381

Village, 43. 201 Varick St ☎ 645-0327

Wall Street, 50.
73 Pine St ☎ 800/ASK-USPS

Washington Bridge, 3.
555 W 180th St ☎ 568-2690

West Village, 41. 527 Hudson St
☎ 645-0347

Yorkville, 16.
1617 Third Ave ☎ 369-2230

MAP 3 Manhattan Neighborhoods

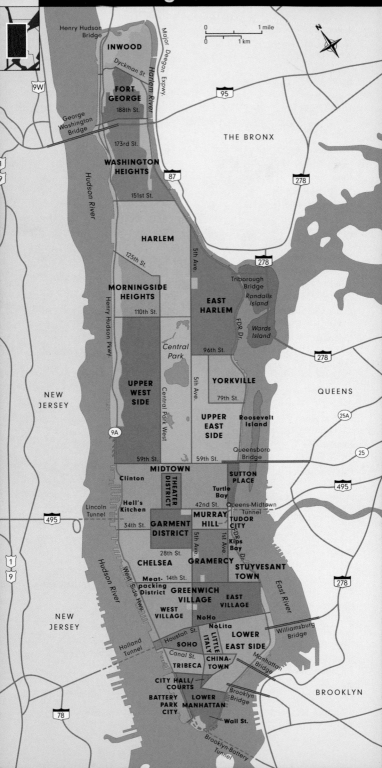

INWOOD

Henry Hudson Bridge

Dyckman St.

FORT GEORGE

188th St.

George Washington Bridge

173rd St.

WASHINGTON HEIGHTS

87

151st St.

Hudson River

Henry Hudson Pkwy.

HARLEM

125th St.

MORNINGSIDE HEIGHTS

110th St.

Central Park

UPPER WEST SIDE

Central Park West

9A

59th St.

NEW JERSEY

THE BRONX

95

278

Major Deegan Expwy.

Harlem River

5th Ave.

278

Triborough Bridge

Randalls Island

EAST HARLEM

Wards Island

96th St.

FDR Dr.

YORKVILLE

79th St.

5th Ave.

UPPER EAST SIDE

Roosevelt Island

Queensboro Bridge

59th St.

QUEENS

25A

25

495

MIDTOWN

Clinton

THEATER DISTRICT

Lincoln Tunnel

495

Hell's Kitchen

42nd St.

GARMENT DISTRICT

34th St.

28th St.

CHELSEA

SUTTON PLACE

Turtle Bay

Queens-Midtown Tunnel

MURRAY HILL

TUDOR CITY

FDR Dr.

5th Ave.

1st Ave.

Kips Bay

GRAMERCY

STUYVESANT TOWN

Meat-packing District

14th St.

West Side Hwy.

Hudson River

WEST VILLAGE

GREENWICH VILLAGE

EAST VILLAGE

NoHo

East River

278

Williamsburg Bridge

NEW JERSEY

1
9

Holland Tunnel

Houston St.

NoLita

SOHO

Canal St.

TRIBECA

LITTLE ITALY

CHINA-TOWN

LOWER EAST SIDE

Manhattan Bridge

CITY HALL/ COURTS

Brooklyn Bridge

BATTERY PARK CITY

LOWER MANHATTAN

Wall St.

BROOKLYN

78

Brooklyn-Battery Tunnel

9W

1
9

0   ½ mile
0   1 km

N

10463

Henry Hudson Bridge

9W

10034

Major Deegan Expwy.

Dyckman St.

10040
188th St.
187th St.

10033

George Washington Bridge

174th St.
173rd St.

Harlem River

N

0   1 mile
0   1 km

95

THE BRONX

278

1 9

10032

87

Hudson River

10039
145th St.

154th St.
153rd St.

St. Nicholas

10031

10030

137th St.
134th St.
133rd

St.
St.

10037

129th St.

10035

Triborough Bridge

Randalls Island

Henry Hudson Pkwy.

10027

120th St.
119th St.

116th St.
115th St.

10026

117th St.

116th St.

10035

Wards Island

278

10025

5th Ave.

97th St.
96th St.

10029

FDR Dr.

278

92nd St.
91st St.

Central Park

10128
87th St.
86th St.
81st St.
80th St.

10028

QUEENS

10024

77th St.

Central Park West

10075

76th St.

Roosevelt Island

25A

NEW JERSEY

9A

10023

60th St.
59th St.

10021

69th St.

10065
61st St.

10044

Queensboro Bridge

25

495

10019

10020

49th St.

10022

50th St.

49th St.

5th Ave.

Lincoln Tunnel

495

10036

48th St.

41st St.

10017
41st St.

10018

40th St.
36th St.
35th St.

40th St.

Queens-Midtown Tunnel

10001

25th St.
24th St.

6th Ave.

10016

27th St.

10010
26th St.
21st St.

10011

14th St.

20th St.

5th Ave.

Hudson River

Greenwich Ave.

10003

1st Ave.

10009

East River

278

10014

4th St.

Charlton

Williamsburg Bridge

Holland Tunnel

10012
Wash. Sq.

Houston St.

10002

Broome St.

Bowery

78

10013

Worth St.

Catherine

Manhattan Bridge

Park Row

10007

10038

Brooklyn Bridge

BROOKLYN

10280/10281/10282
(Battery Park City)

Maiden Lane

10005

278

10006

10041
(55 Water St.)

10004

Brooklyn-Battery Tunnel

MAP 5

Avenue Address Finder

Streets	West End Ave.	Broadway	Amsterdam Ave.	Columbus Ave.	Central Park West
94–96	700–737	2520–2554	702–733	701–740	350–360
92–94	660–699	2476–2519	656–701	661–700	322–336
90–92	620–659	2440–2475	620–655	621–660	300–320
88–90	578–619	2401–2439	580–619	581–620	279–295
86–88	540–577	2361–2400	540–579	541–580	262–275
84–86	500–539	2321–2360	500–539	501–540	241–257
82–84	460–499	2281–2320	460–499	461–500	212–239
80–82	420–459	2241–2280	420–459	421–460	211
78–80	380–419	2201–2240	380–419	381–420	American Museum of Natural History
76–78	340–379	2161–2200	340–379	341–380	
74–76	300–339	2121–2160	300–339	301–340	145–160
72–74	262–299	2081–2114	261–299	261–300	121–135
70–72	221–261	2040–2079	221–260	221–260	101–115
68–70	176–220	1999–2030	181–220	181–220	80–99
66–68	122–175	1961–1998	140–180	141–180	65–79
64–66	74–121	1920–1960	100–139	101–140	50–55
62–64	44–73	Lincoln Center	60–99	61–100	25–33
60–62	20–43	1841–1880	20–59	21–60	15
58–60	2–19	Columbus Circle	1–19	2–20	Columbus Circle

	11th Ave.	Broadway	10th Ave.	9th Ave.	8th Ave.	7th Ave.	6th Ave.
56–58	823–854	1752–1791	852–889	864–907	946–992	888–921	1381–1419
54–56	775–822	1710–1751	812–851	824–863	908–945	842–887	1341–1377
52–54	741–774	1674–1709	772–811	782–823	870–907	798–841	1301–1330
50–52	701–740	1634–1673	737–770	742–781	830–869	761–797	1261–1297
48–50	665–700	1596–1633	686–735	702–741	791–829	720–760	1221–1260
46–48	625–664	1551–1595	654–685	662–701	735–790	701–719	1180–1217
44–46	589–624	1514–1550	614–653	622–661	701–734	Times Square	1141–1178
42–44	553–588	1472–1513	576–613	582–621	661–700		1100–1140
40–42	503–552	1440–1471	538–575	Port Authority	620–660	560–598	1061–1097
38–40	480–502	1400–1439	502–537		570–619	522–559	1020–1060
36–38	431–471	1352–1399	466–501	468–501	520–569	482–521	981–1019
34–36	405–430	Macy's	430–465	432–467	480–519	442–481	Herald Square
32–34	360–404	1260–1282	380–429	412–431	442–479	Penn Station	
30–32	319–359	1220–1279	341–379	Post Office	403–441	362–399	855–892
28–30	282–318	1178–1219	314–340	314–351	362–402	322–361	815–844
26–28	242–281	1135–1177	288–313	262–313	321–361	282–321	775–814
24–26	202–241	1100–1134	239–287	230–261	281–320	244–281	733–774
22–24	162–201	940–1099	210–238	198–229	236–280	210–243	696–732
20–22	120–161	902–939	162–209	167–197	198–235	170–209	656–695
18–20	82–119	873–901	130–161	128–166	162–197	134–169	613–655
16–18	54–81	860–872	92–129	92–127	126–161	100–133	574–612
14–16	26–53	Union Square	58–91	44–91	80–125	64–99	530–573

Crosstown Street Address Finder

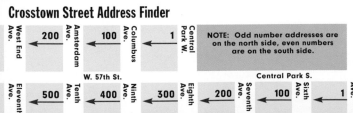

West End Ave. ← 200 Amsterdam Ave. ← 100 Columbus Ave. ← 1 Central Park W.

NOTE: Odd number addresses are on the north side, even numbers are on the south side.

W. 57th St.

Eleventh Ave. ← 500 Tenth Ave. ← 400 Ninth Ave. ← 300 Eighth Ave. ← 200 Seventh Ave. ← 100 Sixth Ave. ← 1 Fifth Ave.

Central Park S.

MAP 5

5th Ave.	Madison Ave.	Park Ave.	Lexington Ave.	3rd Ave.	2nd Ave.	1st Ave.	Streets
1130–1148	1340–1379	1199–1236	1449–1486	1678–1709	1817–1868	1817–1855	**94–96**
1109–1125	1295–1335	1160–1192	1400–1444	1644–1677	1766–1808	1780–1811	**92–94**
1090–1107	1254–1294	1120–1155	1361–1396	1601–1643	1736–1763	1740–1779	**90–92**
1070–1089	1220–1250	1080–1114	1311–1355	1568–1602	1700–1739	1701–1735	**88–90**
1050–1069	1178–1221	1044–1076	1280–1301	1530–1566	1660–1698	1652–1689	**86–88**
1030–1048	1130–1171	1000–1035	1248–1278	1490–1529	1624–1659	1618–1651	**84–86**
1010–1028	1090–1128	960–993	1210–1248	1450–1489	1584–1623	1578–1617	**82–84**
990–1009	1058–1088	916–959	1164–1209	1410–1449	1538–1583	1540–1577	**80–82**
970–989	1012–1046	878–911	1120–1161	1374–1409	1498–1537	1495–1539	**78–80**
950–969	974–1006	840–877	1080–1116	1330–1373	1456–1497	1462–1494	**76–78**
930–947	940–970	799–830	1036–1071	1290–1329	1420–1454	1429–1460	**74–76**
910–929	896–939	760–791	1004–1032	1250–1289	1389–1417	1344–1384	**72–74**
895–907	856–872	720–755	962–993	1210–1249	1328–1363	1306–1343	**70–72**
870–885	813–850	680–715	926–961	1166–1208	1296–1327	1266–1300	**68–70**
850–860	772–811	640–679	900–922	1130–1165	1260–1295	1222–1260	**66–68**
830–849	733–771	600–639	841–886	1084–1129	1222–1259	1168–1221	**64–66**
810–828	690–727	560–599	803–842	1050–1083	1180–1221	1130–1167	**62–64**
790–807	654–680	520–559	770–802	1010–1049	1140–1197	1102–1129	**60–62**
755–789	621–649	476–519	722–759	972–1009	Queensborough Bridge		**58–60**
720–754	572–611	434–475	677–721	942–968	1066–1101	1026–1063	**56–58**
680–719	532–568	408–430	636–665	894–933	1028–1062	985–1021	**54–56**
656–679	500–531	360–399	596–629	856–893	984–1027	945–984	**52–54**
626–655	452–488	320–350	556–593	818–855	944–983	889–944	**50–52**
600–625	412–444	280–300	518–555	776–817	902–943	860–888	**48–50**
562–599	377–400	240–277	476–515	741–775	862–891	827	**46–48**
530–561	346–375	Met Life (200)	441–475	702–735	824–860	785 United Nations	**44–46**
500–529	316–345	Grand Central	395–435	660–701	793–823		**42–44**
460–499	284–315		354–394	622–659	746–773	Tudor City	**40–42**
424–459	250–283	68–99	314–353	578–621	707–747	666–701	**38–40**
392–423	218–249	40–67 Park Ave.	284–311	542–577	666–700	Midtown Tunnel	**36–38**
352–391	188–217	5–35	240–283	508–541	622–659	599–626	**34–36**
320–351	152–184	1–4	196–239	470–507	585–621	556–598	**32–34**
284–319	118–150	444–470 Park Ave. S.	160–195	432–469	543–581	Kips Bay	**30–32**
250–283	79–117	404–431	120–159	394–431	500–541	NYU Hosp.	**28–30**
213–249	50–78	364–403	81–119 Lexington Ave.	350–393	462–499	446–478	**26–28**
201–212	11–37	323–361	40–77	321–355	422–461	411–445	**24–26**
172–200	1–7	286–322	9–39	282–318	382–421	390–410	**22–24**
154–170		251–285	1–8 Irving Pl.	244–281	344–381	315–389	**20–22**
109–153		221–250	70–78	206–243	310–343	310–314	**18–20**
85–127		184–220	40–69	166–205	301–309	280–309	**16–18**
69–108		Union Square	2–30	126–165	230–240	240–279	**14–16**

Fifth Ave. | Madison Ave. | Park Ave. | Lexington Ave. | Third Ave. | Second Ave. | First Ave.

1 → **100** → **140** → **200** → **300** → **400** →

MAP 6

Streetfinder/The Village & Downtown

THE BRONX

Harlem River Dr.

Major Deegan Expwy.

135th St. **2**

278

Triborough Bridge

125th St.

Randal's Island

A.C. Powell Jr. Blvd.

Frederick Douglass Blvd.

Lenox Ave.

3

Ward's Island

FDR Dr.

1

Broadway

Henry Hudson Pkwy.

Riverside Dr.

4

Amsterdam Ave.

Broadway

Columbus Ave.

110th St.

2nd Ave.

3rd Ave.

Park Ave.

Madison Ave.

5

96th St.

5th Ave.

6

7

West End Ave.

8

86th St.

Central Park West

Central Park

79th St.

10

Roosevelt Island

11

13 **12**

72nd St.

15

16

9

Broadway

Park Ave.

14 **17**

18

9A

59th St.

Queensboro Bridge

57th St.

21 **20**

22

Madison Ave.

3rd Ave.

1st Ave.

26

24

19

5th Ave.

23

Ave. of the Americas (6th Ave.)

Queens-Midtown Tunnel

495

Lincoln Tunnel

42nd St.

Lexington Ave.

2nd Ave.

25

East River

34th St.

Park Ave. S.

27

28 **29**

West Side Hwy.

12th Ave.

11th Ave.

10th Ave.

9th Ave.

8th Ave.

7th Ave.

30

23rd St.

Broadway

32

31

33 **34**

37 **35** **36**

14th St.

Ave. A

Ave. B

Ave. C

Ave. D

38

40

39

Hudson St.

Varick St.

Lafayette St.

Bowery

Houston St.

HUDSON RIVER

Canal St.

Williamsburg Bridge

41

42

Manhattan Bridge

NEW JERSEY

Holland Tunnel

Chambers St.

Brooklyn Bridge

43

Broadway

KEY
1 Hospitals
7 Pharmacies

0   1 mile
0   1 km

Brooklyn-Battery Tunnel

MAP 7

Listed Alphabetically
HOSPITALS

Bellevue Hospital Center, 29.
462 First Ave ☎ 562-4141

Beth Israel Med Center, 34.
First Ave at 16th St ☎ 420-2000

Cabrini Med Center, 32. 227 E 19th St
☎ 995-6000

Coler-Goldwater Memorial, 10.
900 Main St, Roosevelt Island
☎ 848-6000

Coler-Goldwater Memorial, 26.
1 Main St, Roosevelt Island
☎ 318-8000

Gouverneur, 42. 227 Madison St
☎ 238-7000

Gracie Square (Psychiatric), 12.
420 E 76th St ☎ 988-4400

Harlem Hospital Center, 2.
506 Lenox Ave ☎ 939-1000

Joint Diseases, 33. 301 E 17th St
☎ 598-6000

Lenox Hill, 11. 100 E 77th St
☎ 434-2000

Manhattan Eye, Ear, & Throat, 18.
210 E 64th St ☎ 838-9200

Memorial Sloan-Kettering (Cancer), 17. 1275 York Ave ☎ 639-2000

Metropolitan, 6. 1901 First Ave
☎ 423-6262

Mount Sinai, 5. Fifth Ave at 100th St
☎ 241-6500

New York Downtown, 43.
170 William St ☎ 312-5000

New York Eye & Ear, 35. 310 E 14th St
☎ 979-4000

New York Foundling (Children), 36.
590 Sixth Ave ☎ 633-9300

North General, 3.
Madison Ave at 122nd St ☎ 423-4000

NY Presbyterian Columbia Med Ctr, 1.
622 W 168th St ☎ 305-2500

NY Presbyterian Cornell-Weill Med Center, 16.
525 E 68th St ☎ 746-5454

NYU Med Center, 27. 550 First Ave
☎ 263-7300

Payne Whitney (Psychiatric), 16.
525 E 68th St ☎ 746-0331

Special Surgery, 15. 535 E 70th St
☎ 606-1000

St Luke's-Roosevelt, 4.
1111 Amsterdam Ave ☎ 523-4000

St Luke's-Roosevelt, 21.
Tenth Ave at 58th St
☎ 523-4000

St Vincent's Midtown, 24.
415 W 51st St ☎ 586-1500

St Vincent's, 38. 153 W 11th St
☎ 604-7000

LATE-NIGHT/24-HOUR PHARMACIES

Apthorp Pharmacy, 9.
2201 Broadway ☎ 800/775-3582

Bigelow Chemists, 40.
414 Sixth Ave ☎ 533-2700

CVS Pharmacy, 8.
1622 Third Ave ☎ 876-7016

CVS Pharmacy, 19.
630 Lexington Ave ☎ 917/369-8688 (24-hour)

CVS Pharmacy, 20.
400 W 58th St ☎ 245-0636 (24-hour)

CVS Pharmacy, 25. 150 E 42nd St
☎ 661-8139 (24-hour)

CVS Pharmacy, 36.
253 First Ave ☎ 254-1454 (24-hour)

Duane Reade, 7. 2522 Broadway
☎ 663-1580 (24-hour)

Duane Reade, 13. 1279 Third Ave
☎ 744-2668 (24-hour)

Duane Reade, 22. 250 W 57th St
☎ 265-2101 (24-hour)

Eckerd Drug, 14. 1299 Second Ave
☎ 772-0104

Rite Aid, 23. 301 W 50th St
☎ 247-8384 (24-hour)

Rite Aid, 28. 542-576 Second Ave
☎ 213-9887

Rite Aid, 41. 408 Grand St
☎ 529-7115 (24-hour)

VA NY Harbor, 30.
423 E 23rd St ☎ 686-7500

Village Apothecary, 39.
346 Bleecker St ☎ 807-7566

Walgreens, 37.
145 Fourth Ave ☎ 677-0214 (24-hour)

MAP 8

Universities, Colleges & Schools

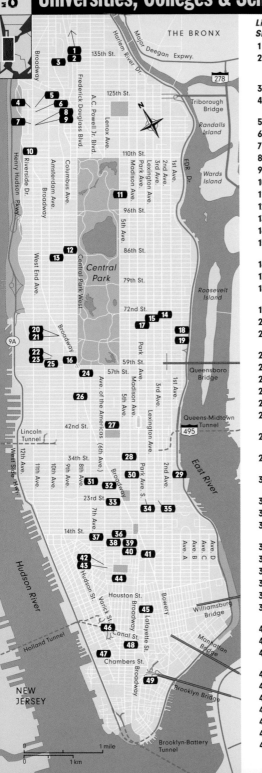

Listed Alphabetically

American Academy of Dramatic Arts, 30. 120 Madison Ave ☎ 800/463-8990

Art Institute of NY, 46. 75 Varick St ☎ 226-5500

Art Students' League, 24. 215 W 57th St ☎ 247-4510

Bank St College of Education, 10. 610 W 112th St ☎ 875-4400

Bard Graduate Center, 12. 18 W 86th St ☎ 501-3000

Barnard College, 7. 3009 Broadway ☎ 854-5262

Baruch College, 34. 55 Lexington Ave ☎ 646/312-1000

Borough of Manhattan Community College, 47. 199 Chambers Street ☎ 220-8000

Cardozo School of Law, 39. 55 Fifth Ave ☎ 790-0200

Circle in the Square Theater School, 26. 1633 Broadway ☎ 307-0388

City College of NY, 3. Convent Ave & 138th St ☎ 650-7000

Columbia University College of Physicians & Surgeons, 2. 630 W 168th St ☎ 305-3806

Columbia University, 8. B'way & 116th St ☎ 854-1754

The Cooper Union, 41. 30 Cooper Sq ☎ 353-4100

CUNY Graduate Center, 28. 365 Fifth Ave ☎ 817-7000

Fashion Institute of Technology, 31. 227 W 27th St ☎ 217-7999

Fordham University School of Law, 23. 140 W 62nd St ☎ 636-6000

Fordham University, 22. 113 W 60th St ☎ 636-6000

The French Culinary Institute, 45. 462 Broadway ☎ 219-8890

Hebrew Union College, 43. 1 W 4th St ☎ 674-5300

Hunter College, 17. 695 Park Ave ☎ 772-4000

Institute of Culinary Education, 33. 50 W 23rd St ☎ 888/354-2433

Jewish Theological Seminary, 5. Broadway & 122nd St ☎ 678-8000

John Jay College, 25. 899 Tenth Ave ☎ 237-8000

Juilliard School, 20. 60 Lincoln Center Plz ☎ 799-5000

Leonard N. Stern School of Business at NYU, 42. 44 W 4th St ☎ 998-0100

Manhattan School of Music, 4. 120 Claremont Ave ☎ 749-2802

Mannes College of Music, 13. 150 W 85th St ☎ 580-0210

Marymount Manhattan College, 14. 221 E 71st St ☎ 517-0400

Mount Sinai School of Medicine, 11. Fifth Ave & 100th St ☎ 241-6691

New School, 38. 66 W 12th St ☎ 229-5600

NY Institute of Technology, 16. 1855 Broadway ☎ 261-1500

NY Law School, 48. 57 Worth St ☎ 431-2100

NY School of Interior Design, 15. 170 E 70th St ☎ 472-1500

NYU, 40. 100 Washington Square E ☎ 998-1212

NYU Law School, 44. 40 Washington Sq S ☎ 998-6060

NYU School of Medicine, 29. 550 First Ave ☎ 263-7300

Pace University, 49. 1 Pace Plaza ☎ 800/847-PACE

Parsons School of Design, 36. 66 Fifth Ave ☎ 229-8900

Pratt Manhattan, 37. 144 W 14th St ☎ 647-7775

Rockefeller University, 19. York Ave & 66th St ☎ 327-8000

School of American Ballet, 21. 70 Lincoln Center Plz ☎ 769-6600

School of Visual Arts, 35. 209 E 23rd St ☎ 592-2000

Stella Adler Studio, 32. 31 W 27th St ☎ 689-0087

SUNY College of Optometry, 27. 33 W 42nd St ☎ 938-4000

Teachers College at Columbia, 9. 525 W 120th St ☎ 678-3000

Union Theological Seminary, 6. 3041 Broadway ☎ 662-7100

Weill Cornell Medical College, 18. 1300 York Ave ☎ 746-1067

Yeshiva University, 1. 500 W 185th St ☎ 960-5400

MAP 9 **Libraries**

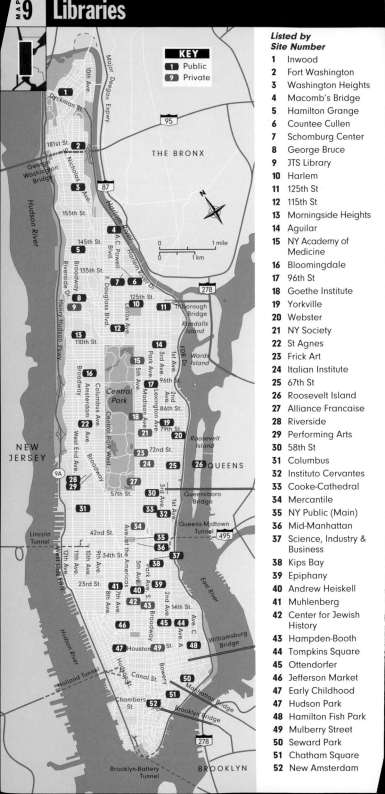

KEY
1 Public
9 Private

THE BRONX

NEW
JERSEY

QUEENS

BROOKLYN

Listed Alphabetically
PUBLIC

Aguilar, 14. 174 E 110th St
☎ 534-2930

Andrew Heiskell Library For the Blind and Physically Handicapped, 40.
40 W 20th St ☎ 206-5400

Bloomingdale, 16. 150 W 100th St
☎ 222-8030

Cardinal Cooke-Cathedral, 33.
560 Lexington Ave ☎ 752-3824

Chatham Square, 51. 33 E Broadway
☎ 964-6598

Columbus, 31. 742 Tenth Ave
☎ 586-5098

Countee Cullen, 6. 104 W 136th St
☎ 491-2070

Early Childhood Resource and Information Ctr, 47. 66 Leroy St
☎ 929-0815

Epiphany, 39. 228 E 23rd St
☎ 679-2645

58th St, 30. 127 E 58th St ☎ 759-7358

Fort Washington, 2. 535 W 179th St
☎ 927-3533

George Bruce, 8. 518 W 125th St
☎ 662-9727

Hamilton Fish Park, 48.
415 E Houston St ☎ 673-2290

Hamilton Grange, 5.
503 W 145th St ☎ 926-2147

Harlem, 10. 9 W 124th St ☎ 348-5620

Hudson Park, 47. 66 Leroy St
☎ 243-6876

Inwood, 1. 4790 Broadway
☎ 942-2445

Instituto Cervantes, 32.
211-215 E 49th St ☎ 308-7720

Jefferson Market, 46. 425 Sixth Ave
☎ 243-4334

Kips Bay, 38. 446 Third Ave
☎ 683-2520

Library for the Performing Arts, 29.
40 Lincoln Center Pl ☎ 870-1630

Macomb's Bridge, 4.
2650 Seventh Ave ☎ 281-4900

Mid-Manhattan, 36. 455 Fifth Ave
☎ 340-0849

Morningside Heights, 13.
2900 Broadway ☎ 864-2530

Muhlenberg, 41. 209 W 23rd St
☎ 924-1585

Mulberry Street, 49.
10 Jersey St ☎ 966-3424

New Amsterdam, 52.
9 Murray St ☎ 732-8186

NY Public (Main), 35.
Fifth Ave & 42nd St ☎ 930-0830

96th St, 17. 112 E 96th St ☎ 289-0908

115th St, 12. 203 W 115th St
☎ 666-9393

125th St, 11. 224 E 125th St
☎ 534-5050

Ottendorfer, 45.
135 Second Ave ☎ 674-0947

Riverside, 28. 127 Amsterdam Ave
☎ 870-1810

Roosevelt Island, 26. 524 Main St
☎ 308-6243

St Agnes, 22. 444 Amsterdam Ave
☎ 877-4380

Schomburg Center, 7.
515 W Malcolm X Blvd ☎ 491-2200

Science, Industry & Business, 37.
188 Madison Ave ☎ 592-7000

Seward Park, 50. 192 E Broadway
☎ 477-6770

67th St, 25. 328 E 67th St ☎ 734-1717

Tompkins Square, 44. 331 E 10th St
☎ 228-4747

Washington Heights, 3.
1000 St Nicholas Ave ☎ 923-6054

Webster, 20. 1465 York Ave
☎ 288-5049

Yorkville, 19. 222 E 79th St
☎ 744-5824

PRIVATE

Alliance Francaise, 27. 22 E 60th St
☎ 646/388-6655

Center for Jewish History, 42.
15 W 16th St ☎ 294-8301

Frick Art, 23. 10 E 71st St ☎ 547-0641

Goethe Institute, 18. 1014 Fifth Ave
☎ 439-8700

Hampden-Booth Theatre Library, 43.
16 Gramercy Pk S ☎ 228-1861

Italian Cultural Institute, 24.
686 Park Ave ☎ 879-4242

Jewish Theological Seminary, 9.
3080 Broadway ☎ 678-8082

Mercantile, 34. 17 E 47th St
☎ 755-6710

NY Academy of Medicine, 15.
1216 Fifth Ave ☎ 822-7300

NY Society, 21. 53 E 79th St
☎ 288-6900

MAP 10 Airport Access

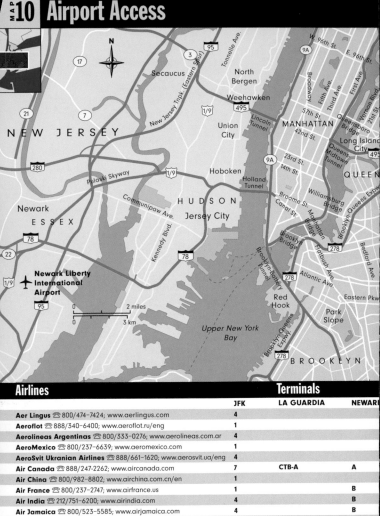

Airlines

Airlines	JFK	LA GUARDIA	NEWARK
Aer Lingus ☎ 800/474-7424; www.aerlingus.com	4		
Aeroflot ☎ 888/340-6400; www.aeroflot.ru/eng	1		
Aerolineas Argentinas ☎ 800/333-0276; www.aerolineas.com.ar	4		
AeroMexico ☎ 800/237-6639; www.aeromexico.com	1		
AeroSvit Ukranian Airlines ☎ 888/661-1620; www.aerosvit.ua/eng	4		
Air Canada ☎ 888/247-2262; www.aircanada.com	7	CTB-A	A
Air China ☎ 800/982-8802; www.airchina.com.cn/en	1		
Air France ☎ 800/237-2747; www.airfrance.us	1		B
Air India ☎ 212/751-6200; www.airindia.com	4		B
Air Jamaica ☎ 800/523-5585; www.airjamaica.com	4		B
AirTran Airways ☎ 800/247-8726; www.airtran.com		CTB-B	A
Alaska Airlines ☎ 800/426-0333; www.alaskaair.com			A
Alitalia ☎ 800/223-5730; www.alitalia.com	1		B
All Nippon Airways ☎ 800/235-9262; www.anaskyweb.com	7		
America West ☎ 800/235-9292; www.usairways.com			A
American ☎ 800/433-7300; www.aa.com	8	CTB-D	A
American Eagle ☎ 800/433-7300; www.aa.com	8	CTB-C	A
Austrian Airlines ☎ 800/843-0002; www.aua.com	1		
Avianca ☎ 800/284-2622; www.avianca.com	4		
Biman Bangladesh ☎ 212/808-4477; www.bimanair.com	4		
British Airways ☎ 800/247-9297; www.britishairways.com	7		B
Caribbean Airlines ☎ 800/538-2942; www.caribbean-airlines.com	4		
Cathay Pacific ☎ 800/233-2742; www.cathaypacific.com	7		
China Airlines ☎ 800/227-5118; www.china-airlines.com/en	1		
Continental ☎ 800/525-0280; www.continental.com	4	CTB-A	A,C
Czech Airlines ☎ 800/223-2365; www.csa.cz/en	4		B
Delta ☎ 800/221-1212; 800/241-4141; www.delta.com	3	Delta	B
Delta Connection ☎ 800/325-5205; www.delta.com	3	Delta	
Delta Shuttle ☎ 800/325-5205; www.delta.com		MAT	
EgyptAir ☎ 212/315-0900; www.egyptair.com	4		
El-Al ☎ 212/768-9200; www.elal.co.il/ELAL/English	4		B
Emirates ☎ 800/777-3999; www.emirates.com	4		

MAP 10

Airlines

Terminals (cont.)

	JFK	LA GUARDIA	NEWARK
Finnair ☎ 800/950-5000; www.finnair.com	8		
Iberia ☎ 800/772-4642; www.iberia.com	7		
Icelandair ☎ 800/223-5500; www.icelandair.com	7		
Japan ☎ 800/525-3663; www.jal.com	1		
JetBlue ☎ 800/538-2583; www.jetblue.com	6	CTB-A,B	A
KLM ☎ 800/374-7747; www.klm.com	4		B
Korean ☎ 800/438-5000; www.koreanair.com	1		
Kuwait ☎ 212/659-4200; www.kuwait-airways.com	4		
LAN ☎ 866/435-9526; www.lan.com	4		
LOT Polish ☎ 212/852-0240; www.lot.com	4		B
Lufthansa ☎ 800/645-3880; www.lufthansa.com	1		B
Malaysia ☎ 800/582-9264; www.malaysiaairlines.com			B
Malev Hungarian ☎ 800/223-6884; www.malev.hu	8		
Mexicana ☎ 800/531-7921; www.mexicana.com	4		B
Midwest ☎ 800/452-2022; www.midwestairlines.com		CTB-B	A
North American ☎ 800/371-6297; www.flynaa.com	4		
Northwest ☎ 800/225-2525; 447-4747; www.nwa.com	4	Delta	B
Olympic ☎ 800/223-1226; www.olympicairlines.com	1		
Pakistan ☎ 212/760-8455; www.piac.com.pk	4		
Qantas ☎ 800/227-4500; www.qantas.com.au	7		
Royal Air Maroc ☎ 800/344-6726; www.royalairmaroc.com	1		
Royal Jordanian ☎ 212/949-0050; www.rj.com	4		
SAS ☎ 800/221-2350; www.flysas.com			B
Saudi Arabian ☎ 718/551-3020; www.saudiairlines.com	1		
Singapore Airlines ☎ 800/742-3333; www.singaporeair.com	4		
South African Airways ☎ 800/722-9675; www.flysaa.com	4		
Spirit ☎ 800/772-7117; www.spiritair.com		CTB-B	
Sun Country ☎ 800/FLY-NSUN; www.suncountry.com	4		
Swiss ☎ 877/359-7947; www.swiss.com	4		
TACA International ☎ 800/535-8780; www.taca.com	4		
TAP Air Portugal ☎ 800/221-7370; www.flytap.com			B
Thai Airways ☎ 800/426-5204; www.thaiair.com	4		

MAP 11 **New York Area Airports**

JFK International Airport

Airlines

Airlines	JFK	LA GUARDIA	NEWARK
Turkish Airlines ☎ 516/247-5402; www.thy.com	1		
United ☎ 800/241-6522; www.united.com	7	CTB-B	A
US Airways ☎ 800/428-4322; 622-1015; www.usairways.com	7	US Airways	A
US Airways Shuttle ☎ 800/428-4322; www.usairways.com		US Airways Shuttle	
Varig ☎ 800/468-2744; www.varig.com	4		
Virgin America ☎ 877/359-8484; www.virginamerica.com	4		
Virgin Atlantic ☎ 800/862-8621; www.virgin-atlantic.com	4		B

Terminals (cont.)

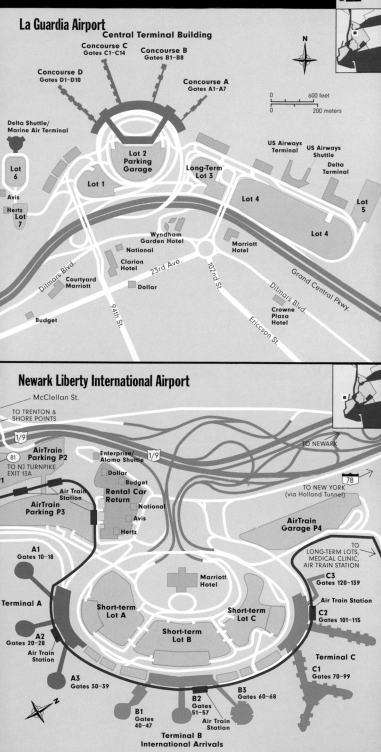

MAP 11

La Guardia Airport

Central Terminal Building

Concourse C
Gates C1–C14

Concourse B
Gates B1–B8

Concourse D
Gates D1–D10

Concourse A
Gates A1–A7

N

Delta Shuttle/
Marine Air Terminal

Lot 6

Avis

Hertz
Lot 7

Lot 2
Parking
Garage

Lot 1

Long-Term
Lot 3

US Airways
Terminal

US Airways
Shuttle

Delta
Terminal

Lot 4

Lot 4

Lot 5

0   600 feet
0   200 meters

Wyndham
Garden Hotel

National

Clarion
Hotel

Marriott
Hotel

Ditmars Blvd.

Courtyard
Marriott

Dollar

23rd Ave.

102nd St.

Grand Central Pkwy.

Ditmars Blvd.

Budget

94th St.

Ericsson St.

Crowne
Plaza
Hotel

Newark Liberty International Airport

McClellan St.

TO TRENTON &
SHORE POINTS

1/9

81   AirTrain
Parking P2

TO NJ TURNPIKE
EXIT 13A

P1

Enterprise/
Alamo Shuttle

1/9

TO NEWARK

Air Train
Station

AirTrain
Parking P3

Dollar

Budget

Rental Car
Return

National

Avis

Hertz

TO NEW YORK
(via Holland Tunnel)

78

AirTrain
Garage P4

TO
LONG-TERM LOTS,
MEDICAL CLINIC,
AIR TRAIN STATION

A1
Gates 10–18

Marriott
Hotel

C3
Gates 120–139

Air Train Station

Terminal A

Short-term
Lot A

Short-term
Lot C

C2
Gates 101–115

A2
Gates 20–28

Short-term
Lot B

Terminal C

Air Train
Station

C1
Gates 70–99

A3
Gates 30–39

B3
Gates 60–68

N

B1
Gates
40–47

B2
Gates
51–57

Air Train
Station

Terminal B
International Arrivals

MAP 12 **Passenger Rail Network**

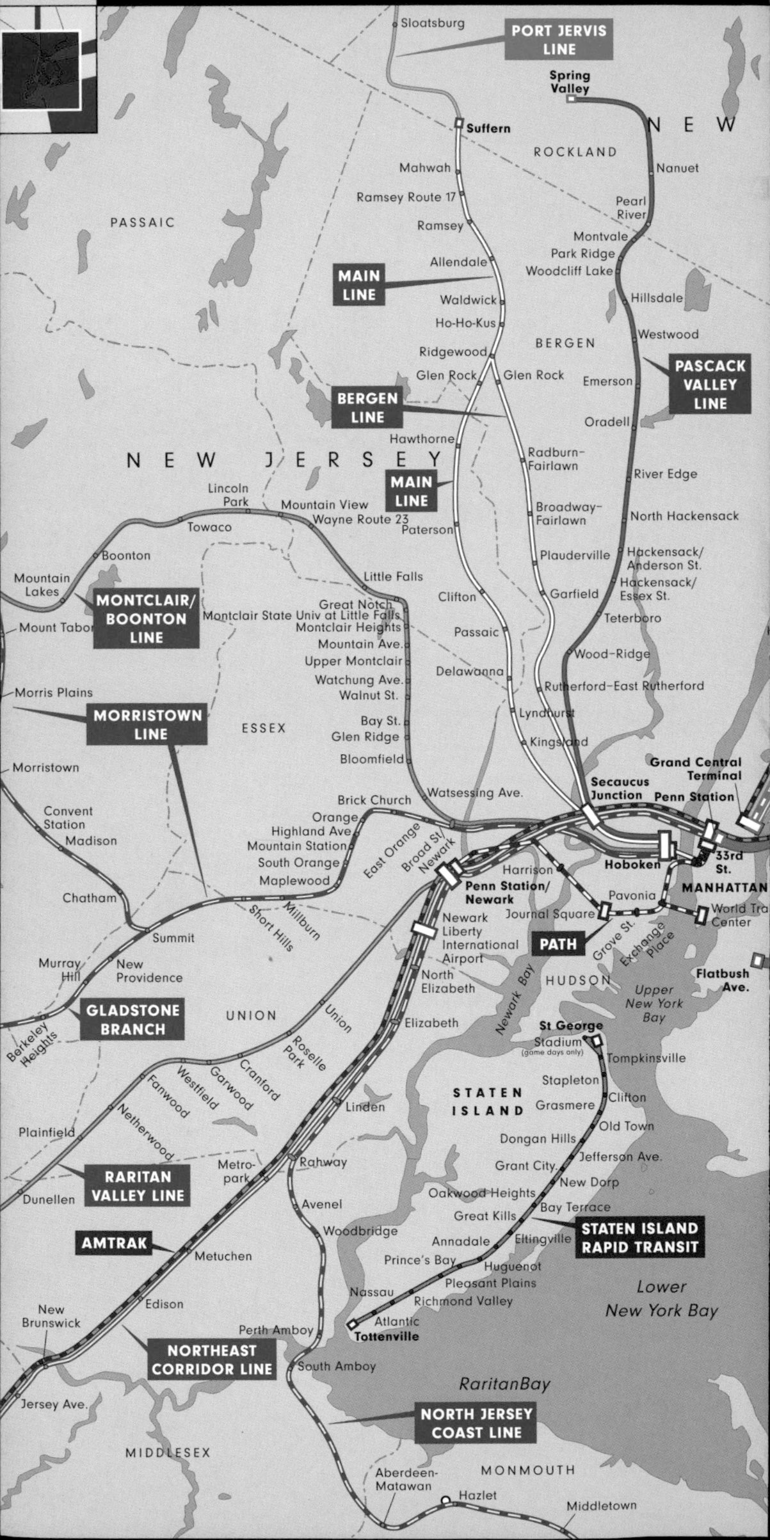

Sloatsburg

PORT JERVIS LINE

Spring Valley

N E W

Suffern

ROCKLAND

Nanuet

Mahwah

Ramsey Route 17

Pearl River

Ramsey

Montvale

Park Ridge

Woodcliff Lake

Allendale

Hillsdale

MAIN LINE

Waldwick

Ho-Ho-Kus

Westwood

Ridgewood

Glen Rock

Glen Rock

BERGEN

Emerson

BERGEN LINE

PASCACK VALLEY LINE

Oradell

Hawthorne

N E W   J E R S E Y

Radburn-Fairlawn

River Edge

MAIN LINE

Lincoln Park

Mountain View

Wayne Route 23

Paterson

Broadway-Fairlawn

North Hackensack

Towaco

Plauderville

Hackensack/ Anderson St.

Boonton

Clifton

Garfield

Hackensack/ Essex St.

Mountain Lakes

Little Falls

Teterboro

Mount Tabor

MONTCLAIR/ BOONTON LINE

Great Notch

Montclair State Univ at Little Falls

Montclair Heights

Mountain Ave.

Upper Montclair

Watchung Ave.

Walnut St.

Passaic

Delawanna

Wood-Ridge

Rutherford–East Rutherford

Morris Plains

MORRISTOWN LINE

ESSEX

Bay St.

Glen Ridge

Bloomfield

Lyndhurst

Kingsland

Grand Central Terminal

Morristown

Brick Church

Watsessing Ave.

Secaucus Junction

Penn Station

Convent Station

Madison

Orange

Highland Ave.

Mountain Station

South Orange

Maplewood

East Orange

Broad St./ Newark

Hoboken

33rd St.

Harrison

MANHATTAN

Chatham

Penn Station/ Newark

Pavonia

Millburn

Short Hills

Journal Square

Grove St.

Exchange Place

World Trade Center

Murray Hill

Summit

New Providence

Newark Liberty International Airport

PATH

Upper New York Bay

Flatbush Ave.

GLADSTONE BRANCH

Berkeley Heights

UNION

North Elizabeth

HUDSON

Union

Roselle Park

Elizabeth

Newark Bay

St George

Stadium (game days only)

Tompkinsville

Cranford

Garwood

Linden

STATEN ISLAND

Stapleton

Clifton

Plainfield

Fanwood

Westfield

Netherwood

Grasmere

Old Town

Dongan Hills

Jefferson Ave.

RARITAN VALLEY LINE

Metro-park

Rahway

Grant City

New Dorp

Dunellen

Avenel

Oakwood Heights

Bay Terrace

Woodbridge

Great Kills

AMTRAK

Metuchen

Eltingville

STATEN ISLAND RAPID TRANSIT

New Brunswick

Edison

Prince's Bay

Huguenot

Pleasant Plains

Lower New York Bay

Nassau

Richmond Valley

Jersey Ave.

NORTHEAST CORRIDOR LINE

Perth Amboy

Atlantic

Tottenville

South Amboy

Raritan Bay

MIDDLESEX

NORTH JERSEY COAST LINE

MONMOUTH

Aberdeen-Matawan

Hazlet

Middletown

PASSAIC

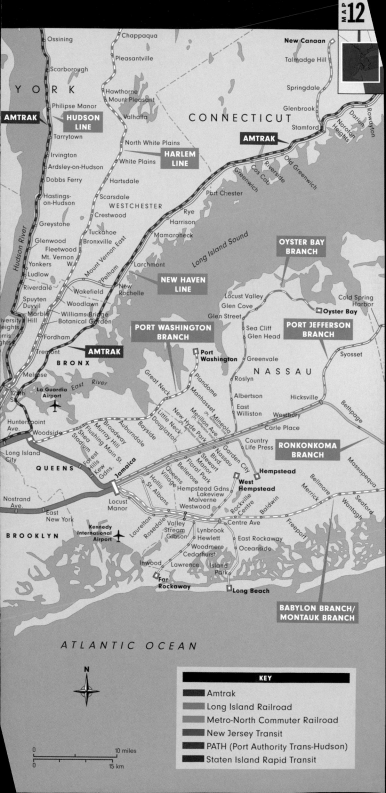

TIMES SQ
42 ST/8 AVE
A
C
E
34 ST/
PENN STN
28 ST
2
3
23 ST
18 ST
14 ST/8 AVE
L
14 ST
6 AVE

CHRISTOPHER ST/
SHERIDAN SQ
1
2
3
HOUSTON ST

CANAL ST

FRANKLIN ST
CHAMBERS ST
CITY HALL
PARK PLACE
WORLD TRADE CENTER
E
BROADWAY/ NASSAU
CORTLANDT ST (CLOSED)
CORTLANDT ST
RECTOR ST
RECTOR ST
J **Z** **BROAD ST**
BOWLING GREEN
WHITEHALL/SOUTH FERRY
SOUTH FERRY

S 42 ST/GRAND CENTRAL
7
42 ST/
6 AVE
5
4
6
B
D
F
V
34 ST/
HERALD SQ
33 ST
28 ST
28 ST
N
Q
R
W
23 ST
23 ST
F
V
14 ST/
UNION SQ
L
Q **N**
W **R**
3
AVE
8 ST/
NYU
AST
PL
B
D
W 4 ST/
WASH SQ
BLEECKER
ST
F
V
B
D
BROADWAY/LAFAYETTE
PRINCE ST
SPRING ST
SPRING ST
BOWERY
CANAL ST
CANAL ST
W
R
6
BROOKLYN BR/
CITY HALL
FULTON
ST
WALL ST
1

Hudson River

N E W
J E R S E Y

0   1500 feet
0   500 meters

KEY
1 Subway line
Terminal
Express stop
Local stop
Express and
local stop
Free transfer
(Local)
Free transfer
(Express)

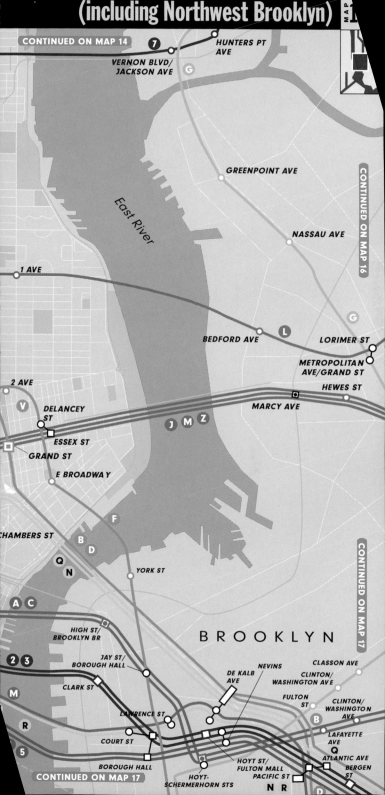

CONTINUED ON MAP 14

7 HUNTERS PT AVE

VERNON BLVD/
JACKSON AVE

G

GREENPOINT AVE

NASSAU AVE

East River

1 AVE

BEDFORD AVE **L** LORIMER ST

G

METROPOLITAN
AVE/GRAND ST

HEWES ST

2 AVE

MARCY AVE

V

DELANCEY
ST

J **M** **Z**

ESSEX ST

GRAND ST

E BROADWAY

F

CHAMBERS ST

B

D

Q **N**

YORK ST

A **C**

HIGH ST/
BROOKLYN BR

B R O O K L Y N

2 **3**

JAY ST/
BOROUGH HALL

CLARK ST

M

R

COURT ST

5

BOROUGH HALL

LAWRENCE ST

DE KALB
AVE

NEVINS

CLASSON AVE

CLINTON/
WASHINGTON AV E

FULTON
ST

CLINTON/
WASHINGTON
AVE

B

LAFAYETTE
AVE

Q ATLANTIC AVE

HOYT ST/
FULTON MALL
PACIFIC ST

BERGEN
ST

HOYT-
SCHERMERHORN STS

N R

D

CONTINUED ON MAP 16

CONTINUED ON MAP 17

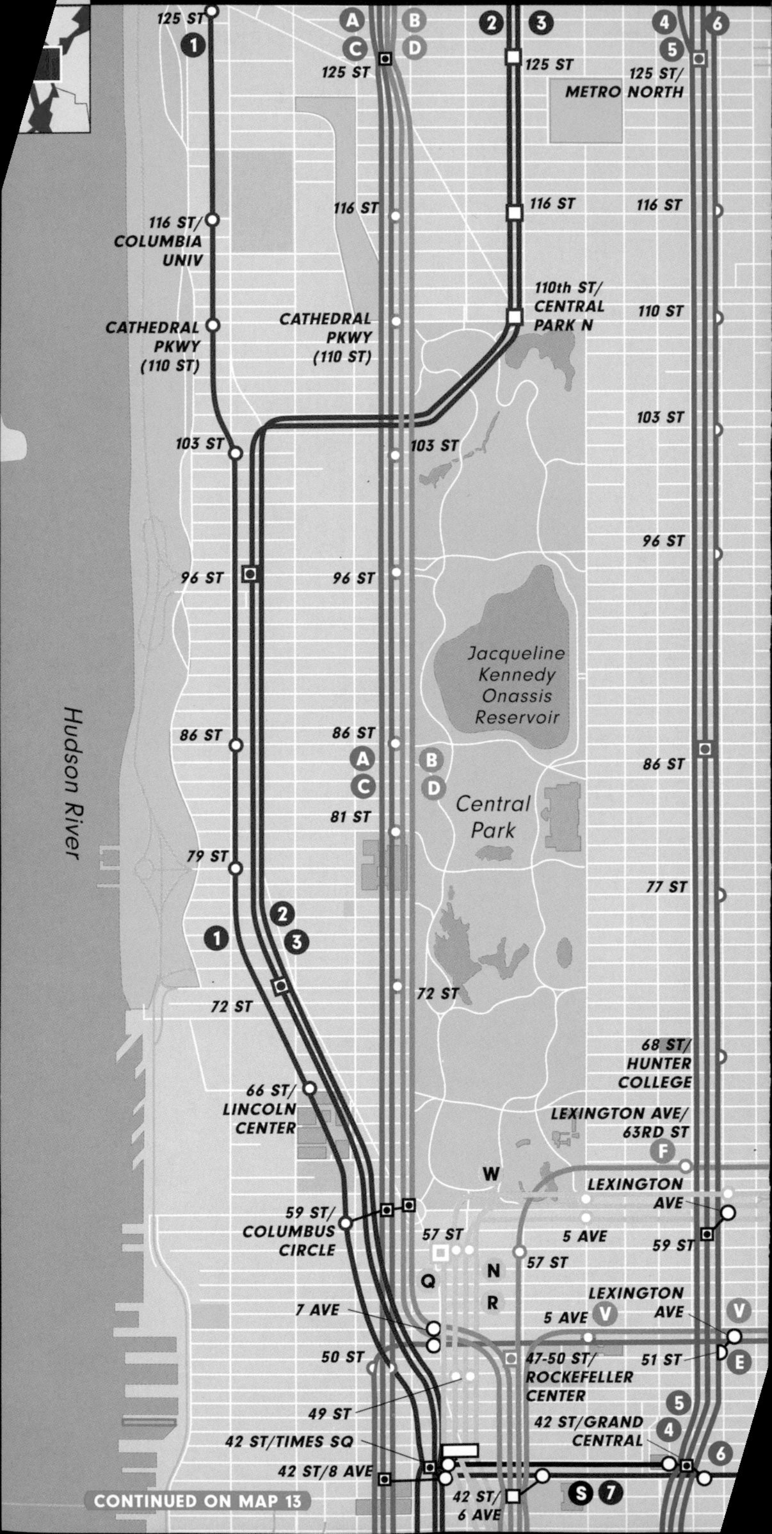

125 ST
Ⓐ Ⓑ ❷ ❸ ❹ ❻
Ⓒ Ⓓ ❺
125 ST
125 ST
125 ST/
METRO NORTH

116 ST
116 ST
116 ST/
COLUMBIA
UNIV
116 ST
116 ST

110th ST/
CENTRAL
PARK N
110 ST

CATHEDRAL
PKWY
(110 ST)
CATHEDRAL
PKWY
(110 ST)

103 ST
103 ST
103 ST

96 ST
96 ST
96 ST

Jacqueline
Kennedy
Onassis
Reservoir

86 ST
86 ST
Ⓐ Ⓑ
Ⓒ Ⓓ
86 ST
81 ST

Central
Park

79 ST

77 ST

❷
❶ ❸

72 ST
72 ST

68 ST/
HUNTER
COLLEGE

66 ST/
LINCOLN
CENTER

LEXINGTON AVE/
63RD ST
Ⓕ

Ⓦ

LEXINGTON
AVE

59 ST/
COLUMBUS
CIRCLE
57 ST
5 AVE
59 ST

Ⓠ Ⓝ
Ⓡ
57 ST
LEXINGTON
AVE
Ⓥ

7 AVE
5 AVE Ⓥ
Ⓔ

50 ST
51 ST

49 ST
47-50 ST/
ROCKEFELLER
CENTER

42 ST/TIMES SQ
42 ST/GRAND
CENTRAL
❺
❹
❻

42 ST/8 AVE

CONTINUED ON MAP 13

42 ST/
6 AVE
Ⓢ ❼

Hudson River

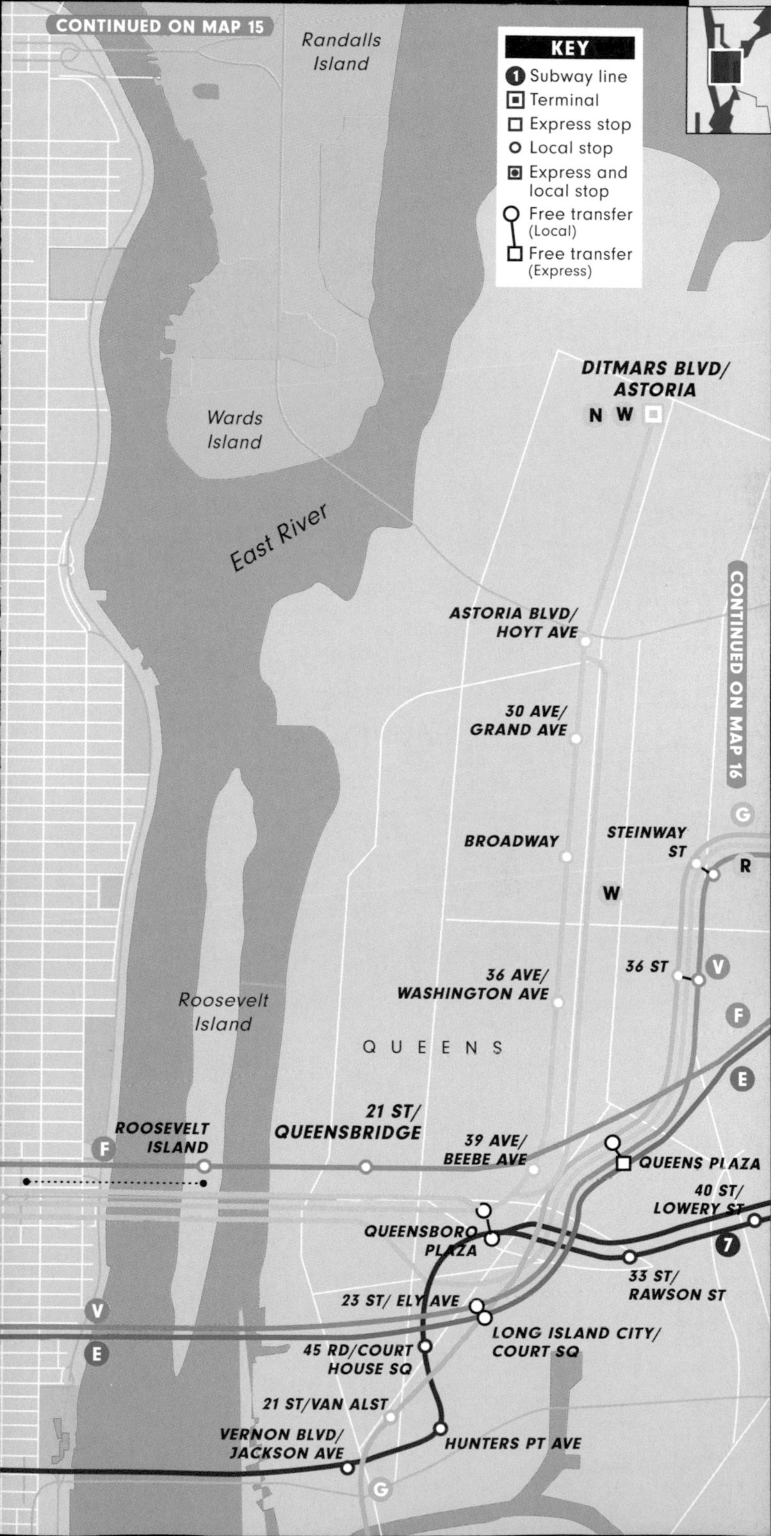

CONTINUED ON MAP 15

Randalls
Island

KEY
- **1** Subway line
- ■ Terminal
- □ Express stop
- ○ Local stop
- ◉ Express and local stop
- ⦁—⦁ Free transfer (Local)
- □—□ Free transfer (Express)

Wards
Island

East River

CONTINUED ON MAP 16

DITMARS BLVD/ ASTORIA
N W ■

ASTORIA BLVD/ HOYT AVE

30 AVE/ GRAND AVE

BROADWAY

STEINWAY ST

W

G

R

36 AVE/ WASHINGTON AVE

36 ST

V

F

E

QUEENS

Roosevelt
Island

21 ST/ QUEENSBRIDGE

39 AVE/ BEEBE AVE

F ROOSEVELT ISLAND

□ QUEENS PLAZA

40 ST/ LOWERY ST

7

QUEENSBORO PLAZA

33 ST/ RAWSON ST

23 ST/ ELY AVE

LONG ISLAND CITY/ COURT SQ

45 RD/COURT HOUSE SQ

V

E

21 ST/VAN ALST

VERNON BLVD/ JACKSON AVE

HUNTERS PT AVE

G

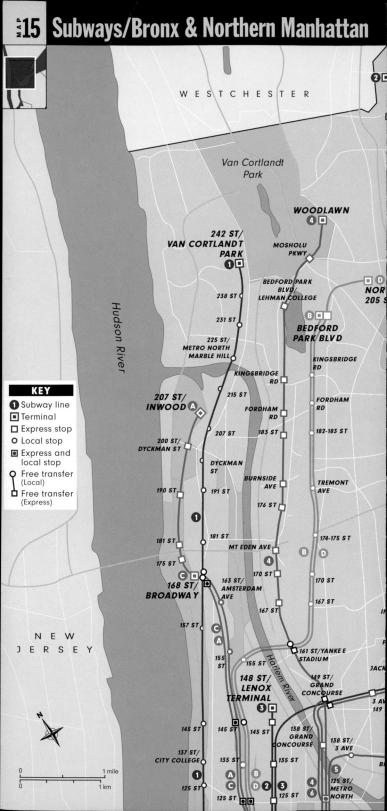

MAP 15 **Subways/Bronx & Northern Manhattan**

WESTCHESTER

Van Cortlandt Park

WOODLAWN
4

242 ST/
VAN CORTLANDT
PARK
1

MOSHOLU
PKWY

2

D
NOR
205 S

BEDFORD PARK
BLVD/
LEHMAN COLLEGE

238 ST

231 ST

B

BEDFORD
PARK BLVD

KINGSBRIDGE
RD

225 ST/
METRO NORTH
MARBLE HILL

Hudson River

KINGSBRIDGE
RD

215 ST

207 ST/
INWOOD **A**

FORDHAM
RD

FORDHAM
RD

182-183 ST

207 ST

183 ST

200 ST/
DYCKMAN ST

DYCKMAN
ST

BURNSIDE
AVE

TREMONT
AVE

190 ST

191 ST

176 ST

1

174-175 S T

181 ST

181 ST

B

D

175 ST

MT EDEN AVE

170 ST

4

170 ST

168 ST/
BROADWAY
C

163 ST/
AMSTERDAM
AVE

167 ST

167 ST

157 ST

C
A

161 ST/YANKE E
STADIUM

I

155
ST

155 ST

JACK

148 ST/
LENOX
TERMINAL

149 ST/
GRAND
CONCOURSE

3 AV
149

145 ST

145 ST

145 ST

138 ST/
GRAND
CONCOURSE

138 ST/
3 AVE

5

3

A
C

B

137 ST/
CITY COLLEGE

135 ST

135 ST

125 ST/
METRO
NORTH

4
6

1

125 ST

125 ST

A
C
E

B
2

3

125 ST

KEY
1 Subway line
⊡ Terminal
☐ Express stop
○ Local stop
⊡ Express and
local stop
○ Free transfer
(Local)
☐ Free transfer
(Express)

NEW
JERSEY

N

0   1 mile
0   1 km

Harlem River

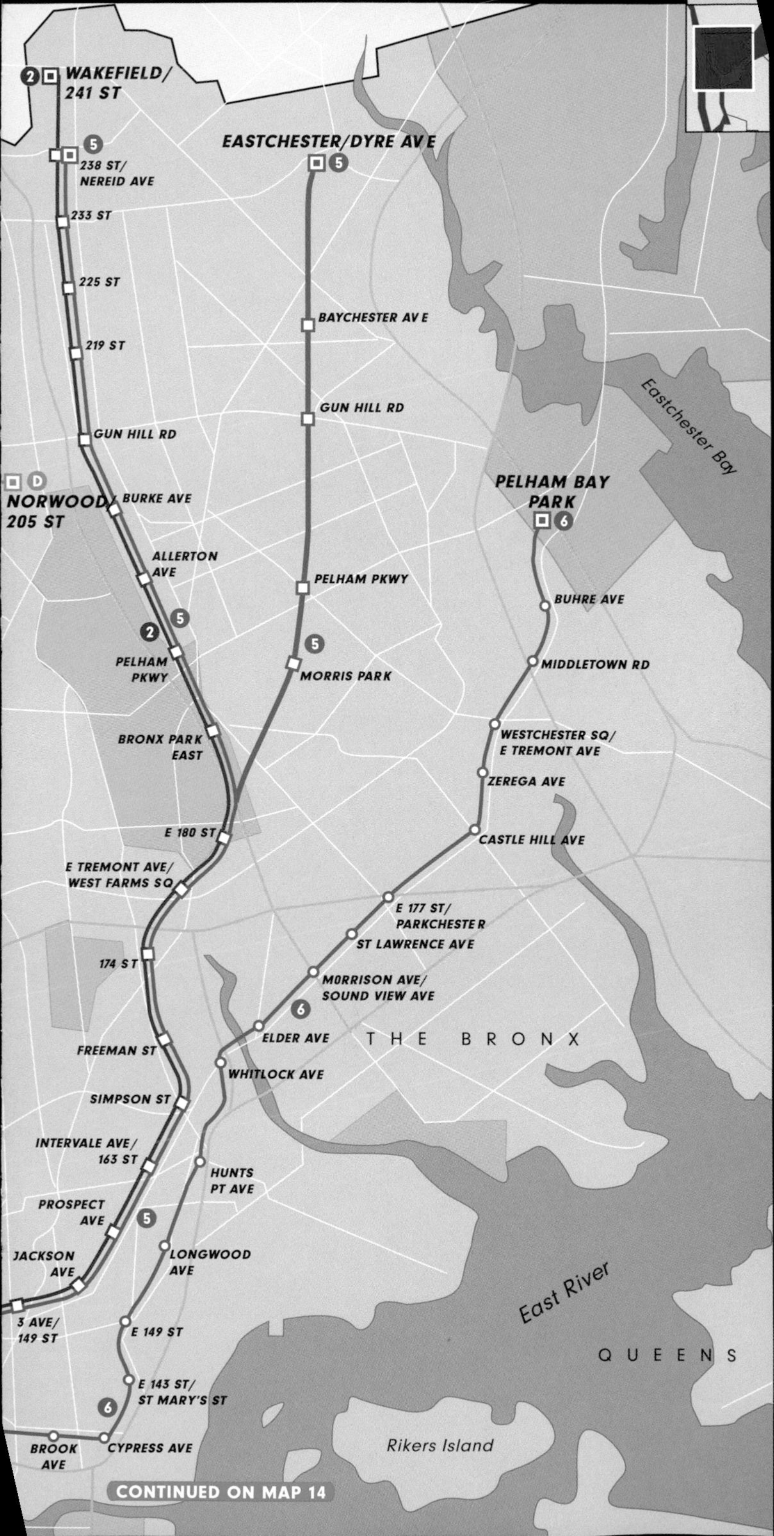

MAP 15

② ■ **WAKEFIELD/
241 ST**

⑤ **238 ST/
NEREID AVE**

233 ST

225 ST

219 ST

EASTCHESTER/DYRE AV E

■ ⑤

GUN HILL RD

⑤ *BAYCHESTER AV E*

⑤ *GUN HILL RD*

■ Ⓓ
**NORWOOD/
205 ST**

BURKE AVE

*ALLERTON
AVE*

② ⑤

**PELHAM
PKWY**

*BRONX PARK
EAST*

PELHAM PKWY

⑤ *MORRIS PARK*

**PELHAM BAY
PARK**

■ ⑥

BUHRE AVE

MIDDLETOWN RD

*WESTCHESTER SQ/
E TREMONT AVE*

ZEREGA AVE

E 180 ST

CASTLE HILL AVE

*E TREMONT AVE/
WEST FARMS SQ*

174 ST

*E 177 ST/
PARKCHESTER
ST LAWRENCE AVE*

*MORRISON AVE/
SOUND VIEW AVE*

⑥

ELDER AVE

T H E   B R O N X

FREEMAN ST

WHITLOCK AVE

SIMPSON ST

*INTERVALE AVE/
163 ST*

*HUNTS
PT AVE*

*PROSPECT
AVE*

⑤

*JACKSON
AVE*

*LONGWOOD
AVE*

East River

*3 AVE/
149 ST*

E 149 ST

Eastchester Bay

Q U E E N S

*E 143 ST/
ST MARY'S ST*

⑥

**BROOK
AVE**

CYPRESS AVE

Rikers Island

CONTINUED ON MAP 14

MAP 16 Subways/Queens & Northeast Brooklyn

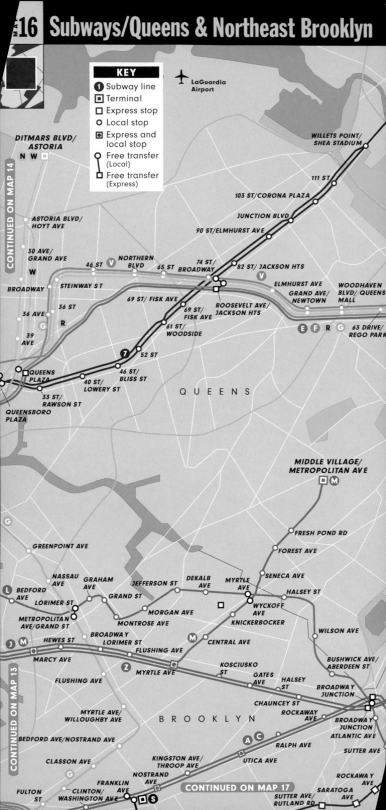

KEY

- **1** Subway line
- **◼** Terminal
- **☐** Express stop
- **○** Local stop
- **◙** Express and local stop
- **○** Free transfer (Local)
- **☐** Free transfer (Express)

LaGuardia Airport

CONTINUED ON MAP 14

DITMARS BLVD/ ASTORIA
N W

WILLETS POINT/ SHEA STADIUM

111 ST

103 ST/CORONA PLAZA

JUNCTION BLVD

90 ST/ELMHURST AVE

ASTORIA BLVD/ HOYT AVE

30 AVE/ GRAND AVE
W

BROADWAY

STEINWAY ST

46 ST

NORTHERN BLVD
V

65 ST

74 ST/ BROADWAY

82 ST/ JACKSON HTS
V

ELMHURST AVE
GRAND AVE/ NEWTOWN

WOODHAVEN BLVD/ QUEENS MALL

E F R G

63 DRIVE/ REGO PARK

36 ST

36 AVE
G R

69 ST/ FISK AVE

69 ST/ FISK AVE

ROOSEVELT AVE/ JACKSON HTS

39 AVE

61 ST/ WOODSIDE

7 52 ST

QUEENS

QUEENS PLAZA

QUEENSBORO PLAZA

40 ST/ LOWERY ST

46 ST/ BLISS ST

33 ST/ RAWSON ST

MIDDLE VILLAGE/ METROPOLITAN AVE
M

G

FRESH POND RD

FOREST AVE

GREENPOINT AVE

NASSAU AVE

GRAHAM AVE

JEFFERSON ST

DEKALB AVE

MYRTLE AVE

SENECA AVE

HALSEY ST

L BEDFORD AVE

LORIMER ST

GRAND ST

MORGAN AVE

WYCKOFF AVE

KNICKERBOCKER

METROPOLITAN AVE/GRAND ST

MONTROSE AVE

CENTRAL AVE

WILSON AVE

J M HEWES ST

BROADWAY LORIMER ST

M

MARCY AVE

FLUSHING AVE

Z MYRTLE AVE

KOSCIUSKO ST

GATES AVE

HALSEY ST

BUSHWICK AVE/ ABERDEEN ST

FLUSHING AVE

MYRTLE AVE/ WILLOUGHBY AVE

CHAUNCEY ST

ROCKAWAY AVE

BROADWAY JUNCTION

BROADWAY JUNCTION ATLANTIC AVE

BEDFORD AVE/NOSTRAND AVE

BROOKLYN

A C

RALPH AVE

SUTTER AVE

CLASSON AVE

KINGSTON AVE/ THROOP AVE

UTICA AVE

ROCKAWAY AVE

G FRANKLIN AVE

NOSTRAND AVE

SARATOGA AVE

FULTON ST

CLINTON/ WASHINGTON AVE

S

SUTTER AVE/ RUTLAND RD

CONTINUED ON MAP 13

CONTINUED ON MAP 17

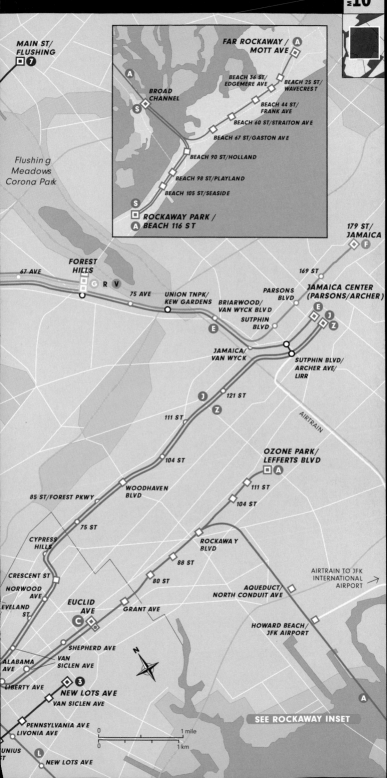

10

MAIN ST/
FLUSHING
7

*Flushing
Meadows
Corona Park*

FAR ROCKAWAY /
MOTT AVE
A

BEACH 36 ST/
EDGEMERE AVE
BEACH 25 ST/
WAVECREST

A
BROAD
CHANNEL

S

BEACH 44 ST/
FRANK AVE
BEACH 60 ST/STRAITON AVE
BEACH 67 ST/GASTON AVE

BEACH 90 ST/HOLLAND

BEACH 98 ST/PLAYLAND

BEACH 105 ST/SEASIDE

S
A
ROCKAWAY PARK /
BEACH 116 ST

179 ST/
JAMAICA
F

67 AVE

FOREST
HILLS
G R V

75 AVE

169 ST

UNION TNPK/
KEW GARDENS

BRIARWOOD/
VAN WYCK BLVD

SUTPHIN
BLVD

E

PARSONS
BLVD

JAMAICA CENTER
(PARSONS/ARCHER)

E J
Z

JAMAICA/
VAN WYCK

SUTPHIN BLVD/
ARCHER AVE/
LIRR

J

121 ST

Z

111 ST

AIRTRAIN

104 ST

OZONE PARK/
LEFFERTS BLVD
A

85 ST/FOREST PKWY

WOODHAVEN
BLVD

111 ST

104 ST

75 ST

CYPRESS
HILLS

ROCKAWAY
BLVD

88 ST

CRESCENT ST

NORWOOD
AVE

80 ST

AQUEDUCT/
NORTH CONDUIT AVE

AIRTRAIN TO JFK
INTERNATIONAL
AIRPORT →

EVELAND
ST

EUCLID
AVE
C

GRANT AVE

HOWARD BEACH/
JFK AIRPORT

SHEPHERD AVE

VAN
SICLEN AVE

ALABAMA
AVE

LIBERTY AVE

NEW LOTS AVE
3
VAN SICLEN AVE

PENNSYLVANIA AVE
LIVONIA AVE

A

UNIUS
ST

L

SEE ROCKAWAY INSET

NEW LOTS AVE

0   1 mile
0   1 km

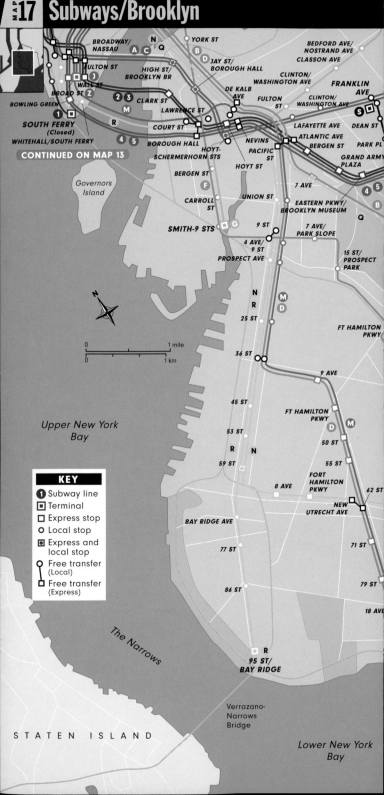

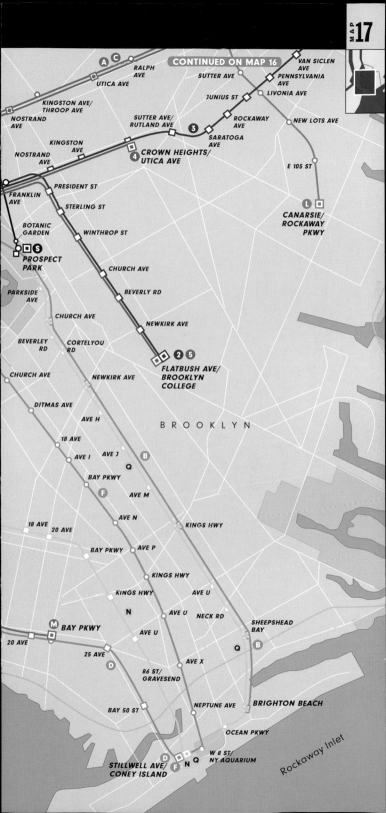

MAP 17

CONTINUED ON MAP 16

VAN SICLEN
AVE

Ⓐ Ⓒ
RALPH
AVE
SUTTER AVE
PENNSYLVANIA
AVE
UTICA AVE
JUNIUS ST
LIVONIA AVE
KINGSTON AVE/
THROOP AVE
ROCKAWAY
AVE
NEW LOTS AVE
NOSTRAND
AVE
SUTTER AVE/
RUTLAND AVE
⓷
SARATOGA
AVE
KINGSTON
AVE
E 105 ST
NOSTRAND
AVE
⓸
CROWN HEIGHTS/
UTICA AVE

FRANKLIN
AVE
PRESIDENT ST
Ⓛ
CANARSIE/
ROCKAWAY
PKWY
STERLING ST
BOTANIC
GARDEN
WINTHROP ST
◧Ⓢ
PROSPECT
PARK
CHURCH AVE
PARKSIDE
AVE
BEVERLY RD
CHURCH AVE
NEWKIRK AVE
BEVERLEY
RD
CORTELYOU
RD
⓶ Ⓢ
FLATBUSH AVE/
BROOKLYN
COLLEGE
CHURCH AVE
NEWKIRK AVE

DITMAS AVE
B R O O K L Y N
AVE H
18 AVE
AVE I
AVE J
Ⓑ
Ⓠ
BAY PKWY
AVE M
Ⓕ
18 AVE 20 AVE
AVE N
KINGS HWY
BAY PKWY
AVE P
KINGS HWY
KINGS HWY
AVE U
KINGS HWY
Ⓝ
AVE U
NECK RD
SHEEPSHEAD
BAY
Ⓜ BAY PKWY
AVE U
Ⓠ
Ⓑ
20 AVE
25 AVE
AVE X
Ⓓ
86 ST/
GRAVESEND
NEPTUNE AVE
BRIGHTON BEACH
BAY 50 ST
OCEAN PKWY
Ⓓ Ⓝ Ⓠ
W 8 ST/
NY AQUARIUM
Ⓕ
STILLWELL AVE/
CONEY ISLAND
Rockaway Inlet

MAP 18 **Entrances, Exits & Bike Paths**

MARBLE HILL

Henry Hudson Br.

INWOOD

Grand Concourse

Bronx River

Bronx Park

1

Tenth Ave.

Broadway

207th St.

University Hts. Br.

9A

Dyckman St./ Riverside Dr. S./ The Cloisters

Dyckman St.

Ft. Tryon Pk./ The Cloisters

Dyckman St.

Harlem River Dr.

St. Nicholas Ave.

Amsterdam Ave.

Tremont Ave.

1

95

Cross Bronx Expwy.

FORT WASHINGTON

Broadway

Washington Br.

181st St.

Hamilton Br.

THE BRONX

Third Ave.

Boston Rd.

W. 179th St./ George Washington Bridge/Riverside Dr./ Cross Bronx Expwy.

W. 165th St.

St. Nicholas Ave.

Broadway

87

Grand

Melrose Ave.

E. 161st St.

Frederick Douglass Blvd.

Macombs Dam Br.

KEY

↳ Northbound Access

↱ Southbound Access

Class 1 Bike Path

Class 2 Bike Path

W. 158th St./ Riverside Drive

W. 155th St.

Edgecombe Ave.

Harlem River Dr.

Concourse

Eugenio Maria de Hostos Blvd.

145th. St. Br.

Willis Ave.

Third Ave.

Hudson River

MANHATTANVILLE

Henry Hudson Pkwy.

Riverside Dr.

Frederick Douglass Blvd.

Adam Clayton Powell Jr. Blvd.

Lenox Ave. / Malcolm X Blvd.

Harlem River

Major Deegan

0   1500 feet
0   500 meters

W. 145th St.

W. 138th St.

Madison Ave. Br.

E. 138th St.

W. 135th St.

W. 135th St.

E. 135th St.

E. 132nd St.

Expwy

87

W. 125th St.

W. 125th St.

3rd Ave. Br.

278

Willis Ave. Br.

Riverside Park

9A

Amsterdam Ave.

Broadway

Manhattan Ave.

Nicholas Ave.

HARLEM

E. 125th St.

Lexington Ave.

SPANISH HARLEM

E. 125th St./ Triborough Br./ Randall's Is.

Randalls Island Park

NEW JERSEY

Riverside Dr.

Cathedral Pkwy.

W. 106th St.

Columbus Ave.

Amsterdam Ave.

Central Park

Harlem Meer

E. 110th St.

E. 106th St.

Fifth Ave.

Madison Ave.

Park Ave.

Third Ave.

Second Ave.

FDR Dr.

E. 116th St.

Wards Island Park

278

W. 96th St.

W. 96th St.

UPPER WEST SIDE

The Reservoir

E. 96th St.

UPPER EAST SIDE

York Ave.

E. 96th St.

QUEENS

East River

Entrances, Exits & Bike Paths

MAP 18

E. 92nd St.

E. 86th St.

Jacqueline Kennedy Onassis Reservoir

Central Park

W. 86th St.

West End Ave.

Amsterdam Ave.

Riverside

The Lake

E. 79th St.

Roosevelt Island

LONG ISLAND CITY

W. 79th St. Boat Basin

Broadway

Columbus Ave.

UPPER WEST SIDE

E. 73rd St.

E. 72nd St.

E. 71st St.

York Ave.

Second Ave.

Lexington Ave.

Third Ave.

Park Ave.

Madison Ave.

Fifth Ave.

UPPER EAST SIDE

East River

FDR Dr.

Vernon Blvd.

W. 72nd St.

9A

Tenth Ave.

The Pond

Central Park S.

E. 65th St.

E. 63rd St.

E. 62nd St.

E. 61st St.

Queensboro Bridge

QUEENS

E. 59th St.

E. 57th St.

W. 57th St.

Ninth Ave.

W. 56th St.

W. 54th St.

W. 52nd St.

W. 50th St.

W. 50th St.

MIDTOWN

TURTLE BAY

E. 53rd St.

E. 48th St.

E. 47th St.

W. 51st St.

W. 49th St.

W. 47th St.

W. 45th St.

W. 48th St.

W. 46th St.

THEATRE DISTRICT

W. 43rd St.

W. 44th St.

W. 42nd St.

E. 42nd St.

E. 42nd St.

495

W. 41st St.

W. 39 St./Javits Center

MURRAY HILL

Queens-Midtown Tunnel

GREENPOINT

Lincoln Tunnel

11th

Eleventh Ave.

E. 37th St.

E. 34th St.

W. 34th St.

Ninth Ave.

Tenth Ave.

W. 30th St.

Seventh Ave.

Fifth Ave.

Madison Ave.

Park Ave. S.

Lexington Ave.

Third Ave.

Second Ave.

First Ave.

E. 25th St.

W. 29th St.

W. 24th St.

W. 26th St.

W. 23rd St.

E. 23rd St.

CHELSEA

GRAMERCY

E. 20th St.

East River

FDR Dr.

W. 18th St.

W. 16th St.

W. 15th St.

W. 14th St.

E. 14th St.

Ave. C

Ave. D

Ave. B

Hudson River Pak

Horatio St.

WEST VILLAGE

GREENWICH VILLAGE

EAST VILLAGE

E. Houston St.

W. 12th St.

Hudson River

W. 11th St.

NOHO

Christopher St.

West Side Hwy.

Varick St.

Clarkson St.

W. Houston St.

Broadway

Bowery

LOWER EAST SIDE

Williamsburg Bridge

NEW JERSEY

SOHO

LITTLE ITALY

Delancey St.

DOWNTOWN

Grand St.

Cherry St.

HOBOKEN

Holland Tunnel

Vestry St.

Laight St.

N. Moore St.

Canal St.

TRIBECA

Canal St.

CHINATOWN

Montgomery St.

Manhattan Bridge

Flatbush Ave.

JERSEY CITY

Chambers St.

Civic Center

278

Brooklyn Bridge

BROOKLYN

World Trade Center Site

FINANCIAL DISTRICT

SOUTH STREET SEAPORT

Brooklyn Bridge

BROOKLYN HEIGHTS

Brooklyn-Queens Expwy.

BATTERY PARK CITY

Whitehall

State St.

Battery Park

N

Brooklyn-Battery Tunnel

KEY

Northbound Access

Southbound Access

Class 1 Bike Path

Class 2 Bike Path

1500 feet

500 meters

MAP 19 | **Buses/Manhattan below 14th Street**

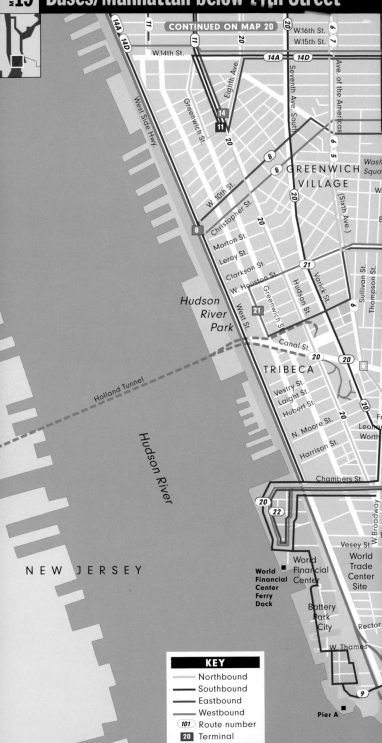

CONTINUED ON MAP 20

W.16th St.
W.15th St.

W.14th St.

GREENWICH
VILLAGE

Wash
Squar

W.

W. 10th St.

Christopher St.

Morton St.

Leroy St.

Clarkson St.

W. Houston St.

Hudson
River
Park

Canal St.

TRIBECA

Vestry St.
Laight St.
Hubert St.

N. Moore St.

Harrison St.

Chambers St.

Hudson River

Holland Tunnel

NEW JERSEY

World
Financial
Center
Ferry
Dock

World
Financial
Center

World
Trade
Center
Site

Battery
Park
City

Rector

W. Thames

Pier A

West Side Hwy.

Greenwich St.

Eighth Ave.

Seventh Ave. South

Ave. of the Americas

Hudson St.

Varick St.

Greenwich St.

West St.

Sullivan St.

Thompson St.

Vesey St.

W. Broadway

Fr
Leona
Worth

Leon
Wort

(Sixth Ave.)

B

KEY

━━━ Northbound
━━━ Southbound
━━━ Eastbound
━━━ Westbound
(101) Route number
[20] Terminal

MAP 20 **Buses/Manhattan 14th St–72nd St**

CONTINUED ON MAP 21

Central Park

Central Park S.

Lincoln Tunnel

CHELSEA

Hudson River

CONTINUED ON MAP 19

W. 72nd St.
W. 70th St.
W. 68th St.
W. 66th St.
W. 65th St.
W. 60th St.
W. 58th St.
W. 57th St.
W. 55th St.
W. 53rd St.
W. 50th St.
W. 49th St.
W. 47th St.
W. 44th St.
W. 42nd St
W. 38th St.
W. 36th St.
W. 34th St.
W. 32nd St.
W. 30th St.
W. 28th St.
W. 25th St.
W. 23rd St.
W. 21st St.
W. 18th St.
W. 15th St.
W. 14th St.

Amsterdam Ave.
West End Ave.
Tenth Ave.
Ninth Ave.
Eighth Ave.
Seventh Ave.
Broadway
(Sixth Ave.)
Ave. of the Americas
Eleventh Ave.
Henry Hudson Pkwy.
West Side Hwy.
Hudson River

9A
495
23
X26
14
14A
14D
Q32

0   1500 feet
0   500 meters

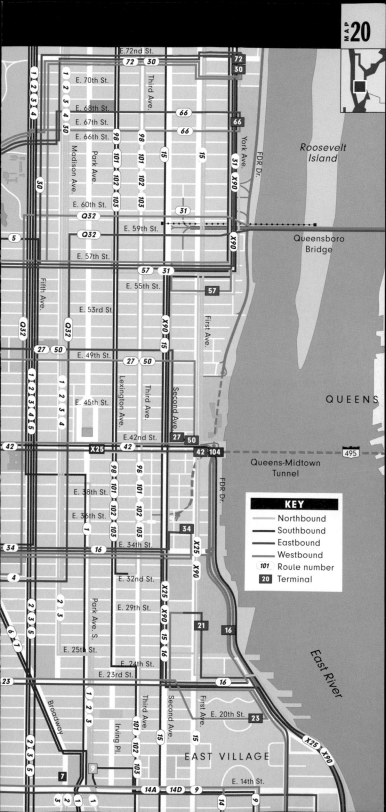

MAP **20**

E. 72nd St.
72 **30**
E. 70th St.
E. 68th St.
E. 67th St.
E. 66th St.
E. 60th St.
E. 59th St.
E. 57th St.
E. 55th St.
E. 53rd St.
E. 49th St.
E. 45th St.
E. 42nd St.
E. 38th St.
E. 36th St.
E. 34th St.
E. 32nd St.
E. 29th St.
E. 25th St.
E. 24th St.
E. 23rd St.
E. 20th St.
E. 14th St.

Third Ave.
Madison Ave.
Park Ave.
Fifth Ave.
York Ave.
FDR Dr.
First Ave.
Lexington Ave.
Second Ave.
Park Ave. S.
Broadway
Irving Pl.

Roosevelt Island

Queensboro Bridge

QUEENS

Queens-Midtown Tunnel

495

FDR Dr.

East River

EAST VILLAGE

72 **30** **66** **31** **X90** **Q32** **57** **31** **X90** **15** **27** **50** **X25** **42** **104** **34** **X25** **X90** **21** **16** **23** **X25** **X90** **9** **14A** **14D** **7**

Route numbers: 1 2 3 4 30 98 101 102 103 15 5 Q32 27 50 96 16 23 14A 14D 9 7 14 6 2 3 5 1 4

KEY

— Northbound
— Southbound
— Eastbound
— Westbound
101 Route number
20 Terminal

MAP **21** **Buses/Manhattan 72nd St–125th St**

HARLEM

CONTINUED ON MAP 22

UPPER
WEST
SIDE

Riverside Park

Hudson River

Central Park

Jacqueline Kennedy Onassis Reservoir

Central Park

CONTINUED ON MAP 20

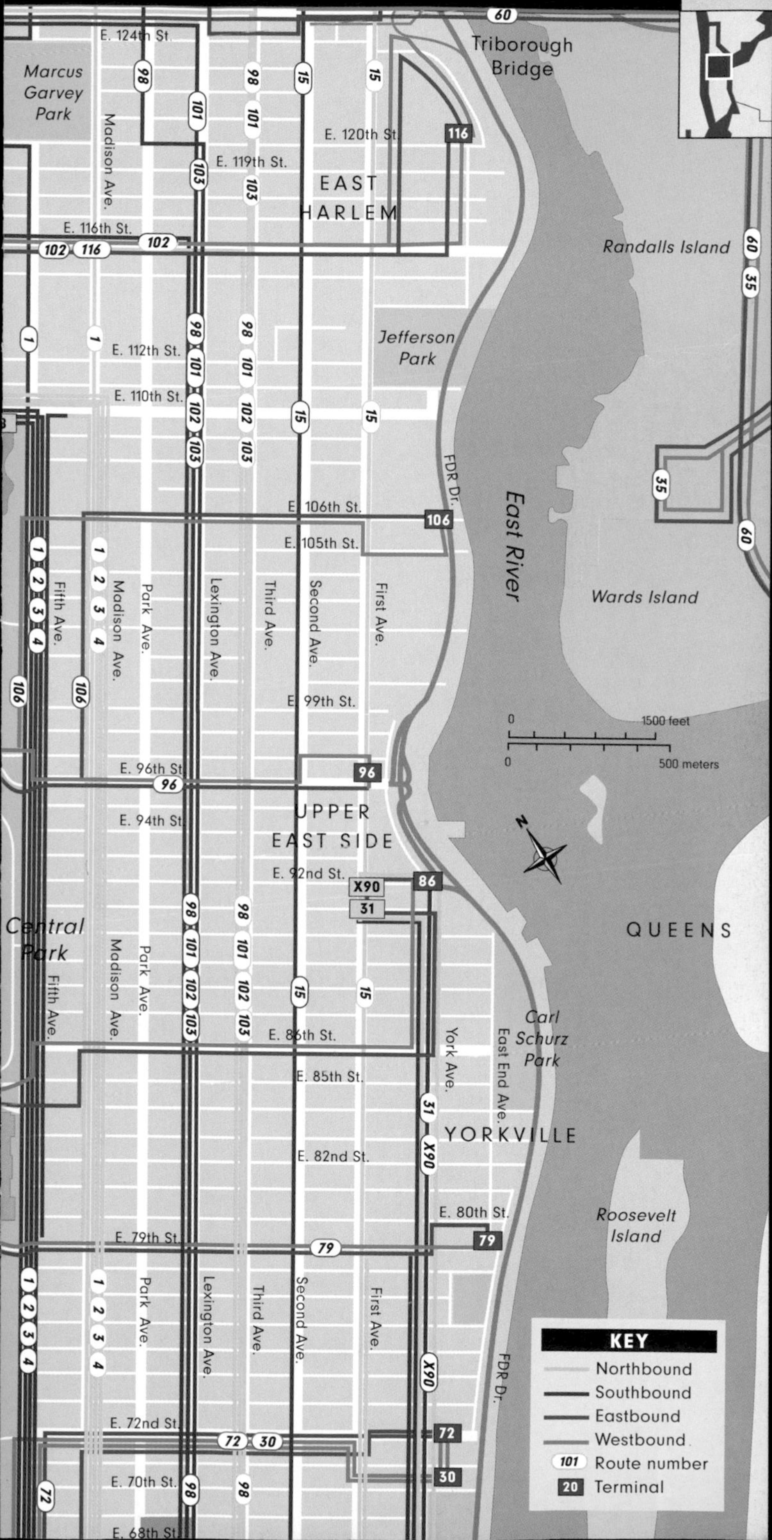

MAP 21

E. 124th St.

Marcus Garvey Park

Madison Ave.

98
98
15
15

Triborough Bridge

E. 120th St.
116

E. 119th St.

101
103

EAST HARLEM

Randalls Island

60
35

E. 116th St.
102 116
102

Jefferson Park

98 101 102 103

E. 112th St.

1
1

98 101 102 103

E. 110th St.

15
15

East River

FDR Dr.

E. 106th St.
106

E. 105th St.

Wards Island

Fifth Ave.
Madison Ave.
Park Ave.
Lexington Ave.
Third Ave.
Second Ave.
First Ave.

1 2 3
1 2 3 4

E. 99th St.

106
106

0   1500 feet
0   500 meters

E. 96th St.
96
96

UPPER EAST SIDE

E. 94th St.

N

E. 92nd St.
X90   86
31

Central Park

98 101 102 103
98 101 102 103
15
15

QUEENS

Fifth Ave.
Madison Ave.
Park Ave.

E. 86th St.

E. 85th St.

Carl Schurz Park

York Ave.
East End Ave.

E. 82nd St.

31
X90

YORKVILLE

E. 80th St.
79

Roosevelt Island

E. 79th St.
79

Fifth Ave.
Park Ave.
Lexington Ave.
Third Ave.
Second Ave.
First Ave.

1 2 3
1 2 3 4

X90

FDR Dr.

E. 72nd St.
72 30
72

E. 70th St.
30

72

E. 68th St.

98
98

KEY

Northbound
Southbound
Eastbound
Westbound
101   Route number
20   Terminal

MAP 22 — Buses/Manhattan above 125th Street

CONTINUED ON MAP 23

Top Sights

MAP 23

MAP 24 **Architecture**

Listed Alphabetically

MAP 25 Churches, Temples & Mosques

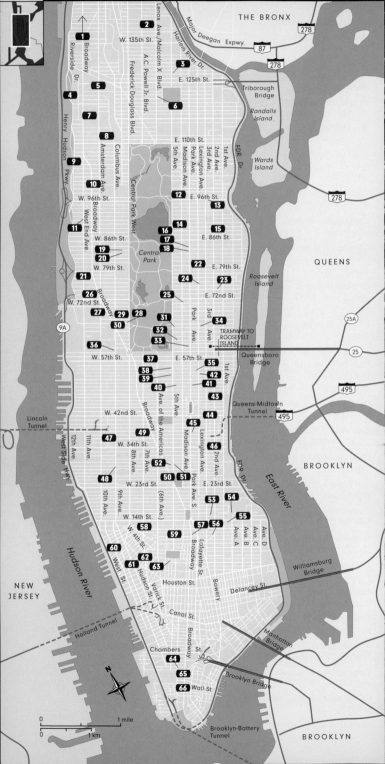

Listed by Site Number

1 Church of the Intercessions
2 Abyssinian Baptist
3 St Andrew's
4 Riverside
5 James Chapel
6 St Martin's Episcopal
7 St Paul's Chapel
8 Cathedral of St John the Divine
9 NY Buddhist Temple
10 St Michael's
11 Church of the Annunciation
12 St Nicholas Russian Orthodox
13 Islamic Center of NY
14 Church of the Heavenly Rest
15 Church of the Holy Trinity
16 Park Ave Synagogue
17 Park Ave Christian
18 St Ignatius Loyola
19 St Matthew & St Timothy
20 Congregation Rodeph Sholom
21 West End Collegiate
22 All Souls Unitarian
23 Holy Trinity Cathedral
24 St Jean Baptiste Church
25 St James
26 Rutgers Presbyterian
27 West End Synagogue
28 Holy Trinity
29 Stephen Wise Free Synagogue
30 Church of Latter Day Saints
31 Temple Emanu-El
32 Fifth Ave Synagogue
33 Christ Church
34 St Vincent Ferrer
35 Central Synagogue
36 St Paul the Apostle
37 Calvary Baptist
38 Fifth Ave Presbyterian
39 St Thomas
40 St Patrick's Cathedral
41 St Bartholomew's
42 St Peter's
43 Holy Family
44 Church of the Covenant
45 Church of Our Saviour
46 St Vartan Armenian
47 Metropolitan Community
48 Holy Apostles
49 Church of the Holy Innocents
50 Cathedral of St Sava
51 Church of the Transfiguration
52 Marble Collegiate
53 Fifteenth Street Meeting
54 Calvary/St George's
55 Immaculate Conception
56 St Mark's in the Bowery
57 Grace Church
58 Metropolitan-Duane
59 Church of the Ascension
60 Congregation Beth Simchat Torah
61 St-Luke-in-the-Fields
62 St John's Lutheran
63 Judson Memorial
64 St Peter's
65 St Paul Chapel
66 Trinity

Listed Alphabetically

Abyssinian Baptist, 2. 132 W 138th St ☏ 862-7474

All Souls Unitarian, 22. 1157 Lexington Ave ☏ 535-5530

Calvary Baptist, 37. 123 W 57th St ☏ 975-0170

Calvary/St George's, 54. 209 E 16th St ☏ 646/723-4184. Episcopal

Cathedral of St John the Divine, 8. Amsterdam Ave & 112th St ☏ 316-7540. Episcopal

Cathedral of St Sava, 50. 16-20 W 25th St ☏ 242-9440. Serbian Orthodox

Central Synagogue, 35. 123 E 55th St ☏ 838-5123. Reform Jewish

Christ Church, 33. 520 Park Ave ☏ 838-3036. Methodist

Church of the Annunciation, 11. 302 W 91st St ☏ 724-2070. Greek Orthodox

Church of the Ascension, 59. 12 W 11th St ☏ 254-8620. Episcopal

Church of the Covenant, 44. 310 E 42nd St ☏ 697-3185. Presbyterian

Church of the Heavenly Rest, 14. 2 E 90th St ☏ 289-3400. Episcopal

Church of the Holy Innocents, 49. 128 W 37th St ☏ 279-5861. Roman Catholic

Church of the Holy Trinity, 15. 316 E 88th St ☏ 289-4100. Episcopal

Church of the Intercessions, 1. B'way & 155th St ☏ 283-6200. Episcopal

Church of Jesus Christ of Latter Day Saints, 30. 125 Columbus Ave ☏ 917/441-8220. Mormon

Church of Our Saviour, 45. 59 Park Ave ☏ 679-8166. Roman Catholic

MAP **25**

Churches, Temples & Mosques

Listed Alphabetically (cont.)

Church of the Transfiguration (Little Church Around the Corner), 51. 1 E 29th St ☎ 684-6770. Episcopal

Congregation Beth Simchat Torah, 60. 57 Bethune St ☎ 929-9498. Gay & Lesbian Synagogue

Congregation Rodeph Sholom, 20. 7 W 83rd St ☎ 362-8800. Reform Jewish

Fifteenth Street Meeting, 53. 15 Rutherford Pl ☎ 475-0466. Quaker

Fifth Ave Presbyterian, 38. Fifth Ave & 55th St ☎ 247-0490

Fifth Ave Synagogue, 32. 5 E 62nd St ☎ 838-2122. Orthodox Jewish

Grace Church, 57. 802 Broadway ☎ 254-2000. Episcopal

Holy Apostles, 48. 296 Ninth Ave ☎ 807-6799. Episcopal

Holy Family, 43. 315 E 47th St ☎ 753-3401. Roman Catholic

Holy Trinity, 28. Central Park W & 65th St ☎ 877-6815. Lutheran

Holy Trinity Cathedral, 23. 319 E 74th St ☎ 288-3215. Greek Orthodox

Immaculate Conception, 55. 414 E 14th St ☎ 254-0200. Roman Catholic

Islamic Center of NY, 13. 1711 Third Ave ☎ 722-5234. Muslim

James Chapel, 5. Union Theological Seminary 3041 Broadway ☎ 662-7100. Inter-Denominational

Judson Memorial, 63. 55 Washington Sq S. ☎ 477-0351. Baptist

Marble Collegiate, 49. Fifth Ave & 29th St ☎ 686-2770. Reformed

Metropolitan Community, 47. 446 W 36th St ☎ 629-7440. Inter-denominational/Gay & Lesbian

Metropolitan-Duane United Methodist, 58. 201 W 13th St ☎ 243-5470.

NY Buddhist Temple, 9. 332 Riverside Dr ☎ 678-0305

Park Ave Christian, 17. 1010 Park Ave ☎ 288-3246. Disciples of Christ

Park Ave Synagogue, 16. 50 E 87th St ☎ 369-2600. Conservative Jewish

Riverside, 4. Riverside Dr & 120th ☎ 870-6700. Inter-Denominational

Rutgers Presbyterian, 26. 236 W 73rd St ☎ 877-8227.

St Andrew's, 3. Fifth Ave & 127th St ☎ 534-0896. Episcopal

St Bartholomew's, 41. 109 E 50th St ☎ 378-0200. Episcopal

St Ignatius Loyola, 18. 980 Park Ave ☎ 288-3588. Roman Catholic

St James, 25. 865 Madison Ave ☎ 288-4100. Episcopal

St Jean Baptiste Church, 24. 76th St & Lexington Ave ☎ 288-5082. Roman Catholic

St John's Lutheran, 62. 81 Christopher St ☎ 242-5737

St Luke-in-the-Fields, 61. 487 Hudson St ☎ 924-0562. Episcopal

St Mark's-in-the-Bowery, 56. Second Ave & 11th St ☎ 674-6377. Episcopal

St Martin's Episcopal, 6. 230 Lenox Ave ☎ 534-4531

St Matthew & St Timothy, 19. 26 W 84th St ☎ 362-6750. Episcopal

St Michael's, 10. 225 W 99th St ☎ 222-2700. Episcopal

St Nicholas Russian Orthodox, 12. 15 E 97th St ☎ 996-6638.

St Patrick's Cathedral, 40. Fifth Ave & 50th St ☎ 753-2261. Roman Cath

St Paul the Apostle, 36. 59th St & Ninth Ave ☎ 265-3495. Roman Catholic

St Paul Chapel, 65. Broadway & Fulton St ☎ 602-0874. Episcopal

St Paul's Chapel, 7. Columbia Univ, Broadway & 117th St ☎ 854-1487. Inter-Denominational

St Peter's, 64. 22 Barclay St ☎ 233-8355. Roman Catholic

St Peter's, 42. 619 Lexington Ave ☎ 935-2200. Lutheran

St Thomas, 39. 1 W 53rd St ☎ 757-7013. Episcopal

St Vartan Armenian Cathedral, 46. 630 Second Ave ☎ 686-0710. Armenian Orthodox

St Vincent Ferrer, 34. Lexington Ave & 66th St ☎ 744-2080. Roman Catholic

Stephen Wise Free Synagogue, 29. 30 W 68th St ☎ 877-4050. Reform Jewish

Temple Emanu-El, 31. 1 E 65th St ☎ 744-1400. Reform Jewish

Trinity, 66. Broadway & Wall St ☎ 602-0800. Episcopal

West End Collegiate, 21. 368 West End Ave ☎ 787-1566. Reformed

West End Synagogue, 27. 190 Amsterdam Ave ☎ 579-0777. Reconstructionist Jewish

W. 101st St.   E. 101st St.
W. 100th St.   E. 100th St.
W. 99th St.   E. 99th St.
W. 98th St.   E. 98th St.
W. 97th St.   E. 97th St.
Transverse
W. 96th St.   E. 96th St.
W. 95th St.   B,C   E. 95th St.
                      E. 94th St.
                      E. 93rd St.
                      E. 92nd St.
                      E. 91st St.
                      E. 90th St.
The Reservoir   E. 89th St.
                      E. 88th St.
W. 87th St.   E. 87th St.   4,5,6
W. 86th St. B,C Transverse   E. 86th St.
W. 85th St.
                      E. 84th St.
W. 83rd St.   E. 83rd St.
W. 82nd St. Great Lawn E. 82nd St.
W. 81st St.   E. 81st St.
             B,C Belvedere Lake E. 80th St.
                      E. 79th St.
W. 77th St. Transverse E. 78th St.
                      E. 77th St.
W. 75th St. Central Park E. 76th St. Lenox Hill Hospital
                      E. 75th St.
W. 73rd St. The Lake   E. 74th St.
W. 72nd St. B,C   E. 73rd St.
W. 71st St.   E. 72nd St.
                      E. 71st St.
W. 69th St.   E. 70th St.
                      E. 69th St. Hunter College
Sheep Meadow The Mall E. 68th St.
W. 67th St.   E. 67th St.
W. 66th St.   E. 66th St.
Transverse   E. 65th St.
Central Park Wildlife Conservation Center
W. 62nd St. Wollman Rink   E. 63rd St. F
A,B,C,D,19   E. 62nd St.
             The Pond   E. 61st St.
Central Park South Grand Army E. 60th St. 4,5,6, N,R,W
Columbus Circle   Plaza N,R,W   E. 59th St.
             W. 58th St. N,R,Q,W   E. 58th St.
W. 57th St. N,R,Q,W   E. 57th St.
Carnegie Hall F (6th Ave.) E. 56th St.
W. 55th St.   E. 55th St.
             B,D,E   E. 54th St. E,V
W. 53rd St.   E. 53rd St.
W. 52nd St. St. Patrick's Cathedral E. 52nd St. E,V
             C,E   B,D,F,V   E. 51st St. 6
W. 49th St. Rockefeller Center E. 50th St.
             N,R   W. 48th St.
W. 47th St.   E. 47th St.
Duffy Sq.   W. 46th St. Grand Central Terminal
8th Ave.   W. 45th St.
W. 45th St.   E. 45th St.
Times Sq.   W. 44th St.
W. 43rd St. B,D,F,V   Ave. E. 43rd St. 4,5, 6,7
A,C,E   W. 42nd St. S
W. 41st St. 12,3   N,Q,R,S,W Bryant Park
Port Authority Bus Terminal of the Americas
W. 39th St. W. 40th St. E. 40th St.
             E. 39th St.
0   1500 feet
0   500 meters   E. 37th St.
             B,D,F,N Empire State E. 36th St.
             Q,R,V,W Building
A,C,E W. 34th St. 12,3 E. 34th St. 6
             E. 33rd St.

MAP 26 **Museums/Elsewhere in Manhattan**

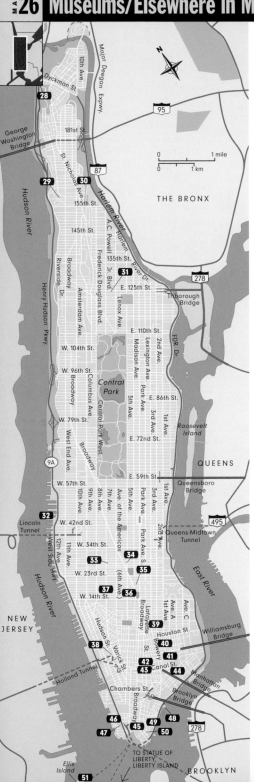

MAP 26

Listed Alphabetically

American Folk Art Museum, 20.
45 W 53rd St ☎ 265-1040

American Folk Art Museum, Feld Gallery, 18. 2 Lincoln Sq ☎ 595-9533

American Mus of Natural History/ Rose Ctr for Earth & Space, 11.
Central Park W & 79th St ☎ 769-5100

The Americas Society, 16.
680 Park Ave ☎ 249-8950

Asia Society, 15.
725 Park Ave ☎ 288-6400

Bard Graduate Center for Decorative Arts and Design, 8.
18 W 86th St ☎ 501-3000

Children's Museum of Manhattan, 9.
212 W 83rd St ☎ 721-1234

Children's Museum of the Arts, 42.
182 Lafayette St ☎ 274-0986

China Institute Gallery, 17.
125 E 65th St ☎ 744-8181

The Cloisters, 28. Fort Tryon Park
☎ 923-3700

Cooper-Hewitt National Design, 4.
2 E 91st St ☎ 849-8400

Ellis Island Immigration, 51.
Ellis Island ☎ 363-3200

Fraunces Tavern, 50.
54 Pearl St ☎ 425-1778

Frick Collection, 14. 1 E 70th St
☎ 288-0700

Guggenheim, 6. 1071 Fifth Ave
☎ 423-3500

Hispanic Society of America, 29.
Broadway & W 155th St ☎ 926-2234

International Ctr of Photography, 25.
1133 Sixth Ave ☎ 857-0000

Intrepid Sea, Air, Space, 32. Pier 86, Twelfth Ave & W 46th St ☎ 245-0072

Japan Society, 24. 333 E 47th St
☎ 832-1155

Jewish Museum, 3. 1109 Fifth Ave
☎ 423-3200

Lower East Side Tenement Museum, 41. 108 Orchard St ☎ 982-8420

Merchant's House, 39.
29 E 4th St ☎ 777-1089

Metropolitan Museum of Art, 10.
1000 Fifth Ave ☎ 535-7710

Morris-Jumel Mansion, 30.
65 Jumel Ter ☎ 923-8008

Mount Vernon Hotel, 19. 421 E 61st St
☎ 838-6878

El Museo del Barrio, 1. 1230 Fifth Ave ☎ 831-7272

Museum at Eldridge St, 44.
12 Eldridge St ☎ 219-0888

Museum at FIT, 33.
27th St & Seventh Ave ☎ 217-4558

Museum of the American Indian, 45.
1 Bowling Green ☎ 514-3700

Museum of Art & Design, 22.
40 W 53rd St ☎ 956-3535

Museum of Chinese in the Americas, 43. 211-215 Centre St ☎ 619-4785

Museum of the City of NY, 2.
1220 Fifth Ave ☎ 534-1672

Museum of Jewish Heritage, 46.
36 Battery Place ☎ 646/437-4200

Museum of Modern Art (MoMA), 21.
11 W 53rd St ☎ 708-9400

Museum of Sex, 34.
233 Fifth Ave ☎ 689-6337

Museum of Television & Radio, 23.
25 W 52nd St ☎ 621-6800

National Academy of Design, 5.
1083 Fifth Ave ☎ 369-4880

Neue Galerie, 7. 1048 Fifth Ave
☎ 628-6200

New Museum, 44. 235 Bowery
☎ 219-1222

NYC Fire Museum, 38. 278 Spring St
☎ 691-1303

NY Historical Society, 12.
170 Central Park W ☎ 873-3400

NY Public Library, 26.
Fifth Ave & 42nd St ☎ 930-0830

Police Museum, 49. 100 Old Slip
☎ 480-3100

Rubin Museum of Art, 37.
150 W 17th St ☎ 620-5000

Skyscraper Museum, 47.
39 Battery Pl ☎ 968-1961

South Street Seaport, 43.
Fulton & South Sts ☎ 748-8600

Studio Museum in Harlem, 31.
144 W 125th St ☎ 864-4500

Theodore Roosevelt Birthplace, 35.
28 E 20th St ☎ 260-1616

Whitney Museum at Altria, 27.
120 Park Ave ☎ 917/663-2453

Whitney Museum of American Art, 13.
945 Madison Ave ☎ 570-3676

Yeshiva University Museum, 36.
15 W 16th St ☎ 294-8330

MAP 27 Art Galleries/Uptown

Metropolitan Museum of Art

Turtle Pond

Transverse

Central Park

The Lake

The Mall

Transverse

Central Park Wildlife Conservation Center

The Pond

Grand Army Plaza

Central Park South

Carnegie Hall

Trump Tower

Fifth Ave.

Madison Ave.

Park Ave.

Lexington Ave.

Seventh Ave.

Sixth Ave.

Park Ave.

1

E. 82nd St.
2

3
E. 81st St.

E. 80th St.

8
6   E. 79th St.
4   13 12
5   7
10
9   11   E. 78th St.

14   E. 77th St.   M 6

15
18 16   E. 76th St.
17

19   E. 75th St.

E. 74th St.
20
21   Madison Ave.   Park Ave.   Lexington Ave.
22

E. 72nd St.

25   E. 70th St.
26

24

27 28   Hunter College

M 6

29   E. 67th St.

30   E. 66th St.

E. 65th St.   32

31   E. 64th St.
33

M F
E. 63rd St.

E. 62nd St.

E. 61st St.

E. 60th St.

4,5,6, N,R,W
M N,R,W   E. 59th St.   M

38
E. 58th St.

42 41
M N,R,Q,W   F   39   36
44 45   43
46 47 48   40   37
49   Trump Tower   E. 57th St.
E. 56th St.
50
E. 55th St.

MAP 27

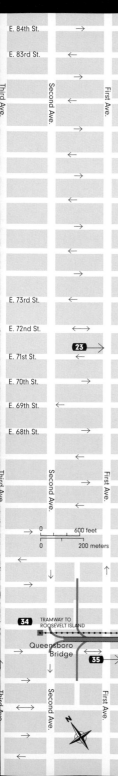

Listed by Site Number

MAP **27** **Art Galleries/Uptown**

Listed Alphabetically

Achim Moeller Fine Art, 33.
36 E 64th St ☎ 644-2133

Acquavella, 6. 18 E 79th St
☎ 734-6300

Adam Baumgold, 13. 74 E 79th St
☎ 861-7338

Allan Stone, 1. 113 E 90th St
☎ 987-4997

Ameringer & Yohe, 48.
20 W 57th St ☎ 445-0051

Anita Shapolsky, 32. 152 E 65th St
☎ 452-1094

Ariadne Galleries, 18.
11 E 76th St ☎ 772-3388

Artemis Greenburg Van Doren, 43.
730 Fifth Ave ☎ 445-0444

Barbara Mathes, 54. 22 E 80th St
☎ 570-4190

Bernarducci Meisel, 44. 37 W 57th St
☎ 593-3757

Bjorn Resie, 5. 16 E 79th St
☎ 744-2266

CDS Gallery, 12. 76 E 79th St
☎ 772-9555

Christie's, 50. 20 Rockefeller
Plaza ☎ 636-2000

D Wigmore, 43. 730 Fifth Ave
☎ 581-1657

DC Moore, 49. 724 Fifth Ave
☎ 247-2111

David Findlay Jr, 39. 41 E 57th St
☎ 486-7660

Davis & Langdale, 34. 231 E 60th St
☎ 838-0333

Dickinson Roundell, 30. 19 E 66th St
☎ 772-8083

Edwynn Houk, 42. 745 Fifth Ave
☎ 750-7070

E&J Frankel, 8. 1040 Madison Ave
☎ 879-5733

Elkon, 3. 18 E 81st St
☎ 535-3940

Fitch-Febvrel, 41. 5 E 57th St
☎ 688-8522

Flowers, 14. 1000 Madison Ave
☎ 439-1700

Forum, 42. 745 Fifth Ave ☎ 355-4545

Frank J. Miele, 2. 1086 Madison Ave
☎ 249-7250

Franklin Parrasch, 48. 20 W 57th St
☎ 246-5360

Gagosian, 16. 980 Madison Ave
☎ 744-2313

Galerie St Etienne, 47. 24 W 57th St
☎ 245-6734

Gallery Schlesinger, 22. 24 E 73rd St
☎ 734-3600

Garth Clark, 47. 24 W 57th St
☎ 246-2205

Gering & López, 43. 730 Fifth Ave
☎ 646/336-7183

Hammer, 45. 33 W 57th St
☎ 644-4400

Helly Nahmad, 17. 975 Madison Ave
☎ 879-2075

Hirschl & Adler, 26. 21 E 70th St
☎ 535-8810

Howard Greenberg, 39. 41 E 57th St
☎ 334-0010

James Goodman, 39. 41 E 57th St
☎ 593-3737

James Graham & Sons, 6.
1014 Madison Ave ☎ 535-5767

Jane Kahan, 20. 922 Madison Ave
☎ 744-1490

Joan Washburn, 48. 20 W 57th St
☎ 397-6780

Jonathan O'Hara, 39. 41 E 57th St
☎ 644-3533

Katharina Rich Perlow, 39.
41 E 57th St ☎ 644-7171

Knoedler, 25. 19 E 70th St
☎ 794-0550

Kouros, 21. 23 E. 73rd St
☎ 288-5888

L&M Arts, 11. 45 E 78th St
☎ 861-0020

Laurence Miller, 48. 20 W 57th St
☎ 397-3930

Leigh Keno American Antiques, 24.
127 E 69th St ☎ 734-2381

Leo Castelli, 15. 18 E 77th St
☎ 249-4470

Marian Goodman, 47. 24 W 57th St
☎ 977-7160

Marlborough, 46. 40 W 57th St
☎ 541-4900

Mary Boone, 42. 745 Fifth Ave
☎ 752-2929

Maxwell Davidson, 49. 724 Fifth Ave
☎ 759-7555

McKee, 42. 745 Fifth Ave ☎ 688-5951

Michael Rosenfeld, 47. 24 W 57th St
☎ 247-0082

Mireille Mosler, 29. 35 E 67th St
☎ 249-4195

MAP 27

Listed Alphabetically (cont.)

Mitchell-Innes & Nash, 7.
1018 Madison Ave ☎ 744-7400

Nohra Haime, 39. 41 E 57th St
☎ 888-3550

Owen, 19. 19 E 75th St ☎ 879-2415

Pace/MacGill, 40. 32 E 57th St
☎ 759-7999

PaceWildenstein, 40. 32 E 57th St
☎ 421-3292

Peter Findlay, 39. 41 E 57th St
☎ 644-4433

The Project, 44. 37 W 57th St
☎ 688-1585

Reece, 47. 24 W 57th St ☎ 333-5830

Richard Gray, 7. 1018 Madison Ave
☎ 472-8787

Richard L. Feigen, 28. 34 E 69th St
☎ 628-0700

Shepherd & Derom, 10. 58 E 79th St
☎ 861-4050

Skarskedt, 7. 20 E 79th St
☎ 737-2060

Sotheby's, 23. 1334 York Ave
☎ 606-7010

Soufer, 9. 1015 Madison Ave
☎ 628-3225

Spanierman, 38. 45 E 58th St
☎ 832-0208

Throckmorton, 36. 145 E 57th St
☎ 223-1059

Tibor de Nagy, 49. 724 Fifth Ave
☎ 262-5050

Ubu, 35. 416 E 59th St ☎ 753-4444

Wally Findlay, 37. 124 E 57th St
☎ 421-5390

Wildenstein, 31. 19 E 64th St
☎ 879-0500

Zabriskie, 39. 41 E 57th St
☎ 752-1223

Zwirner & Wirth, 27. 32 E 69th St
☎ 517-8677

MAP 28 **Art Galleries/Chelsea**

Listed by Site Number

1 Martos	**16** Mitchell, Innes & Nash	**26** McKenzie
2 Sean Kelly	**17** Galerie Lelong	**26** Alan Klotz
3 Dieu Donné	**18** Greene Naftali	**26** SoHo 20
4 Broadway 1602	**18** Nicole Klagsbrun	**26** Luise Ross
5 Schroeder Romero	**18** G.R. N'Namdi	**27** Cavin-Morris
6 Clementine	**18** Michael Steinberg	**27** Robert Mann
7 ATM	**19** Robert Miller	**27** Chambers Fine Art
8 Ceres	**20** Bose Pacia	**27** Edward Thorp
8 Sundaram Tagore	**21** P.P.O.W	**27** Fischbach
9 Paul Kasmin	**22** Cheim & Reid	**28** Gagosian
10 Paul Kasmin	**23** PaceWildenstein	**29** Marlborough
11 Roebling Hall	**24** Blue Mountain	**29** Elizabeth Dee
12 Tony Shafrazi	**24** Stefan Stux	**30** Mary Boone
13 Stephen Haller	**24** Viridian	**31** Silverstein Photography
14 Lehmann Maupin	**25** Yossi Milo	**32** Fredericks & Freiser
15 James Cohan		

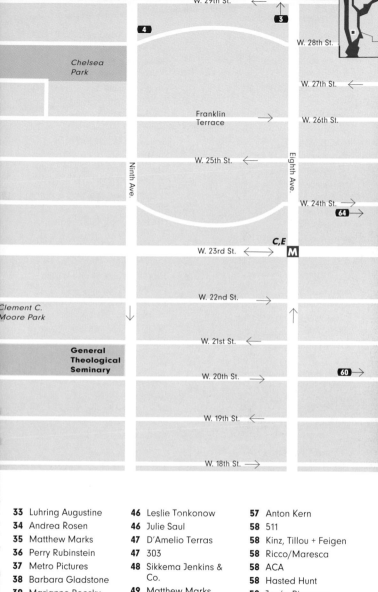

MAP 28 **Art Galleries/Chelsea**

Listed Alphabetically

ACA, 58. 529 W 20th St
☎ 206-8080

Alan Klotz, 26. 511 W 25th St
☎ 741-4764

Andrea Rosen, 34. 525 W 24th St
☎ 627-6000

Anton Kern, 57. 532 W 20th St
☎ 367-9663

ATM, 7. 619b W27th St ☎ 375-0349

Barbara Gladstone, 38.
515 W 24th St ☎ 206-9300

Bellwether, 63. 134 Tenth Ave
☎ 929-5959

Bitforms, 58. 529 W 20th St
☎ 366-6939

Blue Mountain, 24. 530 W 25th St
☎ 646/486-4730

Bose Pacia, 20. 508 W 26th St
☎ 989-7074

Broadway 1602, 4. 1182 Broadway
☎ 481-0362

Caren Golden, 40. 539 W 23rd St
☎ 727-8304

Casey Kaplan, 53. 525 W 21st St
☎ 645-7335

Cavin-Morris, 27. 210 Eleventh Ave
☎ 226-3768

Ceres, 8. 547 W 27th St
☎ 947-6100

Chambers Fine Art, 27. 210
Eleventh Ave ☎ 414-1169

Cheim & Reid, 22. 547 W 25th St
☎ 242-7727

Clementine, 6. 623 W 27th St
☎ 243-5937

D'Amelio Terras, 47. 525 W 22nd St
☎ 352-9460

David Zwirner, 61. 525 W 19th St
☎ 727-2070

Demisch Danant, 44. 542 W 22nd St
☎ 989-5750

Dieu Donné, 3. 315 W 36th St
☎ 226-0573

Edward Thorp, 27. 210 Eleventh Ave
☎ 691-6565

Elizabeth Dee, 29. 545 W 20th St
☎ 924-7545

Fischbach, 27. 210 Eleventh Ave
☎ 759-2345

511 Gallery, 58. 529 W 20th St
☎ 255-2885

Frederieke Taylor, 46. 535 W 22nd St
☎ 646/230-0992

Fredericks & Freiser, 32. 536
W 24th St ☎ 633-6555

Friedrich Petzel, 46. 535 W 22nd St
☎ 680-9467

Gagosian, 28. 555 W 24th St
☎ 741-1111

Gagosian, 52. 522 W 21st St
☎ 741-1717

Galerie Lelong, 17. 528 W 26th St
☎ 315-0470

G.R. N'Namdi, 18. 526 W 26th St
☎ 929-6645

Greene Naftali, 18. 526 W 26th St
☎ 463-7770

Hasted Hunt, 58. 529 W 20th St
☎ 627-0006

Jack Shainman, 59. 513 W 20th St
☎ 645-1701

James Cohan, 15. 533 W 26th St
☎ 714-9500

Josée Bienvenu, 58. 529 W 20th St
☎ 206-7990

Julie Saul, 46. 535 W 22nd St
☎ 627-2410

Kathryn Markel, 58. 529 W 20th St
☎ 366-5368

Kinz, Tillou + Feigen, 58. 529
W 20th St ☎ 929-0500

Lehmann Maupin, 14. 540 W 26th St
☎ 255-2923

Leslie Tonkonow, 46. 535 W 22nd St
☎ 255-8450

Luise Ross, 26. 511 W 25th St
☎ 343-2468

Luhring Augustine, 33. 531 W 24th St
☎ 206-9100

Lyons Weir Ortt, 60. 175 Seventh Ave
☎ 242-6220

Marianne Boesky, 39. 509 W 24th St
☎ 680-9889

Marlborough, 29. 545 W 25th St
☎ 463-8634

Martos Gallery, 1. 540 W 29th St
☎ 560-0670

Mary Boone, 30. 541 W 24th St
☎ 752-2929

Matthew Marks, 35. 523 W 24th St
☎ 243-0200

Matthew Marks, 49. 522 W 22nd St
☎ 243-0200

MAP **28**

Listed Alphabetically (cont.)

Matthew Marks, 52. 521 W 21st St
☎ 243-0200

Max Protetch, 51. 511 W 22nd St
☎ 633-6999

Maya Stendhal, 56. 545 W 20th St
☎ 366-1549

McKenzie Fine Art, 26. 511 W 25th St
☎ 989-5467

Metro Pictures, 37. 519 W 24th St
☎ 206-7100

Michael Steinberg, 18. 526 W 26th St
☎ 924-5770

Mitchell, Innes & Nash, 16. 534
W 26th St ☎ 744-7400

Newman Popiashvili, 50. 504
W 22nd St ☎ 274-9166

Nicole Klagsburn, 18. 526 W 26th St
☎ 243-3335

PaceWildenstein, 23. 534 W 25th St
☎ 929-7000

PaceWildenstein, 43. 545 W 22nd St
☎ 989-4258

Paul Kasmin, 9. 511 27th St
☎ 563-4474

Paul Kasmin, 10. 293 Tenth Ave
☎ 563-4474

Paula Cooper, 54. 534 W 21st St
☎ 255-1105

Perry Rubinstein, 36. 526 W 24th St
☎ 627-8000

Perry Rubinstein, 41. 527 W 23rd St
☎ 627-8000

Postmasters, 62. 459 W 19th St
☎ 727-3323

P.P.O.W, 21. 555 W 25th St
☎ 647-1044

Ricco/Maresca, 58. 529 W 20th St
☎ 627-4819

Robert Mann, 27. 210 Eleventh Ave
☎ 989-7600

Robert Miller, 19. 524 W 26th St
☎ 366-4774

Ruebling Hall, 11. 606 W 26th St
☎ 929-8180

Schroeder Romero, 5. 637 W 27th St
☎ 630-0722

Sean Kelly, 2. 528 W 29th St
☎ 239-1181

Sepia, 64. 148 W 24th St ☎ 645-9444

Sikkema Jenkins & Co., 48. 530
W 22nd St ☎ 929-2262

Silverstein Photography, 31.
535 W 24th St ☎ 627-3930

SoHo 20, 26. 511 W 25th St
☎ 367-8994

Sonnabend, 45. 536 W 22nd St
☎ 627-1018

Stefan Stux, 24. 530 W 25th St
☎ 352-1600

Stephen Haller, 13. 542 W 26th St
☎ 741-7777

Sundaram Tagore, 8. 547 W 27th St
☎ 677-4520

Tanya Bonakdar, 52. 521 W 21st St
☎ 414-4144

Tony Shafrazi, 12. 544 W 26th St
☎ 274-9300

303, 47. 525 W 22nd St ☎ 255-1121

Van de Weghe, 42. 521 W 23rd St
☎ 929-6633

Viridian Artists, 24. 530 W 25th St
☎ 414-4040

Yancey Richardson, 46.
535 W 22nd St ☎ 646/230-9610

Yossi Milo, 25. 525 W 25th St
☎ 414-0370

Yvon-Lambert, 55. 550 W 21st St
☎ 242-3611

MAP **29** **Exploring the Bronx**

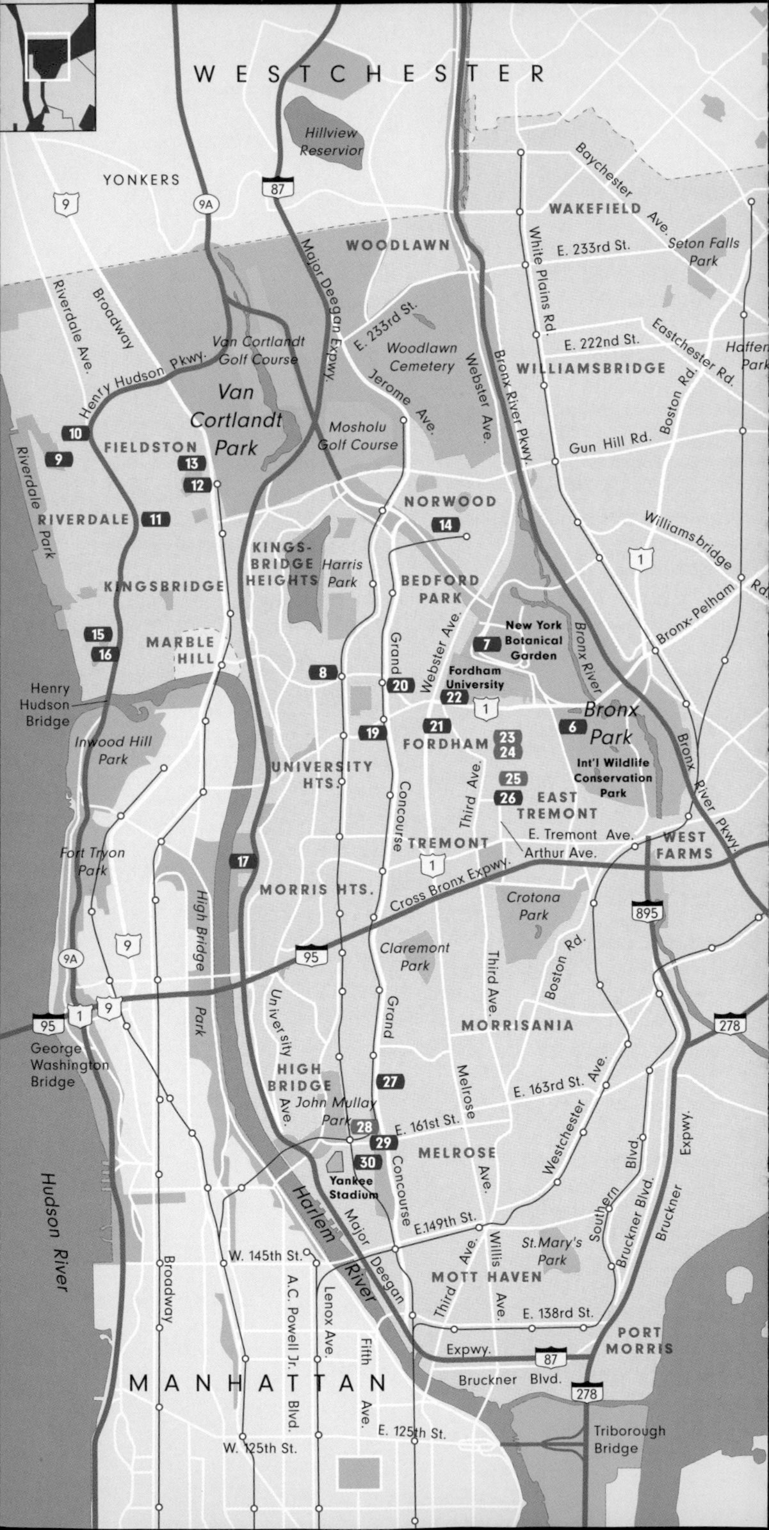

WESTCHESTER

Hillview
Reservoir

YONKERS

WOODLAWN

WAKEFIELD

E. 233rd St.

Seton Falls
Park

Baychester Ave.

Riverdale Ave.

Broadway

Henry Hudson Pkwy.

Van Cortlandt
Golf Course

Van
Cortlandt
Park

E. 233rd St.

Woodlawn
Cemetery

Jerome Ave.

White Plains Rd.

E. 222nd St.

WILLIAMSBRIDGE

Haffen

Eastchester Rd.

Boston Rd.

Webster Ave.

Bronx River Pkwy.

Gun Hill Rd.

10

9

FIELDSTON

13

12

RIVERDALE

11

Riverdale
Park

KINGSBRIDGE

KINGS-
BRIDGE
HEIGHTS

Harris
Park

Mosholu
Golf Course

NORWOOD

14

BEDFORD
PARK

New York
Botanical
Garden

7

Williams
bridge

Bronx-Pelham

1

Henry
Hudson
Bridge

15

16

MARBLE
HILL

Inwood Hill
Park

8

Grand Ave.

Webster Ave.

20

Fordham
University

22

1

Bronx River

Bronx
Park

6

Int'l Wildlife
Conservation
Park

Bronx River Pkwy.

UNIVERSITY
HTS.

19

21

FORDHAM

23
24

25

26

EAST
TREMONT

Third Ave.

Concourse

TREMONT

E. Tremont Ave.

Arthur Ave.

WEST
FARMS

Fort Tryon
Park

17

MORRIS HTS.

Cross Bronx Expwy.

Crotona
Park

Boston Rd.

895

95

9A

9

High Bridge
Park

Claremont
Park

Third Ave.

Grand Ave.

MORRISANIA

Westchester Ave.

278

George
Washington
Bridge

95

1

9

University Ave.

HIGH
BRIDGE

John Mullaly
Park

27

28

29

30

Yankee
Stadium

E. 161st St.

MELROSE

Melrose Ave.

E. 163rd St.

Southern Blvd.

Bruckner Blvd.

Bruckner Expwy.

Hudson
River

Harlem River

Broadway

A.C. Powell Jr. Blvd.

Lenox Ave.

Major Deegan

Concourse

W. 145th St.

E. 149th St.

Third Ave.

Willis Ave.

St. Mary's
Park

MOTT HAVEN

E. 138th St.

PORT
MORRIS

MANHATTAN

Fifth Ave.

W. 125th St.

E. 125th St.

Bruckner Blvd.

Expwy.

87

278

Triborough
Bridge

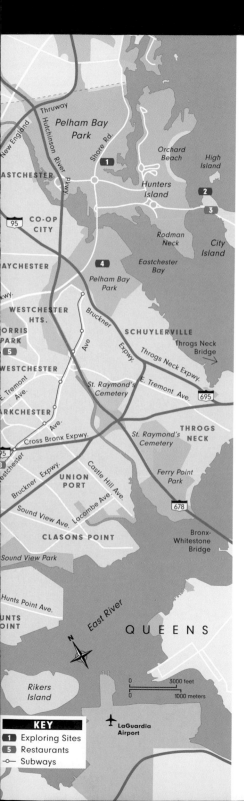

MAP **29**

MAP **30** **Exploring Brooklyn**

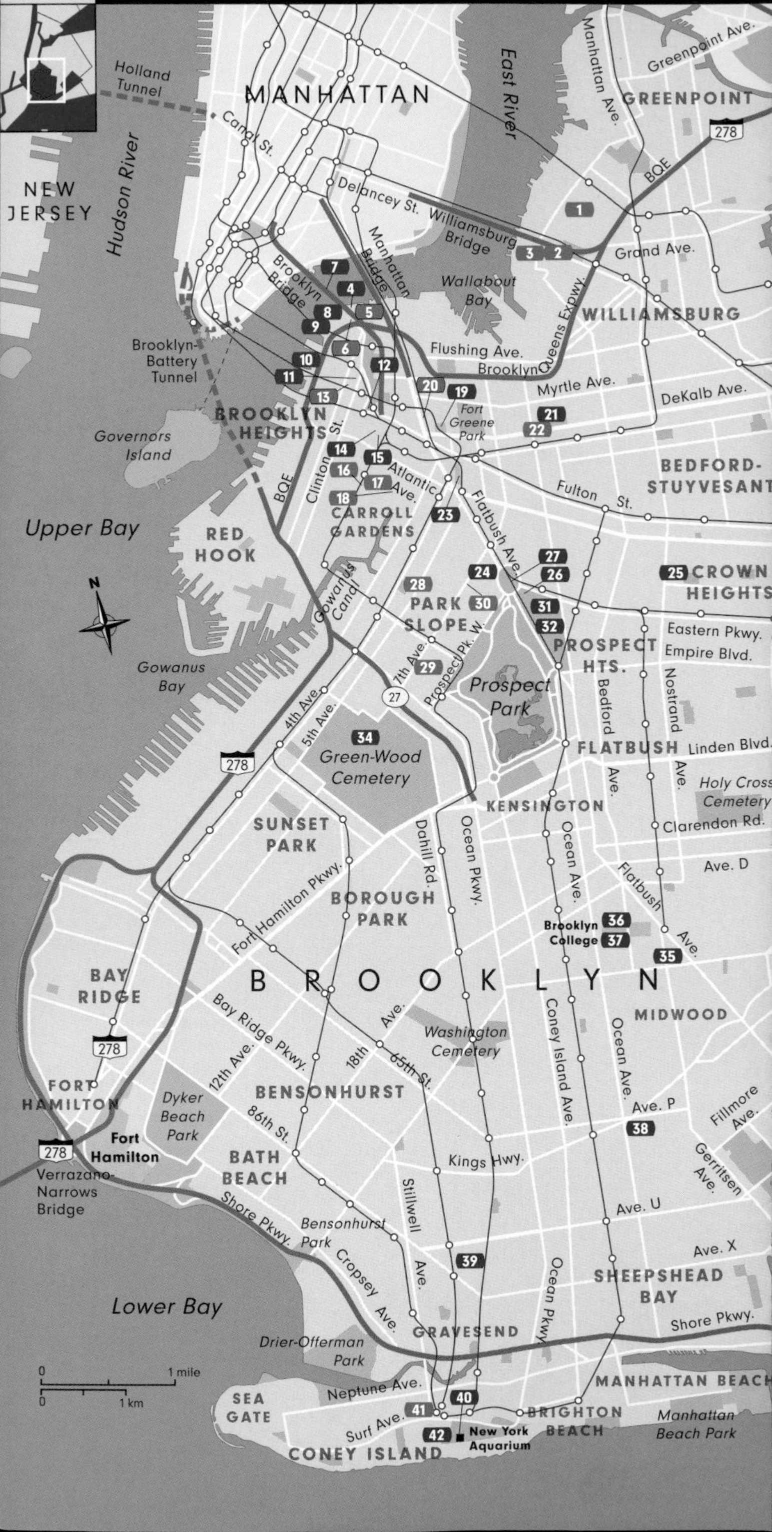

NEW JERSEY

Holland Tunnel

Hudson River

MANHATTAN

East River

Manhattan Ave.

Greenpoint Ave.

GREENPOINT

278

BQE

Canal St.

Delancey St.

Williamsburg Bridge

1

3 2

Grand Ave.

Queens Expwy.

WILLIAMSBURG

Brooklyn Bridge

7

4

Manhattan Bridge

8
9

5

Wallabout Bay

Flushing Ave.

Brooklyn

Myrtle Ave.

DeKalb Ave.

Brooklyn-Battery Tunnel

10

6

11

12

13

20 19

Fort Greene Park

21

22

Clinton St.

BROOKLYN HEIGHTS

Fulton St.

BEDFORD-STUYVESANT

Governors Island

15

16

Atlantic Ave.

18 17

CARROLL GARDENS

23

Flatbush Ave.

BQE

Upper Bay

RED HOOK

Gowanus Canal

28

24

27
26

25 CROWN HEIGHTS

N

Gowanus Bay

4th Ave.

5th Ave.

30

7th Ave.

29

27

Prospect Pk. W.

31
32

PROSPECT HTS.

Eastern Pkwy.
Empire Blvd.

Bedford Ave.

Nostrand Ave.

34

Green-Wood Cemetery

Prospect Park

FLATBUSH

Linden Blvd.

Holy Cross Cemetery

278

SUNSET PARK

Dahill Rd.

Ocean Pkwy.

KENSINGTON

Ocean Ave.

Clarendon Rd.

Ave. D

BOROUGH PARK

Flatbush Ave.

B R O O K L Y N

Brooklyn College

36
37

35

BAY RIDGE

278

Fort Hamilton Pkwy.

Bay Ridge Pkwy.

18th Ave.

65th St.

Ave.

Washington Cemetery

Coney Island Ave.

Ocean Ave.

MIDWOOD

Ave. P

FORT HAMILTON

278

Fort Hamilton

12th Ave.

DYKER BEACH PARK

86th St.

BENSONHURST

Fillmore Ave.

Gerritsen Ave.

38

Verrazano-Narrows Bridge

BATH BEACH

Stillwell Ave.

Kings Hwy.

Ave. U

Shore Pkwy.

Bensonhurst Park

Cropsey Ave.

39

Ocean Pkwy.

Ave. X

SHEEPSHEAD BAY

Shore Pkwy.

Lower Bay

Drier-Offerman Park

Neptune Ave.

GRAVESEND

40

MANHATTAN BEACH

SEA GATE

0   1 mile
0   1 km

Surf Ave.

41

42 ■ New York Aquarium

BRIGHTON BEACH

Manhattan Beach Park

CONEY ISLAND

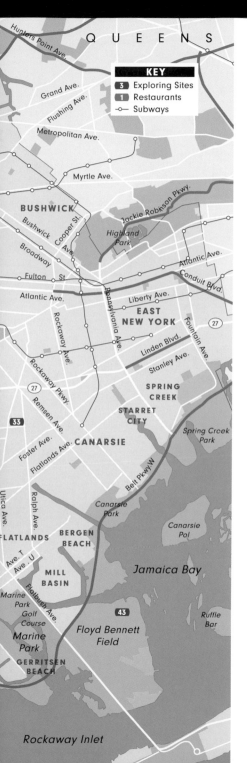

MAP 30

KEY
3 Exploring Sites
1 Restaurants
○—○ Subways

MAP 31 **Exploring Queens**

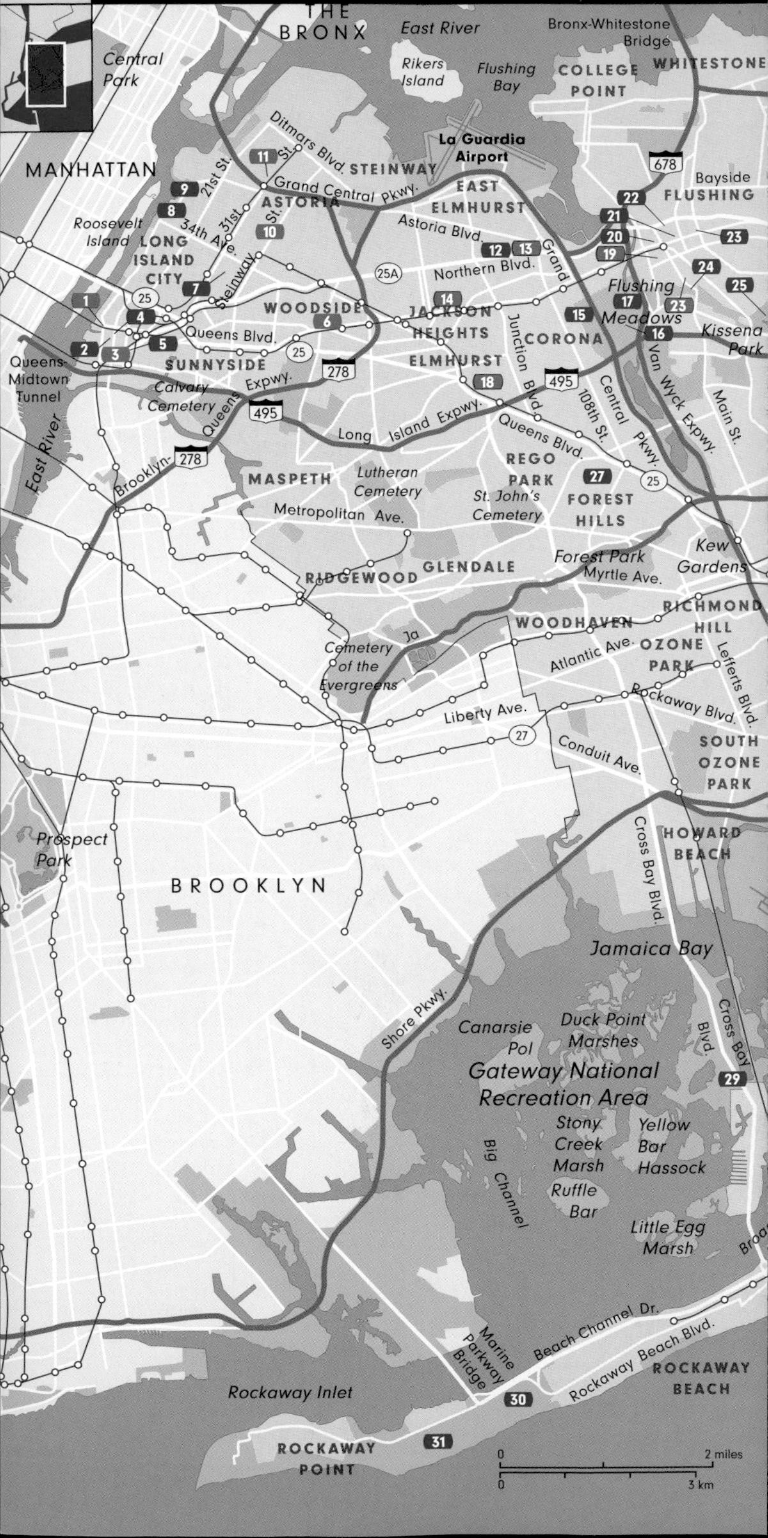

THE BRONX

East River

Rikers Island

Flushing Bay

Bronx-Whitestone Bridge

COLLEGE POINT

WHITESTONE

Central Park

11 Ditmars Blvd. St.

STEINWAY

La Guardia Airport

678

Bayside

MANHATTAN

21st St.

Grand Central Pkwy.

9 34th Ave.

8

ASTORIA

10

EAST ELMHURST

Astoria Blvd.

Northern Blvd.

22

21

20

19

FLUSHING

23

Roosevelt Island

LONG ISLAND CITY

7

Steinway

25A

12 **13**

14

Grand

17

Flushing Meadows

24

25

1

25

WOODSIDE

6

Queens Blvd.

JACKSON HEIGHTS

15

CORONA

23

Kissena Park

16

2

4

5

3

SUNNYSIDE

25

ELMHURST

18

Junction Blvd.

495

Central Pkwy.

Van Wyck Expwy.

Main St.

Queens-Midtown Tunnel

278

Calvary Cemetery

Queens Expwy.

495

Long Island Expwy.

Queens Blvd.

108th St.

25

East River

Brooklyn

278

MASPETH

Lutheran Cemetery

St. John's Cemetery

REGO PARK

27

FOREST HILLS

Kew Gardens

Metropolitan Ave.

RIDGEWOOD

GLENDALE

Forest Park

Myrtle Ave.

RICHMOND HILL

Cemetery of the Evergreens

Ja

WOODHAVEN

OZONE PARK

Lefferts Blvd.

Atlantic Ave.

Rockaway Blvd.

Liberty Ave.

27

Conduit Ave.

SOUTH OZONE PARK

Prospect Park

BROOKLYN

HOWARD BEACH

Cross Bay Blvd.

Jamaica Bay

Shore Pkwy.

Canarsie Pol

Duck Point Marshes

Gateway National Recreation Area

Cross Bay Blvd.

29

Stony Creek Marsh

Yellow Bar Hassock

Big Channel

Ruffle Bar

Little Egg Marsh

Broad

Beach Channel Dr.

Marine Parkway Bridge

Rockaway Beach Blvd.

ROCKAWAY BEACH

30

Rockaway Inlet

31

0 2 miles

0 3 km

ROCKAWAY POINT

MAP 31

KEY

2 Exploring Sites
1 Restaurants
—o— Subways

MAP 32 **Exploring Staten Island**

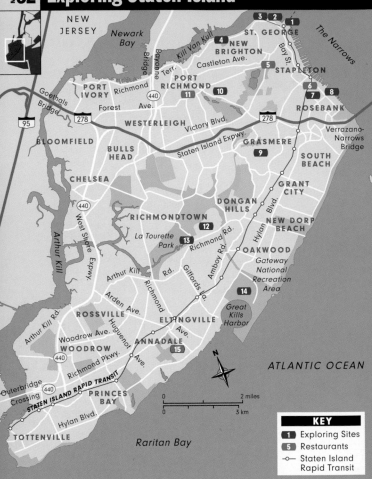

NEW
JERSEY

Newark
Bay

ST. GEORGE

The Narrows

3 2 1

NEW
BRIGHTON

Castleton Ave.

4

Bay St.

STAPLETON

5

Kill Van Kull

Bayonne Bridge

Richmond Terr.

PORT
RICHMOND

11

10

6
7

8

ROSEBANK

PORT
IVORY

Richmond Ave.

Forest Ave.

Goethals
Bridge

95

278

WESTERLEIGH

Victory Blvd.

278

Verrazano-
Narrows
Bridge

Staten Island Expwy.

BLOOMFIELD

BULLS
HEAD

GRASMERE

9

SOUTH
BEACH

CHELSEA

440

GRANT
CITY

DONGAN
HILLS

RICHMONDTOWN

12

NEW DORP
BEACH

West Shore Expwy.

La Tourette
Park

13

Richmond Rd.

Hylan Blvd.

OAKWOOD

Gateway
National
Recreation
Area

Arthur Kill

Rd.

Arthur Kill Rd.

Amboy Rd.

Giffords La.

14

Great
Kills
Harbor

Arden Ave.

ROSSVILLE

ELTINGVILLE

Huguenot Ave.

ANNADALE

N

WOODROW

Woodrow Ave.

15

ATLANTIC OCEAN

440

Richmond Pkwy.

Amboy Ave.

Outerbridge
Crossing

440

STATEN ISLAND RAPID TRANSIT

PRINCES
BAY

0   2 miles

0   3 km

TOTTENVILLE

Hylan Blvd.

Raritan Bay

KEY
1 Exploring Sites
5 Restaurants
—o— Staten Island
Rapid Transit

Staten Island Listed by Site Number

1 Staten Island Ferry

2 Staten Island
Yankees/Richmond
County Bank
Ballpark

3 Staten Island
Museum

4 Staten Island
Botanical Garden

4 Snug Harbor Cultural
Center

5 Enoteca Maria

6 Aesop's Tables

7 Garibaldi-Meucci
Museum

8 Alice Austin House

9 Carol's Cafe

10 Staten Island Zoo

11 Denino's Pizzeria

12 Jacques Marchais
Museum of Tibetan
Art

13 Historic
Richmondtown/
Staten Island
Historical Society

14 Gateway National
Recreation Area

15 Angelina's

MAP **29**

Outer Boroughs Listed Alphabetically

BRONX SITES

Arthur Ave Italian Market, 26.
Arthur Ave, betw E Fordham Rd &
E Tremont Ave

Bartow-Pell Mansion, 1.
895 Shore Rd N & Pelham Bay Pkwy
☎ 718/885-1461

Bronx County Courthouse, 29.
851 Grand Concourse

Bronx Museum of the Arts, 27.
1040 Grand Concourse ☎ 718/681-6000

Bronx Zoo (IWCP), 6. Fordham Rd &
Bronx River Pkwy ☎ 718/367-1010

Christ Church Riverdale, 10.
Henry Hudson Pkwy & 252nd St
☎ 718/543-1011.

City Island, 2. Long Island Sound

Creston Ave Baptist Church, 19.
114 E 188th St ☎ 718/367-1754

Edgar Allan Poe Cottage, 20.
Grand Concourse & Kingsbridge Rd
☎ 718/881-8900

Edgehill Church, 16.
2550 Independence Ave ☎ 718/549-7324

**Enrico Fermi Cultural Center/Library,
21.** 610 E 186th St ☎ 718/933-6410

Fordham University, 22.
441 E Fordham Rd ☎ 718/817-1000

Henry Hudson Memorial, 15.
Independence Ave & W 227th St

Kingsbridge Armory, 8.
Kingsbridge Rd & Jerome Ave

Manhattan College, 13.
Manhattan College Pkwy & W 242nd St
☎ 718/862-8000

**Museum of Bronx History/Valentine-
Varian House, 14.** 3266 Bainbridge
Ave ☎ 718/881-8900

NY Botanical Garden, 7.
Southern Blvd & 200th St
☎ 718/817-8700

Pelham Bay Park, 4. Pelham Bay

Roberto Clemente State Park, 17.
W Tremont Ave & Matthewson Rd
☎ 718/299-8750

Van Cortlandt House Museum, 12.
B'way & W 246th St
☎ 718/543-3344

Wave Hill, 9. W 249th St &
Independence Ave ☎ 718/549-3200

World War I Memorial Tower, 11.
Riverdale Ave & 239th St

BRONX RESTAURANTS

Dominick's, 24. 2335 Arthur Ave
☎ 718/733-2807. Italian. $-$$$

Enzo's, 5. 1998 Williamsbridge Rd
☎ 718/409-3828. Italian. $-$$

The Feeding Tree, 28.
982 Gerard Ave ☎ 718/293-5025.
Jamaican. ¢-$

Joe's Place, 18. 1841 Westchester Ave
☎ 718/918-2947. Caribbean. ¢-$$

Le Refuge Inn, 3. 586 City Island Ave
☎ 718/885-2478. French. $$$$

Mario's, 23. 2342 Arthur Ave
☎ 718/584 1188. Italian. $-$$

Press Café, 30. 114 E 157th St
☎ 718/401-0545. Italian. ¢-$

Roberto's Restaurant 25.
603 Crescent Ave ☎ 718/33-9503.
Italian. $$-$$$

BROOKLYN SITES

Bargemusic, Ltd, 6. Fulton Ferry
Landing, Old Fulton St & Waterfront
☎ 718/624-2083

Bklyn Acad of Music (BAM), 23.
30 Lafayette Ave ☎ 718/636-4100

Bklyn Borough Hall, 15.
Joralemon St ☎ 718/802-3700

Bklyn Botanic Garden, 33. 1000
Washington Ave ☎ 718/623-7200

Bklyn Bridge, 3. Cadman Plaza,
Bklyn, to City Hall Park, Manhattan

**Bklyn Center for Performing
Arts, 37.** Brooklyn College,
2900 Campus Rd ☎ 718/951-4500

Bklyn Children's Museum, 29.
145 Brooklyn Ave ☎ 718/735-4400

Bklyn College CUNY, 36. 2900
Bedford Ave ☎ 718/951-5000

209

MAP **30**

$$$$ = *over $40* $$$ = *$30–$40* $$ = *$20–$29* $ = *$10–$19*   ¢ = *under $10*
Based on cost per person for an entrée.

Outer Boroughs Listed Alphabetically (Cont.)

BROOKLYN SITES (cont.)

Brooklyn Historical Society, 11.
128 Pierrepont St ☎ 718/222–4111

Brooklyn Museum of Art, 31.
200 Eastern Pkwy ☎ 718/638–5000

Brooklyn Public Library, 26.
Grand Army Plaza ☎ 718/230–2100

Coney Island Amusement Park, 42.
1000 Surf Ave ☎ 718/372–0275

Empire-Fulton Ferry State Park, 8.
26 New Dock St ☎ 718/858–4708

Gateway National Recreation Area, 43. Floyd Bennett Field, Flatbush Ave & Shore Pkwy ☎ 718/338–3799

Green-Wood Cemetery, 34.
Fifth Ave & 25th St ☎ 718/768–7300

Long Island Univ, 19. Univ Plaza, DeKalb & Flatbush Aves
☎ 718/488–1011

Montauk Club, 24. 25 Eighth Ave
☎ 718/638–0800

NY Aquarium, 40. Boardwalk & W 8th St
☎ 718/265–FISH

NY Transit Museum, 14. Boerum Pl & Schermerhorn St ☎ 718/694–1600

Old Gravesend Cemetery, 39.
Gravesend Neck Rd & MacDonald Ave

Pratt Institute, 21. 200 Willoughby Ave
☎ 718/636–3600

The Promenade, 10. Between Montague & Clark Sts

St Ann's Warehouse, 4.
38 Water St ☎ 718/254–8779

Soldiers' & Sailors' Memorial Arch, 27.
Flatbush Ave & Eastern Pkwy

State St Houses, 15. 290-324 State St

Van Nuyse-Coe House, 35.
1128 E 34th St

Wyckoff House/Pieter Claesen, 33.
5816 Clarendon Rd ☎ 718/629–5400

Wyckoff-Bennett Homestead, 38.
1669 E 22nd St

BROOKLYN RESTAURANTS

al di la, 30. 248 Fifth Ave
☎ 718/783–4565. Italian. $

Applewood 29. 501 11th St
☎ 718/768–2044. New American. $$

Chestnut, 16. 271 Smith St
☎ 718/243–0049. New American. $-$$

Dressler, 3. 149 Broadway
☎ 718/384–6343. New American. $-$$

Fette Sau, 1. 354 Metropolitan Ave
☎ 718/963–3404. Barbecue. $-$$

Gargiulo's Restaurant, 41.
2911 W 15th St ☎ 718/266–4891. Italian.
¢-$$$

Grimaldi's Pizzeria, 6.
19 Old Fulton St ☎ 718/858–4300.
Pizza. $-$$

The Grocery, 18. 288 Smith St
☎ 718/596–3335. American. $$$

Henry's End, 13. 44 Henry St
☎ 718/834–1776. New American. $-$$

Junior's Restaurant, 20. 386 Flatbush Ave ☎ 718/852–5257. American. $

Madiba, 22. 195 DeKalb Ave
☎ 718/855–9190. South African. $-$$

Peter Luger Steak House, 2. 178 B'way
☎ 718/387–7400. Steak. $$$$

River Cafe, 5. 1 Water St
☎ 718/522–5200. Contemporary. $$$$

Saul, 17. 140 Smith St ☎ 718/935–9844.
Contemporary. $$

QUEENS SITES

American Museum of the Moving Image, 7. 35th Ave & 36th St ☎ 718/784–0077

Bowne House Historical Society, 21.
37-01 Bowne St ☎ 718/359–0528

Court House Square, 4.
45th Ave & 21st St

Flushing Meadows-Corona Park, 17.
College Point Blvd & Grand Central Pkwy ☎ 718/760–6565

Fort Tilden, 33. Breezy Pt,
Gateway NRA ☎ 718/318–4300

Flushing Meeting House, 22.
137-16 Northern Blvd ☎ 718/358–9636

Hunter's Point Historic District, 5.
45th Ave & 21st–23rd Sts

Isamu Noguchi Garden Museum, 8.
9-01 33rd Rd ☎ 718/204–7088

Jacob Riis Park, 32. Marine Bridge Pkwy at Rockaway Pt Blvd,
Gateway NRA ☎ 718/318–4300

Jamaica Bay Wildlife Refuge, 31.
Broad Channel & First Rd,
Gateway NRA ☎ 718/318–4340

Louis Armstrong House, 12.
34-56 107th St ☎ 718/478–8274

Kissena Park, 26.
Rose Ave & Parsons Blvd

Outer Boroughs Listed Alphabetically (Cont.)

QUEENS SITES (cont.)

NY Hall of Science, 15. 47-01 111th St
☎ 718/699-0005

PS 1 Contemporary Art Center, 2.
22-25 Jackson Ave ☎ 718/784-2084

Queens Botanical Gardens, 24.
43-50 Main St ☎ 718/886-3800

Queens Historical Society, 20.
143-35 37th Ave ☎ 718/939-0647

Queens Museum of Art, 16. Flushing
Meadows-Corona Park ☎ 718/592-9700

Socrates Sculpture Park, 9.
32-01 Vernon Blvd ☎ 718/956-1819

St John's University, 28.
8000 Utopia Pkwy ☎ 718/990-2000

West Side Tennis Club, 27.
1 Tennis Pl ☎ 718/268-2300

QUEENS RESTAURANTS

Elias Corner, 11. 24-02 31st St
☎ 718/932-1510. Greek Seafood. $-$$

Green Field, 13. 108-01 Northern Blvd
☎ 718/672-5202. Brazilian. $$

Jackson Diner, 14. 37-47 74th St
☎ 718/672-1232. Indian. $-$$

Joe's Shanghai, 23.
136-21 37th Ave
☎ 718/539-3838. Chinese $-$$

Manducatis, 3. 13-27 Jackson Ave
☎ 718/729-4602. Italian. $-$$

Mombar, 10. 25-22 Steinway St
☎ 718/726-2356. Middle Eastern.
$-$$

My Uncle's Steakhouse, 18.
89-08 Queens Blvd ☎ 718/426-8080.
South American/Steak. $

Sentosa, 19. 39-07 Prince St
☎ 718/886-6331. Malaysian. ¢-$

Spicy & Tasty, 19. 39-07 Prince St
☎ 718/359-1601. Chinese. ¢-$

Sripraphai, 6. 64-13 39th Ave
☎ 718/899-9599. Thai. ¢-$

Uncle Jack's Steakhouse, 26.
39-40 Bell Blvd ☎ 718/229-1100.
Steak. $$$$

Water's Edge Restaurant, 1.
44th Dr at Vernon Blvd
☎ 718/482-0033. American. $$$$

STATEN ISLAND SITES

Alice Austin House Museum, 8.
2 Hylan Blvd ☎ 718/816-4506

Garibaldi-Meucci Museum, 7.
420 Tompkins Ave ☎ 718/442-1608

**Gateway National Recreation Area,
14.** Fort Wadsworth
☎ 718/354-4500

**Historic Richmondtown/Staten Island
Historical Society, 13.**
441 Clarke Ave ☎ 718/351-1611

**Jacques Marchais Museum of Tibetan
Art, 12.** 338 Lighthouse Ave
☎ 718/987-3500

Snug Harbor Cultural Center, 4.
1000 Richmond Ter ☎ 718/448-2500

Staten Island Botanical Garden, 4.
1000 Richmond Terrace
☎ 718/273-8200

Staten Island Ferry, 1.
St George Terminal, Richmond
Terrace/Bay St ☎ 718/876-8441

Staten Island Museum, 3.
75 Stuyvesant Pl ☎ 718/727-1135

**Staten Island Yankees/ Richmond
County Bank Ballpark, 2.**
75 Richmond Terrace
☎ 718/720-9265

Staten Island Zoo, 10.
614 Broadway ☎ 718/442-3100

STATEN ISLAND RESTAURANTS

Aesop's Tables, 6. 1233 Bay St
☎ 718/720-2005. New American. $-$$

Angelina's, 15. 26 Jefferson Blvd
☎ 718/227-7100. Italian. $-$$$

Carol's Cafe, 9. 1571 Richmond Rd
☎ 718/979-5600. Eclectic. $-$$$$

Denino's Pizzeria, 11.
524 Port Richmond Ave
☎ 718/442-9401. Pizza. $

Enoteca Maria, 5. 27 Hyatt St
☎ 718/447-2777. Italian. $-$$

$$$$ = *over $40* $$$ = *$30–$40* $$ = *$20–$29* $ = *$10–$19*   ¢ = *under $10*
Based on cost per person for an entrée.

MAP 33 **Parks/Uptown**

KEY

- Playing Fields
- Vest-Pocket Parks
- Swimming Pools
- Tennis Courts

MARBLE HILL

Kingsbridge Rd.

Baker Field

INWOOD

Isham Park

Inwood Hill Park

Tenth Ave.

207th St.

Broadway

Dyckman St.

Nagle Ave.

UNIVERSITY HTS

Grand Concourse

Bronx River

Bronx Park

Fort Tryon Park

Highbridge Park

St. Nicholas Ave.

Amsterdam Ave.

Harlem River Dr.

MORRIS HTS

TREMONT

Tremont Ave.

95

Fort Washington Park

WASHINGTON HEIGHTS

W. 181st St.

Cross Bronx Expwy.

Claremont Park

Crotona Park

Third Ave.

Boston Rd.

95

1

George Washington Bridge

J. Hood Wright Park

Fort Washington Ave.

Audubon Ave.

University Ave.

MORRISANIA

THE BRONX

Highbridge Park

HIGH BRIDGE

John Mullaly Park

E. 163rd St.

Melrose Ave.

Westchester Ave.

87

Macombs Dam Park

Concourse

Grand

E. 161st St.

MELROSE

0   1500 feet
0   500 meters

Broadway

St. Nicholas Ave.

W. 155th St.

Trinity Cemetery

Franz Sigel Park

Major Deegan

Eugenio Maria de Hostos Blvd.

St. Mary's Park

Southern Blvd.

Bruckner Blvd.

Fort Washington Park

Jackie Robinson Park

Edgecombe Ave.

Convent Ave.

Amsterdam Ave.

W. 145th St.

Colonel Young Park

Harlem River

Harlem River Dr.

MOTT HAVEN

Third Ave.

Willis Ave.

E. 138th St.

PORT MORRIS

Riverbank State Park

Henry Hudson Pkwy.

Hudson River

St. Nicholas Park

W. 138th St.

Lenox Ave.

Malcolm X Blvd.

Expwy.

Bruckner Blvd.

87

278

Riverside Dr.

W. 135th St.

Sheltering Arms Park

Frederick Douglass Blvd.

Adam Clayton Powell Jr. Blvd.

Harlem River Drive Park

Randalls Island Park

Sakura Park

W. 125th St.

Riverside Park

9A

MORNINGSIDE HEIGHTS

Morningside Ave.

Amsterdam Ave.

Manhattan Ave.

St. Nicholas Ave.

Marcus Garvey Park

HARLEM

E. 125th St.

Triborough Bridge

Broadway

Morningside Park

Cathedral Pkwy.

Central Park W.

E. 110th St.

Lexington Ave.

EAST HARLEM

Thomas Jefferson Park

E. 110th St. Recreation Pier

FDR Dr.

278

Wards Island Park

West End Ave.

W. 106th St

Columbus Ave.

Central Park

Fifth Ave.

Madison Ave.

Park Ave.

E. 106th St.

Third Ave.

Second Ave.

First Ave.

East River

East River

Riverside Dr.

W. 96th St.

UPPER WEST SIDE

W. 96th St.

UPPER EAST SIDE

York Ave.

Esplanade

Carl Schurz Park

QUEENS

W. 86th St.

Jacqueline Kennedy Onassis Reservoir

E. 86th St.

Riverside Park

West End Ave.

W. 86th St.

Jacqueline Kennedy Onassis Reservoir

E. 86th St.

Carl Schurz Park

Riverside Dr.

W. 79th St.

Amsterdam Ave.

Broadway

Central Park

E. 79th St.

John Jay Park

East River Esplanade

York Ave.

First Ave.

Second Ave.

Third Ave.

FDR Dr.

East River

Roosevelt Island

Theodore Roosevelt Park

W. 72nd St.

The Lake

E. 72nd St.

UPPER WEST SIDE

Columbus Ave.

Central Park W.

Children's Zoo

E. 65th St.

UPPER EAST SIDE

Lexington Ave.

Park Ave.

Madison Ave.

Fifth Ave.

LONG ISLAND CITY

Damrosch Park

Central Park Wildlife Conservation Center

The Pond

Ninth Ave.

Central Park S.

E. 59th St.

TRAMWAY

E. 57th St.

Queensboro Bridge

QUEENS

W. 57th St.

DeWitt Clinton Park

W. 50th St.

Tenth Ave.

Eighth Ave.

E. 53rd St.

9A

Eleventh Ave.

THEATER DISTRICT

Bryant Park

W. 42nd St.

E. 42nd St.

495

Lincoln Tunnel

495

HELL'S KITCHEN

St. Vartan's Park

MURRAY HILL

Queens-Midtown Tunnel

BROOKLYN

East River

W. 34th St.

E. 34th St.

Tenth Ave.

Ninth Ave.

Eighth Ave.

Seventh Ave.

Ave. of the Americas

Fifth Ave.

Madison Ave.

Park Ave.

Lexington Ave.

Third Ave.

Second Ave.

First Ave.

FDR Dr.

Chelsea Park

Madison Square Park

W. 23rd St.

E. 23rd St.

CHELSEA

Gramercy Park

GRAMERCY

Union Square Park

Stuyvesant Square Park

E. 14th St.

W. 14th St.

Ave. A

Ave. B

Ave. C

Ave. D

Jefferson Market Garden

Greenwich Ave.

GREENWICH VILLAGE

Tompkins Square Park

EAST VILLAGE

East River Park

WEST VILLAGE

Washington St.

Washington Square Park

Sixth Ave.

Fourth Ave.

Lafayette

HUDSON RIVER

Hudson River

J.J. Walker Park

Hudson St.

Bedford St.

Houston St.

W.

SOHO

E. Houston St.

LOWER EAST SIDE

Williamsburg Bridge

NEW JERSEY

Hudson River Park

Varick St.

Greenwich St.

West Side Hwy.

Broadway

Bowery

Sara D. Roosevelt Park

Corlears Hook Park

HOBOKEN

Holland Tunnel

Canal St.

LITTLE ITALY

E. Broadway

Seward Park

278

TRIBECA

Church St.

CHINATOWN

Manhattan Bridge

Chambers St.

Columbus Park

Gov. Smith Park

North Park

City Hall Park

Brooklyn Bridge

Flatbush Ave.

BATTERY PARK CITY

FINANCIAL DISTRICT

Wall St.

BROOKLYN

BROOKLYN HEIGHTS

Robert F. Wagner Jr. Park

Battery Park

Brooklyn-Battery Tunnel

Brooklyn Queens Expwy.

Adams St.

Joralemon St.

0   1500 feet
0   500 meters

MAP 35 Central Park/North

A.C. Powell Blvd.
W. 111th St.
Lenox Ave.
Central Park North
Duke Ellington Circle
E. 110th St.
M 2,3
(Warriors' Gate)
(Pioneers' Gate)
Frederick Douglass Circle
M B,C
Harlem Meer
W. 106th St. (Strangers' Gate)
E. 106th St.
Great Hill
Conservatory Garden
El Museo del Barrio
The Ravine
Museum of The City of New York
M B,C
The Loch
W. 103rd St.
E. 102nd St (Girls' Gate)
The Pool
Central Park West
0 600 feet
0 200 meters
W. 100th St. (Boys' Gate)
North Meadow
East Meadow
97th St.
Transverse
← E. 97th St.
M B,C
E. 96th St. (Woodman's Gate)
W. 96th St. (Gate of All Saints)
North Gate House
Jewish Museum
Cooper-Hewitt Museum
Central Park West
(Runners' Gate)
E. 90th St.
W. 90th St.
National Academy of Design
Guggenheim Museum
Fifth Ave.
Jacqueline Kennedy Onassis Reservoir
South Gate House
85th St. Transverse
W. 86th St.
M B,C
W. 85th St. (Mariners' Gate)
E. 85th St.
E. 84th St.
KEY
Playground
Restrooms
Tennis Courts
Bridle Path
Metropolitan Museum of Art
W. 81st St. (Hunters' Gate)
E. 81st St.
M

Central Park/South

MAP 35

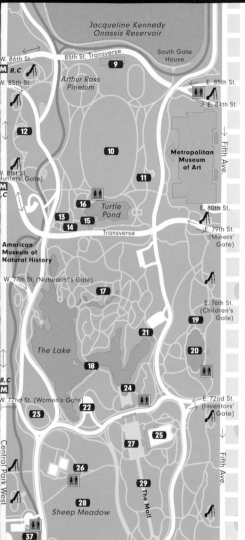

MAP
36 Stadiums & Arenas

Flushing Bay

Whitestone Expwy.

Northern Blvd.

Grand Central Pkwy.

126th Pl.

127th Pl.

34th Ave.

35th Ave.

36th Ave.

127th St.

37th Ave.

Shea Stadium

126th St.

38th Ave.

Willets Point Blvd.

Van Wyck Expwy.

River

39th Ave.

Roosevelt Ave.

M 7

Flushing

678

Corona Rail Road Yard

U.S. Tennis Association Arena/ Arthur Ashe Stadium

Meridian Rd.

N

Flushing Meadows - Corona Park

300 feet

100 meters

Shea Stadium & U.S. Tennis Association Arena

Yankee Stadium

E. 162nd St.

Jerome Ave.

Macombs Dam Park

E. 162nd St.

E. 161st St.

Macombs Dam Bridge Approach

B, D, 4 M

Babe Ruth Plaza

Rupert Pl.

Yankee Stadium

Lou Gehrig Plaza

Major Deegan Expwy.

E. 157th St.

Bronx Boro Hall

Harlem River

E. 153rd St.

River Ave.

Gerard Ave.

Walton Ave.

Franz Sigel Park

N

87

Grand Concourse

300 feet

100 meters

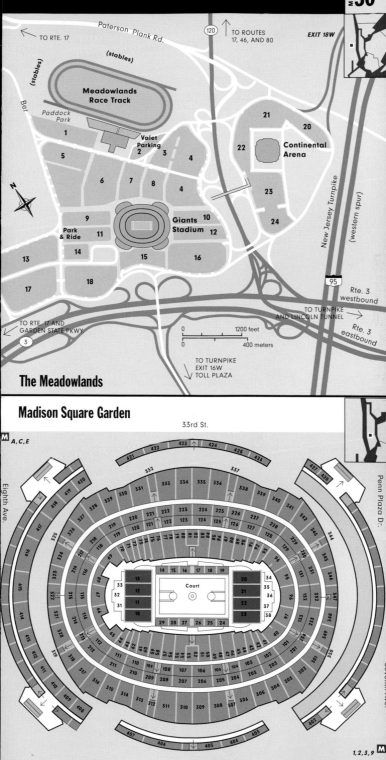

MAP **36**

TO RTE. 17

Paterson Plank Rd.

120

TO ROUTES
17, 46, AND 80

EXIT 18W

(stables)

(stables)

Ber

**Meadowlands
Race Track**

*Paddock
Park*

1

**Valet
Parking**

2   3

4

5

6   7   8

4

N

9

**Park
& Ride**   11

14

**Giants
Stadium**   10

12

13

15   16

17

18

21

22

20

**Continental
Arena**

23

24

New Jersey Turnpike

(western spur)

95   Rte. 3
westbound

TO TURNPIKE
AND LINCOLN TUNNEL

Rte. 3
eastbound

TO RTE. 17 AND
GARDEN STATE PKWY

3

0   1200 feet
0   400 meters

TO TURNPIKE
EXIT 16W
TOLL PLAZA

The Meadowlands

Madison Square Garden

33rd St.

M A,C,E

Eighth Ave.

Penn Plaza Dr.

421   422   423   424   425   426

427   428

352   337

333   334   335   336   338   339   340   341   342

329   330   331   343

219   220   221   222   225   224   225   226   227   228   344

119   120   121   122   123   124   125   126   127   128   345

129   130   346

14   15   16   17   18   19

13   20   34

Court

33   32   31   12   21   35

11   22   36

10   23   37

38

29   28   27   26   25   24

211   210   209   208   207   206   205   204   203   202

314   313   312   311   310   309   308   307   306   305   304   303   302

407   404   405   404   403

1, 2, 3, 9   M

31st St.

MAP 37 Shopping Highlights

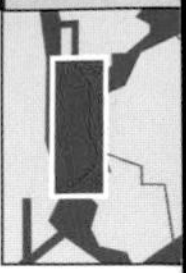

MAP **37**

Listed Alphabetically

ABC Carpet & Home, 36.
881 & 888 Broadway ☎ 473-3000

Alessi, 42. 130 Greene St ☎ 941-7300, Home

Apple Store, 22. 767 Fifth Ave
☎ 336-1440

Apple Store, 34. W 14th St
☎ 444-3400

B&H Photo-Video, 31.
420 Ninth Ave ☎ 444-6615

Barneys NY, 7.
660 Madison Ave ☎ 826-8900

Bed, Bath & Beyond, 35.
620 Sixth Ave ☎ 255-3550

Bergdorf Goodman, 14.
754 Fifth Ave ☎ 753-7300

Bloomingdale's, 10.
59th St & Lexington Ave ☎ 705-2000

Bridge Kitchenware, 23.
711 Third Ave ☎ 688-4220

Brooks Brothers, 28.
346 Madison Ave ☎ 682-8800

Century 21, 48.
22 Cortlandt St ☎ 227-9092

Crate & Barrel, 8.
650 Madison Ave ☎ 308-0011, Home

Dean & Deluca, 44.
560 Broadway ☎ 226-6800, Gourmet

Dylan's Candy Bar, 9. 1011 Third Ave
☎ 646/735-0078, Sweets

Grand Central Terminal Shops, 30.
Park Ave & 42nd St

Henri Bendel, 18.
712 Fifth Ave ☎ 247-1100

J & R Music and Computer, 49.
23 Park Row ☎ 238-9000

Jeffrey NY, 39.
449 W 14th St ☎ 206-1272, Clothing

Kalustyan's, 32. 123 Lexington Ave
☎ 685-3451, Gourmet

Kitchen Arts & Letters, 1.
1435 Lexington Ave ☎ 876-5550

La Maison du Chocolat, 3.
1018 Madison Ave ☎ 744-7117

Lord & Taylor, 29.
424 Fifth Ave ☎ 391-3344

Macy's, 30.
Herald Sq & 34th St ☎ 695-4400

Manhattan Art & Antiques Center, 19.
1050 Second Ave ☎ 355-4400

Museum of Modern Art Design Store, 20.
44 W 53rd St ☎ 767-1050

Paragon, 37. 867 Broadway
☎ 255-8036, Sporting Goods

Pearl Paint, 46. 308 Canal St
☎ 431-7932, Art Supplies

Pearl River, 45. 477 Broadway
☎ 431-4770, Asian Department Store

Petrossian, 13.
911 Seventh Ave ☎ 245-2217,
Caviar/Gourmet

Polo/Polo Sport, 6.
867 Madison Ave ☎ 606-2100;
888 Madison Ave ☎ 606-2100

Prada, 43. 575 Broadway
☎ 334-8888

Rizzoli, 13. 31 W 57th St
☎ 759-2424, Bookstore

Rockefeller Center, 24.
30 Rockefeller Plaza ☎ 632-3975

Saks Fifth Ave, 25.
611 Fifth Ave ☎ 753-4000

Shops at Columbus Circle, 12.
10 Columbus Circle ☎ 823-6300

Strand Books, 41.
828 Broadway ☎ 473-1452

Takashimaya, 21. 693 Fifth Ave
☎ 350-0100, Japanese Style

Terence Conran Shop, 11.
407 E 59th St ☎ 755-9079, Home

Tiffany & Co, 15.
727 Fifth Ave ☎ 755-8000

Torneau, 16.
12 E 57th St ☎ 758-7300, Watches

Virgin Megastore, 26.
1540 Broadway ☎ 921-1020

Whole Foods, 47. 95 E Houston St
☎ 420-1320

Zabar's, 2. 2245 Broadway
☎ 787-2000, Gourmet

MARKETS

Annex Antiques Fair & Flea Market, 33. 112 W 25th St.
Open Sat, Sun

IS 44 Market, 4. Columbus Ave betw 76th & 77th Sts. Open Sun

PS 41 Market, 40. Greenwich Ave & Charles St. Open Sat

PS 183 Market, 5. 419 E 66th St.
Open Sat

Union Square Greenmarket, 38.
Union Sq & 14th St. Open Mon, Wed, Fri, Sat

MAP 38 Shopping/Madison Avenue

E. 76th St.

8

1 – 7

E. 75th St.

9
10
11

Whitney
Museum of
American Art

E. 74th St.

0   600 feet
0   200 meters

12

E. 73rd St.

Madison Ave.

Park Ave.

N

E. 72nd St.

13

E. 71st St.

14 15
16 17
18

Frick
Collection

E. 70th St.

19 20
21
22

E. 69th St.

23
24

Hunter
College

E. 68th St.

25 26
27

E. 67th St.

28

E. 66th St.

29
30

Children's
Zoo

31
32
34   33

Central Park
Wildlife
Conservation
Center

35

E. 64th St.

36

E. 63rd St.

37

E. 62nd St.

38
39

E. 61st St.

41   40
42

44   43

Grand
Army
Plaza

45
46   47
48

N,R,W

M   E. 59th St.

50

51

49

Plaza
Hotel

E. 58th St.

Fifth Ave.

Central Park

Conservatory
Water

E. 65th St.

Listed by Site Number

1 Corner Bookstore
2 Crawford Doyle Booksellers
3 Lady M Cake Boutique
4 Missoni
5 La Maison du Chocolat
6 Vera Wang
7 Michael Kors
8 Florian Papp
9 Bang & Olufsen
10 Jo Malone
11 Christian Louboutin
12 Reinstein/Ross
13 Polo/Polo Sport
14 Gianfranco Ferre
15 Yves St Laurent
16 Juicy Couture
17 Asprey
18 Tom Ford
19 Chloé
20 Prada
21 Gucci
22 Pratesi
23 Debauve & Gallais
24 Dolce & Gabbana
25 JM Weston
26 La Perla
27 Issey Miyake
28 Emanuel Ungaro
29 Fred Leighton
30 Krizia
31 Julie Artisans' Gallery
32 Giorgio Armani
33 Valentino
34 Mitchel London
35 Chanel
36 Jimy Choo
37 Hermès
38 Georg Jensen
39 Taryn Rose
40 Alicia Mugetti
41 Barneys NY
42 Cole-Haan
43 DKNY
44 Calvin Klein
45 Nicole Farhi
46 Tod's
47 Ann Taylor
48 Crate & Barrel
49 Sherry-Lehmann Inc
50 Baccarat
51 Bally of Switzerland

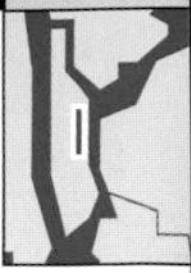

MAP 38

Listed Alphabetically

Alicia Mugetti, 40. 675 Madison Ave
☎ 355-4059, Womenswear

Ann Taylor, 47. 645 Madison Ave
☎ 832-9114, Womenswear

Asprey New York, 17. 853 Madison
Ave ☎ 688-1811, Jewelry

Baccarat, 50.
625 Madison Ave ☎ 826-4100

Bally of Switzerland, 51.
628 Madison Ave ☎ 751-9082, Shoes

Bang & Olufsen, 9.
952 Madison Ave ☎ 879-6161, Audio

Barneys NY, 41.
660 Madison Ave ☎ 826-8900

Calvin Klein, 44.
654 Madison Ave ☎ 292-9000

Chanel, 35.
737 Madison Ave. ☎ 535-5505

Chloé, 19. 850 Madison Ave
☎ 717-8220, Womenswear

Christian Louboutin, 11.
941 Madison Ave ☎ 396-1884, Shoes

Cole-Haan, 42.
667 Madison Ave ☎ 421-8440, Shoes

Corner Bookstore, 1.
1313 Madison Ave ☎ 831-3554

Crate & Barrel, 48.
650 Madison Ave. ☎ 308-0011, Home

Crawford Doyle Booksellers, 2.
1082 Madison Ave ☎ 288-6300

DKNY, 43. 655 Madison Ave
☎ 223-3569, Clothing

Debauve & Gallais, 23. 20 E 69th St
☎ 734-8880, Chocolates

Dolce & Gabbana, 24.
825 Madison Ave ☎ 249-4100

Emanuel Ungaro, 28.
792 Madison Ave ☎ 249-4090

Florian Papp, 8. 962 Madison Ave
☎ 288-6770, Antiques

Fred Leighton, 29. 773 Madison Ave
☎ 288-1872, Jewelry

Georg Jensen, 38.
685 Madison Ave ☎ 759-6457

Gianfranco Ferre, 14.
870 Madison Ave ☎ 717-5430,
Clothing

Giorgio Armani, 32.
760 Madison Ave ☎ 988-9191

Gucci, 18.
840 Madison Ave ☎ 717-2619

Hermès, 37.
691 Madison Ave ☎ 751-3181

Issey Miyake, 27.
802 Madison Ave ☎ 439-7822

JM Weston, 25. 812 Madison
Ave ☎ 535-2100, Mens Shoes

Jimmy Choo, 36. 716 Madison
Ave ☎ 759-7078, Shoes

Jo Malone, 10. 946 Madison Ave
☎ 472-0074, Perfume

Juicy Couture, 16. 860 Madison Ave
☎ 327-2398, Clothiing

Julie Artisans' Gallery, 31.
762 Madison Ave ☎ 717-5959,
Wearable Art

Krizia, 30.
769 Madison Ave ☎ 879-1211,
Womenswear

La Maison du Chocolat, 5.
1018 Madison Ave ☎ 744-7117

La Perla, 26. 803 Madison Ave.
☎ 570-0050, Lingerie

Lady M Cake Boutique, 3.
41 E 78th St ☎ 452-2222

Michael Kors, 7. 974 Madison Ave
☎ 452-4685

Missoni, 4.
1009 Madison Ave ☎ 517-9339

Mitchel London Foods, 34.
22A E 65th St ☎ 737-2850

Nicole Farhi, 45.
10 E 60th St ☎ 223-8811

Polo/Polo Sport, 13.
867 Madison Ave ☎ 606-2100 and
888 Madison Ave ☎ 434-8000

Reinstein/Ross, 12.
29 E 73rd St ☎ 722-1901, Jewelry

Prada, 20.
841 Madison Ave ☎ 327-4200

Pratesi, 22. 829 Madison Ave
☎ 288-2315, Linens

Sherry-Lehmann Inc, 49.
505 Park Ave ☎ 838-7500, Wine

Steuben Glass, 42. 667 Madison Ave
☎ 752-1441

Taryn Rose, 39. 681 Madison Ave
☎ 753-3939, Shoes

Tod's, 46. 650 Madison Ave
☎ 644-5945, Shoes

Tom Ford, 18. 845 Madison Ave
☎ 359-0300, Menswear

Valentino, 33.
747 Madison Ave ☎ 772-6969

Vera Wang, 6.
991 Madison Ave ☎ 628-3400

Yves St Laurent, 15.
855 Madison Ave ☎ 988-3821

MAP 39 **Shopping/Fifth Avenue & 57th Street**

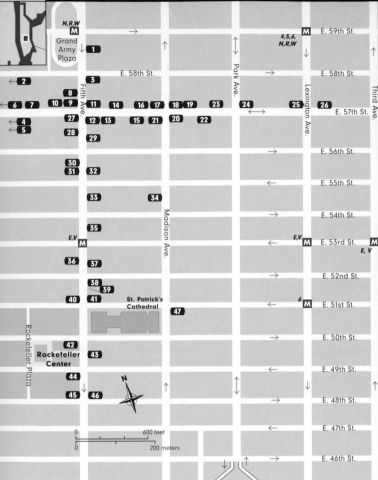

MAP **39**

Listed Alphabetically

Alfred Dunhill, 32. 711 Fifth Ave
☎ 753-9292, Leather Goods

American Girl Place, 46. 604 Fifth Ave
☎ 371-2220, Dolls

Apple Store, 1. 767 Fifth Ave
☎ 336-1440

Barnes & Noble, 45. 600 Fifth Ave
☎ 765-0592

Bergdorf Goodman, 3. 754 Fifth Ave
☎ 753-7300

Bergdorf Men's, 1. 745 Fifth Ave
☎ 753-7300

Borders Books, 24.
461 Park Ave ☎ 980-6785

Brooks Brothers, 36.
666 Fifth Ave ☎ 261-9440

Buccellati, 22. 46 E 57th St
☎ 308-2900, Jewelry

Bulgari, 27. 730 Fifth Ave
☎ 315-9000, Jewelry

Burberry, 14. 9 E 57th St ☎ 407-7100

Cartier, 38. 653 Fifth Ave ☎ 753-0111

Chanel, 16. 15 E 57th St ☎ 355-5050

Christian Dior, 17. 21 E 57th St
☎ 931-2950

Coach, 18.
595 Madison Ave ☎ 754-0041

Daffy's, 25. 125 E 57th St ☎ 376-4477,
Discount Clothing

Dana Buchman, 23. 65 E 57th St
☎ 319-3257

Destination Maternity, 21.
28 E 57th St ☎ 588-0220

F.A.O Schwartz, 1. 767 8th Ave
☎ 644-9400

Fendi, 29. 677 Fifth Ave ☎ 759-4646

Fortunoff, 10. 3 W 57th St
☎ 292-8800, Jewelry/Tableware

Gianni Versace Boutique, 39.
647 Fifth Ave ☎ 317-0224

Gucci, 29. 725 Fifth Ave ☎ 826-2600

H & M, 40. 640 Fifth Ave ☎ 489-0390

H Stern Jewelers, 41. 645 Fifth Ave
☎ 688-0300

Hammacher Schlemmer, 26.
147 E 57th St ☎ 421-9000

Harry Winston, 30. 718 Fifth Ave
☎ 245-2000, Jewelry

Henri Bendel, 31. 712 Fifth Ave
☎ 247-1100

Kate's Paperie, 5. 140 W 57th St
☎ 459-0700, Stationery

Lee's Art Shop, 4. 220 W 57th St
☎ 247-0110

Louis Vuitton, 11. 1 E 57th St
☎ 758-8877

Mikimoto, 27. 730 Fifth Ave
☎ 457-4600, Jewelry

Minamoto Kitchoan, 44.
608 Fifth Ave ☎ 489-3747,
Japanese Bakery

NBA Store, 36. 666 Fifth Ave
☎ 515-6221

NikeTown, 13. 6 E 57th St
☎ 891-6453

Petrossian, 2. 911 Seventh Ave
☎ 245-2217, Caviar/Gourmet

Prada, 19. 45 E 57th St ☎ 308-2332

Prada, 28. 724 Fifth Ave ☎ 664-0010

Rizzoli, 7. 31 W 57th St ☎ 759-2424,
Bookstore

Saks Fifth Ave, 43. 611 Fifth Ave
☎ 753-4000

Salvatore Ferragamo, 37.
661 Fifth Ave ☎ 759-3882

Sony Style, 34. 550 Madison Ave
☎ 833-8800, Electronics

Steinway & Sons, 6. 109 W 57th St
☎ 246-1100, Pianos

Takashimaya, 33. 693 Fifth Ave.
☎ 350-0100, Japanese Style

Teuscher Chocolates, 42. 620 Fifth Ave
☎ 246-4416

Tiffany & Co, 12. 727 Fifth Ave
☎ 755-8000

Torneau, 15. 12 E 57th St ☎ 758-7300,
Watches

Urban Center Books, 47.
457 Madison Ave ☎ 935-3595

Van Cleef & Arpels, 9.
744 Fifth Ave ☎ 644-9500

Victoria's Secret, 20. 34 E 57th St
☎ 758-5592

MAP 40 **Shopping/Upper West Side**

Listed by Site Number

1 Albee Baby	18 Eileen Fisher	36 Sean
2 West Side Kids	19 IS 44 Market	37 Lucky Brand Dungarees
3 Harry's Shoes	20 Sacco	38 Magnolia Bakery
4 Barnes & Noble	21 Gotham Gardens	39 Reebok
5 Avventura	22 Barney's CO-OP	40 Ann Taylor
6 April Cornell	23 Citarella	41 Gracious Home
7 Penny Whistle Toys	24 Fairway	42 67 Wine & Spirits
8 Daphne	25 Jacques Torres	43 Pottery Barn
9 Patagonia	26 Loehmann's	44 Balducci's
10 Berkley Girl	27 Really Great Things	45 Kiehl's
11 AMNH Shop	28 Verve	46 Banana Republic
12 Zabar's	29 Roslyn	47 Barnes & Noble
13 H & H Bagels	30 Swatch Shop	48 American Folk Art Museum Shop
14 Filene's Basement	31 Betsey Johnson	
15 LainaJane	32 Acker Merrall & Condit	49 Bed, Bath & Beyond
16 Sephora	33 Theory	50 Lululemon Athletica
17 Kenneth Cole	34 Brief Encounters	
18 Design Within Reach	35 FACE Stockholm	

MAP 40

Listed Alphabetically

Acker Merrall & Condit, 32.
160 W 72nd St ☎ 787-1700, Wine

Albee Baby, 1. 715 Amsterdam Ave
☎ 662-5740

**American Folk Art Museum Shop,
48.** 2 Lincoln Sq ☎ 595-9533, Crafts

**American Museum of Natural History
Shop, 11.** Central Park W & 79th St
☎ 800/671-7035

Ann Taylor, 40. 2017 Broadway
☎ 873-7344, Womenswear

April Cornell, 6.
487 Columbus Ave ☎ 799-1110,
Womenswear/Linens

Avventura, 5.
463 Amsterdam Ave ☎ 769-2510,
Tableware

Balducci's, 44. 155A W 66th St
☎ 653-8320, Gourmet

Banana Republic, 46.
1976 Broadway ☎ 362-7370

Berkley Girl, 10. 410 Columbus Ave
☎ 877-4770, Girls' Clothing

Barnes & Noble, 4.
2289 Broadway ☎ 362-8835

Barnes & Noble, 47.
1972 Broadway ☎ 595-6859

Barney's CO-OP, 22.
2151 Broadway ☎ 646/335-0978

Bed, Bath & Beyond, 49. 1932
Broadway ☎ 917/441-9391, Home

Betsey Johnson, 31. 248 Columbus Ave
☎ 362-3364, Womenswear

Brief Encounters, 34. 239 Columbus
Ave ☎ 496-5649, Lingerie

Citarella, 23. 2135 Broadway
☎ 874-0383, Gourmet

Daphne, 8. 467 Amsterdam Ave
☎ 877-5073, Full-figured
Womenswear

Design Within Reach, 18. 341
Columbus Ave ☎ 799-5900, Furniture

Eileen Fisher, 18.
341 Columbus Ave ☎ 362-3000

FACE Stockholm, 35. 226 Columbus
Ave ☎ 769-1420, Cosmetics

Fairway, 24.
2127 Broadway ☎ 595-1888, Gourmet

Filene's Basement, 14.
2222 Broadway ☎ 873-8000

Gotham Gardens, 21.
325 Amsterdam Ave ☎ 877-8908

Gracious Home, 41.
1992 Broadway ☎ 231-7800

H & H Bagels 13. 2239 Broadway
☎ 595-8003

Harry's Shoes, 3.
2299 Broadway ☎ 874-2035

IS 44 Market, 19.
Columbus Ave between 76th &
77th Sts. Sundays

Jacques Torres Chocolates, 25.
285 Amsterdam Ave ☎ 414-2462

Kenneth Cole, 17.
353 Columbus Ave ☎ 873-2061,
Shoes/Clothing

Kiehl's, 45. 1541 Columbus Ave
☎ 799-3438, Beauty

LainaJane, 15. 416 Amsterdam Ave
☎ 875-9168, Lingerie

Loehmann's, 26. 2101 Broadway
☎ 882-9990, Discount Fashion

Lucky Brand Dungarees, 37.
216 Columbus Ave ☎ 579-1760

Lululemon Athletica, 50.
1928 Broadway ☎ 712-1767

Magnolia Bakery, 38.
200 Columbus Ave ☎ 724-8101

Patagonia, 9. 426 Columbus Ave
☎ 917/441-0011, Activewear

Penny Whistle Toys, 7.
448 Columbus Ave ☎ 873-9090

Pottery Barn, 43.
1965 Broadway ☎ 579-8477

Really Great Things, 27.
284 Columbus Ave ☎ 787-5354,
Womenswear

Reebok, 39. 160 Columbus Ave
☎ 595-1480, Athleticwear

Roslyn, 29. 276 Columbus Ave
☎ 496-5050, Jewelry

Sacco, 20. 324 Columbus Ave
☎ 799-5229, Shoes

Sean, 36. 224 Columbus Ave
☎ 769-1489, Menswear

Sephora, 16. 2164 Broadway
☎ 717/441-4760, Cosmetics

67 Wines & Spirits, 42.
179 Columbus Ave ☎ 724-6767

Swatch Shop, 30. 100 W 72nd St
☎ 595-9640

Theory, 33. 230 Columbus Ave
☎ 362-3676, Womenswear

Verve, 28. 282 Columbus Ave
☎ 580-7150, Accessories

West Side Kids, 2.
498 Amsterdam Ave ☎ 496-7282,
Toys

Zabar's, 12. 2245 Broadway
☎ 787-2000, Gourmet

MAP 41 **Shopping/23rd St to Houston St**

W. 24th St.

Madison Square Park

W. 23rd St.

C,E

W. 22nd St.

Flatiron Building

N,R

F,V

Broadway

W. 21st St.

Seventh Ave.

W. 20th St.

W. 19th St.

W. 18th St.

Ave. of the Americas

W. 17th St.

W. 16th St.

Ninth Ave.

Eighth Ave.

W. 15th St.

A,C,E,L

1,2,3, L

F,L,V

W. 14th St.

Fifth Ave.

W. 13th St.

W. 12th St.

Greenwich Ave.

Seventh Ave. S.

W. 11th St.

Little W. 12th St.

Gansevoort St.

Horatio St.

Jane St.

Abingdon Sq.

W. 12th St.

Bethune St.

Bank St.

W. 4th St.

Waverly Pl.

Perry St.

W. 11th St.

Charles St.

W. 10th St.

Milligan Pl.

Patchin Pl.

W. 10th St.

W. 9th St.

GREENWICH VILLAGE

Gay St.

W. 8th St.

MacDougal Alley

Washington Mews

Sheridan Sq.

Waverly Pl.

Washington Sq. N.

W. Washington Pl.

Washington Square Park

Hudson River Park

West St.

Washington St.

Greenwich St.

Christopher St.

Grove St.

Jones St.

Cornelia St.

A,B,C, D,E,F,V

Washington Sq. S.

New York University

West Side Hwy.

Barrow St.

Morton St.

Leroy St.

Hudson St.

St. Luke's Pl.

Commerce St.

Bedford St.

Bleecker St.

Carmine St.

Downing St.

Sixth Ave.

Minetta La.

Father Demo Sq.

Sullivan St.

MacDougal St.

LaGuardia Pl.

W. Houston St.

Bleeck

Listed by Site Number

1 Jazz Record Center	**20** Bed, Bath & Beyond	**37** Banana Rep Men's
2 Whole Foods	**21** A.I. Friedman	**38** Kenneth Cole
3 City Quilters	**22** Books of Wonder	**39** Banana Republic Women's
4 Tekserve	**23** Academy Records & CDs	**40** Loehmann's
5 Barnes & Noble	**24** Skyline Books & Records	**41** Williams-Sonoma
6 Reminiscence	**25** Daffy's	**42** Sacco
7 NY Cake & Baking	**26** ABC Carpet	**43** Chelsea Market
8 Jo Malone	**27** Barnes & Noble	**44** Alexander McQueen
9 Shakespeare & Co	**28** Paragon	**45** Ten Thousand Things
10 Restoration Hardware	**29** Greenmarket	**46** La Perla
11 M.A.C.	**30** Aveda	**47** Stella McCartney
12 Otto Tootsi Plohound	**31** Puma Store	**48** Jeffrey NY
13 Fishs Eddy	**32** Sound by Singer	**49** Apple Store
14 Sam Flax	**33** Beads of Paradise	**50** Henry Beguelin
15 Comme des Garçons	**34** J Crew	**51** Catharine Malandrino
16 192 Books	**35** Kidding Around	**52** An Earnest Cut & Sew
17 Printed Matter	**36** Paul Smith	**53** Christian Louboutin
18 Barneys CO-OP		
19 Miya Shoji		

MAP 41

PETER COOPER VILLAGE

Gramercy Park

Beth Israel Medical Center

STUYVESANT TOWN

Stuyvesant Square

Union Square Park

ALPHABET CITY

Tompkins Square Park

EAST VILLAGE

St. Marks Pl.

Cooper Sq.

Hamilton Fish Park

Samuel Gompers Houses

MAP 41 Shopping/23rd St to Houston St

Listed Alphabetically

ABC Carpet, 26. 888 Broadway
☎ 473–3000, Home

A.I. Friedman, 21. 44 W 18th St
☎ 243–9000, Stationary/Office

Academy Records & CDs, 23. 12 W
18th St ☎ 242–3000
Used Music

Alpana Bawa, 95. 70 E First St
☎ 254–1249, Womenswear

Alphabets, 69. 115 Avenue A
☎ 475–7250, Gifts

Alexander McQueen, 44.
417 W 14th St ☎ 645–1797
Womenswear

An Earnest Cut & Sew 52.
821 Washington St ☎ 242–3414,
Jeans

Apple Store, 49. 401 W 14th St
☎ 444–3400

Astor Wines & Spirits, 92.
399 Lafayette St ☎ 674–7500

Aveda, 30. 22 E 17th St ☎ 675–7735,
Cosmetcs/Skin Care

Banana Republic Men's, 37.
114 Fifth Ave ☎ 366–4691

Banana Republic Women's, 39.
89 Fifth Ave ☎ 366–4630

Barnes & Noble, 5. 675 Sixth Ave
☎ 727–1227

Barnes & Noble, 27. 33 E 17th St
☎ 253–0810

Barnes & Noble, 89. 396 Sixth Ave
☎ 674–8780

Barneys CO-OP, 18. 236 W 18th St
☎ 593–7800, Clothing

Beads of Paradise, 33. 16 E 17th St
☎ 620–0642

Bed, Bath & Beyond, 20.
620 Sixth Ave ☎ 255–3550

Biography Bookstore, 81.
400 Bleecker St ☎ 807–8655

Black Hound, 67. 170 Second Ave
☎ 979–9505, Bakery

Bleecker Bob's, 103. 118 W Third St
☎ 475–9677, Records

Blick Art Materials, 99. 1–5 Bond St
☎ 533–2444

Books of Wonder, 22. 16 W 18th St
☎ 989–3270

Broadway Panhandler, 73.
65 E 8th St ☎ 966–3434, Kitchenware

C O Bigelow, 76. 414 Sixth Ave
☎ 533–2700, Pharmacy/Cosmetics

Catherine Malandrino, 51. 652
Hudson St ☎ 929–8710, Womenswear

Chelsea Market, 43.
75 Ninth Ave ☎ 243–6005

Christian Louboutin, 53.
59 Horatio St ☎ 255–1910, Shoes

City Quilters, 3.
133 W 25th St ☎ 807–0390

Comme des Garçons, 15.
520 W 22nd St ☎ 604–9200,
Clothing

Cones, 105. 272 Bleeker St
☎ 414–1795, Ice Cream

Crate & Barrel, 108. 611 Broadway
☎ 780–0004, Home

Daryl K, 100. 21 Bond St ☎ 529–8790,
Womenswear

Diesel, 58. 1 Union Sq W
☎ 646/336–8552, Jeans

Dinosaur Hill, 70. 306 E Ninth St
☎ 473–5850, Toys

Discovery Wines, 96. 10 Avenue A
☎ 674–7833

East West Books, 57. 78 Fifth Ave
☎ 243–5994, New Age Books

Elan, 101. 345 Lafayette ☎ 529–2724,
Antiques

Fishs Eddy, 13. 889 Broadway
☎ 420–9020, Kitchen

Flight 001, 55. 96 Greenwich Ave
☎ 989–0001, Luggage

Forbidden Planet, 62. 840 Broadway
☎ 473–1576, Comics/Sci Fi

Geppetto's Toy Box, 88.
10 Christopher St ☎ 620–7511, Toys

Greenmarket at Union Square, 29.
17th St at Broadway ☎ 788–7476

Hable Construction, 85. 117 Perry St
☎ 989–2375, Home

Henry Beguelin, 50. 18 Ninth Ave
☎ 647–8415, Leather Goods

House of Oldies, 107. 35 Carmine St
☎ 243–0500, Used Records

[hus], 87. 11 Christopher St
☎ 620–5430, Scandinavian Design

Hyde Park Antiques, 63.
836 Broadway ☎ 477–0033

J Crew, 34. 91 Fifth Ave ☎ 255–4848,
Clothing

Jazz Record Center, 1.
236 W 26th St ☎ 675–4480

Jeffrey NY, 48. 449 W 14th St
☎ 206–1272, Clothing

Jo Malone, 8. 949 Broadway
☎ 673–2220, Scent

John Derian Company, 97.
6 E Second St ☎ 677–3917, Home

Kate's Paperie, 56. 8 W 13th St
☎ 633–0570, Stationery

Listed Alphabetically (cont.)

MAP 42 Shopping/SoHo

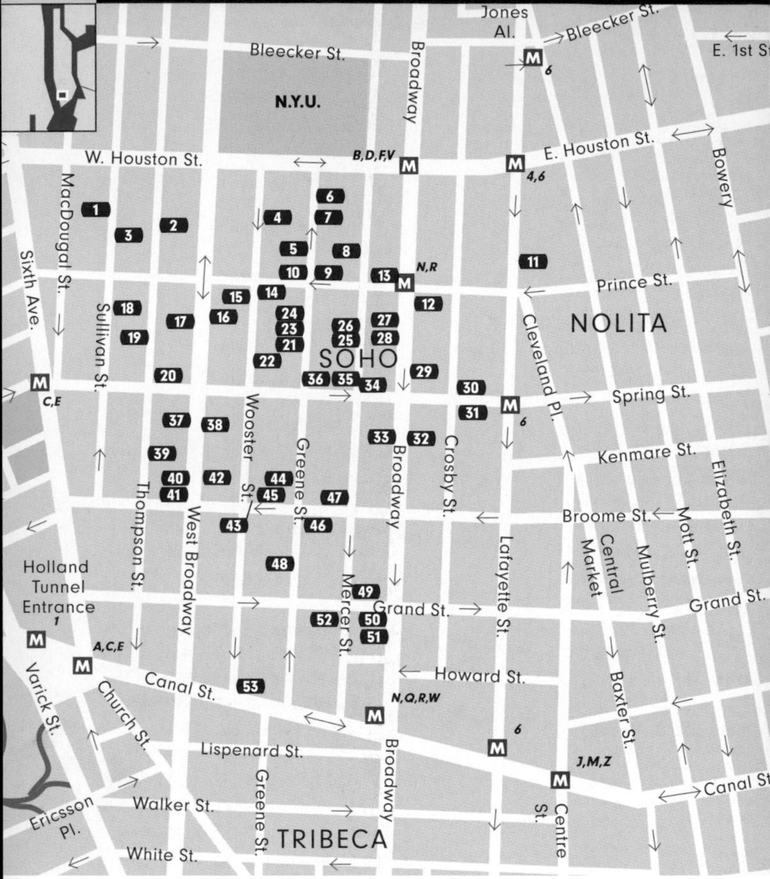

Jones Al.

Bleecker St.

Bleecker St.

E. 1st St

M 6

Broadway

N.Y.U.

W. Houston St.

B,D,F,V

E. Houston St.

M 4,6

Bowery

MacDougal St.

Sixth Ave.

1

2

3

6

7

4

5

8

10 9

13

N,R

M

11

Prince St.

NOLITA

Sullivan St.

18

17

15

16

14

24 25 23 21

26

27 28

12

Cleveland Pl.

19

22

SOHO

29

M C,E

20

36 35 34

30

31

M 6

Spring St.

37 38

Wooster St.

33 32

Kenmare St.

Elizabeth St.

39

Greene St.

Broadway

Crosby St.

Broome St.

Central Market

Mott St.

Mulberry St.

40 42

44

Lafayette St.

41

45

43

47

46

Thompson St.

West Broadway

48

Baxter St.

Grand St.

Holland Tunnel Entrance

Mercer St.

49

Grand St.

1

52

50

51

M A,C,E

M

Canal St.

53

Howard St.

N,Q,R,W

6

Varick St.

Church St.

Lispenard St.

Greene St.

Broadway

Centre St.

M

J,M,Z

M

Canal St

Ericson Pl.

Walker St.

White St.

TRIBECA

Listed by Site Number

Listed Alphabetically

Adidas Originals, 4.
136 Wooster St ☎ 777-2005

AG Adriano Goldschmied, 21.
111 Greene St ☎ 680-0581, Jeans

Agatha Ruiz de la Prada, 10.
135 Wooster St ☎ 598-4078, Clothing

Agent Provocateur, 25.
133 Mercer St ☎ 965-0229, Lingerie

Agnès b, 23. 103 Greene St
☎ 925-4649, Womenswear

Anna Sui, 24. 113 Greene St
☎ 941-8406, Womenswear

Apple Store, 9. 103 Prince St
☎ 226-3126

Anthropologie, 42. 375 W Broadway
☎ 343-7070, Womenswear/Home

APC, 26. 131 Mercer St ☎ 966-9685,
Clothing

Bloomingdales, 32.
504 Broadway ☎ 729-5900

Boca Grande Furnishings, 46.
54 Greene St ☎ 226-8766, Home

Burton, 34. 106 Spring St
☎ 966-8068, Snowboarding

Camper, 15.
125 Prince St ☎ 358-1842, Shoes

CB2, 51. 451 Broadway
☎ 219-1454, Home

Cite, 33. 131 Greene St
☎ 431-7272, Home

Clio, 20. 92 Thompson St
☎ 966-8991, Home

Costume National, 22.
108 Wooster St ☎ 431-1530, Clothing

D&G, 17. 434 W Broadway
☎ 965-8000, Clothing

Dean & DeLuca, 12. 560 Broadway
☎ 226-6800, Gourmet

Depression Modern, 1.
150 Sullivan St ☎ 982-5699, Antiques

Eileen Fisher, 38. 395 W Broadway
☎ 431-4567, Womenswear

French Connection, 16. 435 W
Broadway ☎ 219-1197, Clothing

Hilfiger, 41. 372 W Broadway
☎ 917/237-0983

Global Table, 18. 107-109 Sullivan St
☎ 431-5839, Tableware

Jonathan Adler, 48.
47 Greene St ☎ 941-8950, Home

Kate Spade, 47. 454 Broome St
☎ 274-1991, Accessories

Kate's Paperie, 31.
72 Spring St ☎ 941-9816

Kee's Chocolate, 39.
80 Thompson St
☎ 334-3284

Kirna Zabete, 36. 96 Greene St
☎ 941-9656, Womenswear

Luce Plan, 44. 49 Greene St
☎ 966-1399, Lighting

Marc Jacobs, 8. 163 Mercer
☎ 343-1490

MarieBelle, 45. 484 Broome St
☎ 923-6999, Chocolate

Moss, 6. 150 Greene St ☎ 204-7100,
Home

Muji, 50. 455 Broadway
☎ 334-2002, Home/Office

Paul Smith, 7. 142 Greene St
☎ 613-3060, Clothing

Pearl River Mart, 33. 477 Broadway
☎ 431-4770, Asian Department Store

Peter Fox, 19. 105 Thompson St
☎ 431-7426, Shoes

Pleats Please Issey Miyake, 14.
128 Wooster St ☎ 226-3600, Clothing

Prada, 13.
575 Broadway ☎ 334-8888

Purl, 3. 137 Sullivan St
☎ 420-8796, Knitting

Robert Lee Morris, 37.
400 W Broadway ☎ 431-9405,
Jewelry

Santa Maria Novella, 11.
285 Lafayette St ☎ 925-0001,
Cosmetics

Scholastic Store, 28. 557 Broadway
☎ 343-6166, Children's Books

Sean, 2. 132 Thompson St
☎ 598-5980, Menswear

Sephora, 27. 555 Broadway
☎ 625-1309, Cosmetics

Sur La Table, 30. 75 Spring St
☎ 966-3375, Kitchen/Tableware

Te Casan 40. 382 W Broadway
☎ 584-8000, Shoes

3.1 Phillip Lim, 35. 115 Mercer St
☎ 334-1160, Clothing

Traveler's Choice Bookstore, 53.
2 Wooster St ☎ 941-1535

Uniqlo 29. 546 Broadway
☎ 917/237-8800, Clothing

Vivienne Tam, 49.
40 Mercer ☎ 966-2398, Clothing

Vintage New York, 43. 482 Broome St
☎ 226-9463, Wine

Yohji Yamamoto, 52.
103 Grand St ☎ 966-9066, Clothing

MAP 43 **Shopping/Lower East Side & NoLita**

Listed by Site Number

1	Femmegems
2	Groupe 16sur20
3	Area I.D. Moderne
4	Mayle
5	Whole Foods
6	Seize sur Vingt
7	Me + Ro
8	Le Labo
9	Sigerson Morrison
10	McNally Robinson
11	Bess
12	Triple Five Soul
13	Eileen's Special Cheesecake
14	Ceci-cela
15	Tracy Feith
16	Resurrection
17	Zero + Maria Cornejo
18	Hollywould

19	Erica Tanov
20	Doyle & Doyle
21	Russ and Daughters
22	Las Venus
23	Blibetroy
23	September
24	Ludlow Guitars
25	Foley + Corinna
26	The Light Fantastic
27	20 Peacocks
28	de-vino
29	Economy Candy
30	Sugar Sweet Sunshine
31	Dolce Vita
32	Bluestockings
33	Jutta Newman
34	Frock
35	Babeland

36	Essex Market
37	Ekovaruhuset
38	Lower East Side Tenement Museum Gift Shop
39	il Laboratorio del Gelato
40	Guss' Pickles
41	Kossar's Bialys
42	Doughnut Plant

Listed Alphabetically

Area I.D. Moderne, 3.
262 Elizabeth St ☎ 219–9903,
Antiques/Home

Babeland, 35. 94 Rivington St
☎ 375–1701, Adult Toys

Bess, 11. 292 Lafayette St
☎ 219–0723, Jewelry

Bilbetroy, 23. 100 Stanton St
☎ 979–5250, Handbags

Bluestockings, 32. 172 Allen St
☎ 777–6028, Radical Books

Ceci-cela, 14. 55 Spring St
☎ 274–9179, Bakery

de-vino, 28. 30 Clinton St
☎ 228–0073, Wine

Dolce Vita, 31. 149 Ludlow St
☎ 529–2111, Shoes

Doughnut Plant, 42. 379 Grand St
☎ 505–3700

Doyle & Doyle, 20. 189 Orchard St
☎ 677–9991, Antique Jewelry

Economy Candy, 29. 108 Rivington St
☎ 254–1531

Eileen's Special Cheesecake, 13.
17 Cleveland Pl ☎ 966–5585

Ekovaruhuset, 37. 123 Ludlow St
☎ 673–1753, Organic/Fair Trade
Clothing

Erica Tanov, 19 204 Elizabeth St
☎ 334–8020, Clothing

Essex Street Market, 36. 120 Essex St
☎ 312–3603, Gourmet

Femmegems, 1. 280 Mulberry St
☎ 625–1611, Jewelry

Foley + Corinna, 25. 114 Stanton St
☎ 529–2338, Womenswear

Frock, 34. 148 Orchard St
☎ 594–5380, Vintage

Groupe 16sur20, 2. 267 Elizabeth St
☎ 343–0007, Menswear

Guss' Pickles, 40. 85 Orchard St
☎ 334–3616

Hollywould, 18. 198 Elizabeth St
☎ 219–1905, Shoes

il Laboratorio del Gelato, 39.
95 Orchard St ☎ 343–9922,
Ice Cream

Jutta Newman, 33. 158 Allen St
☎ 982–7048, Leather Goods

Kossar's Bialys, 41. 367 Grand St
☎ 473–4810

Las Venus, 22. 163 Ludlow St
☎ 982–0608, 20th Century Furniture

Le Labo, 8. 233 Elizabeth St
☎ 219–2230, Scent

The Light Fantastic, 26.
37–39 Clinton St ☎ 772–2502, Lamps

**Lower East Side Tenement Museum
Gift Shop, 38.** 108 Orchard St
☎ 431–0233

Ludlow Guitars, 24. 164 Ludlow St
☎ 353–1775

Mayle, 4. 242 Elizabeth St
☎ 625–0406, Womenswear

McNally Robinson, 10. 52 Prince St
☎ 274–1160, Books

Me + Ro, 7. 241 Elizabeth St
☎ 917/237–9215, Jewelry

Resurrection, 16. 217 Mott St
☎ 625–1374, Vintage

Russ and Daughters, 21.
179 E Houston St ☎ 475–4880,
Gourmet

September Wines & Spirits, 23.
100 Stanton St ☎ 388–0770

Seize sur Vingt, 6.
243 Elizabeth St ☎ 343–0476,
Custom Tailoring/Menswear

Sigerson Morrison, 9 28 Prince St
☎ 219–3893, Shoes

Sugar Sweet Sunshine, 30.
126 Rivington St ☎ 995–1960, Bakery

Tracy Feith, 15. 209 Mulberry St
☎ 334–3097, Womenswear

Triple Five Soul, 12. 290 Lafayette St
☎ 431–0404, Clothing

20 Peacocks, 27. 20 Clinton St
☎ 387–8660, Menswear

Whole Foods, 5. 95 E Houston St
☎ 420–1320

Zero + Maria Cornejo, 17.
225 Mott St ☎ 925–3849,
Womenswear

MAP 44 **Restaurants/Midtown**

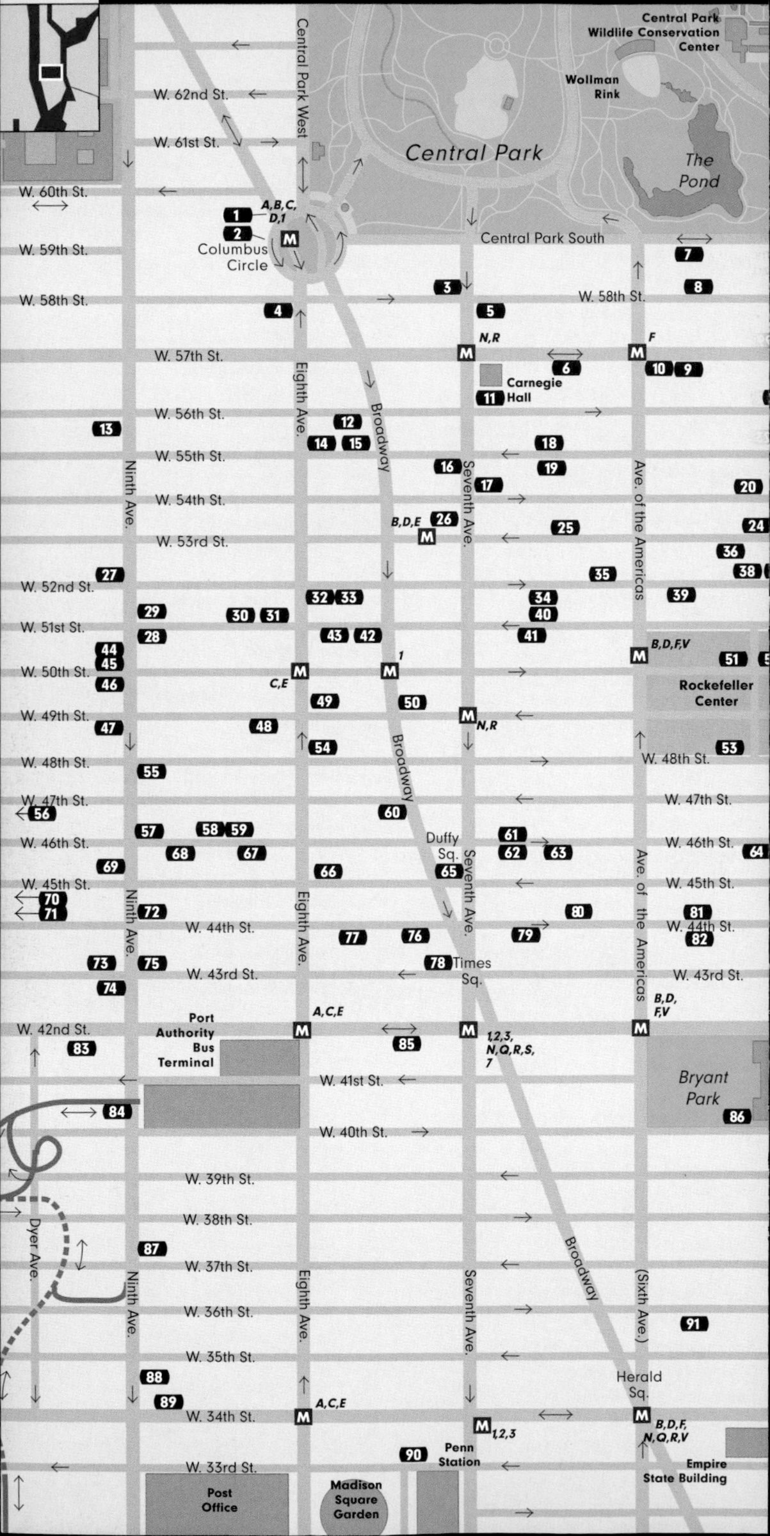

Central Park West

W. 62nd St.

W. 61st St.

W. 60th St.

W. 59th St.

1
2

Columbus Circle

M

W. 58th St.

4

3

5

Central Park

Central Park Wildlife Conservation Center

Wollman Rink

The Pond

Central Park South

7

8

W. 58th St.

W. 57th St.

Eighth Ave.

Broadway

N,R

M

6

F

M

Carnegie Hall

10 **9**

11

W. 56th St.

13

12

W. 55th St.

14 **15**

18

16

19

Seventh Ave.

W. 54th St.

17

W. 53rd St.

B,D,E **26**

M

Ninth Ave.

20

Ave. of the Americas

24

25

W. 52nd St.

27

35

36

38

39

W. 51st St.

29

30 **31**

32 **33**

34

40

W. 50th St.

28

43 **42**

41

B,D,F,V

M

51

Rockefeller Center

44
45
46

M

C,E

49

1

M

50

W. 49th St.

47

48

M N,R

W. 48th St.

54

53

W. 48th St.

W. 47th St.

55

60

W. 47th St.

56

W. 46th St.

57

58 **59**

61

W. 46th St.

64

68

67

62 **63**

W. 45th St.

69

66

Duffy Sq.

65

80

81

W. 44th St.

82

70
71

72

77 **76**

79

W. 45th St.

73

75

W. 44th St.

Eighth Ave.

Ninth Ave.

Seventh Ave.

Ave. of the Americas

78 Times Sq.

W. 43rd St.

74

W. 43rd St.

B,D, F,V

W. 42nd St.

83

Port Authority Bus Terminal

A,C,E

M

85

M 1,2,3, N,Q,R,S, 7

84

W. 41st St.

Bryant Park

86

W. 40th St.

W. 39th St.

Dyer Ave.

W. 38th St.

87

W. 37th St.

Eighth Ave.

Ninth Ave.

Seventh Ave.

(Sixth Ave.)

Broadway

91

W. 36th St.

W. 35th St.

88

Herald Sq.

89

A,C,E

M

W. 34th St.

M B,D,F, N,Q,R,V

Empire State Building

W. 33rd St.

90

Penn Station

M 1,2,3

Post Office

Madison Square Garden

Fifth Ave.

E. 63rd St.

B,Q
Ⓜ

E. 62nd St.

E. 61st St.

E. 60th St.

E. 59th St.

4,5,6,
N,R
Ⓜ

TRAMWAY TO
ROOSEVELT
ISLAND

N,R

Ⓜ

Plaza

Madison Ave.

E. 58th St.

92

Park Ave.

94

93 **95**

96

First Ave.

Lexington Ave.

Third Ave.

Second Ave.

99

97

E. 57th St.

98

22

100

E. 56th St.

23

E. 55th St.

101

102

103

105

E. 54th St.

104

E,V

E. 53rd St.

106

E,V
Ⓜ

107

108

Ⓜ

113

111 **110**

115

E. 52nd St.

114

112

109

St. Patrick's
Cathedral

E. 51st St.

6
Ⓜ

122

123

116

E. 50th St.

117

118 **119**

E. 49th St.

121

120

127

126 **124**

125

129

E. 48th St.

128

130

E. 47th St.

United Nations Plaza

Beekman Pl.

United
Nations
Headquarters

131

E. 46th St.

134 **135**

136

138

E. 45th St.

137

Madison Ave.

Vanderbilt Ave.

E. 44th St.

Grand Central
Terminal

E. 43rd St.

139

132 **133**

Ⓜ
S

Ⓜ
4,5,
6,7

Chrysler
Building

E. 42nd St.

First Ave.

140

N.Y. Public
Library
(Main)

E. 41st St.

FDR Dr.

NYU
Medical
Center

Fifth Ave.

E. 40th St.

E. 39th St.

141

N

E. 38th St.

142

Park Ave.

Lexington Ave.

Third Ave.

E. 37th St.

143

E. 36th St.

Madison Ave.

Second Ave.

E. 35th St.

First Ave.

0   7500 feet

0   250 meters

E. 34th St.

E. 33rd St.

6
Ⓜ

E. 32nd St.

Kips
Bay
Plaza

NYU
Medical
Center

MAP **44** **Restaurants/Midtown**

Listed by Site Number

1 Asiate
2 Bouchon Bakery
2 Landmarc
2 Masa
2 Per Se
2 Porter House
3 Le Pain Quotidien
4 Blue Ribbon Sushi Bar & Grill
5 Petrossian
6 Burger Joint
7 Mickey Mantle's
8 Quality Meats
9 Mangia
10 Rue 57
11 Molyvos
12 Patsy's
13 Puttanesca
14 Nocello
15 Sugiyama
16 Carnegie Deli
17 Abboccato
18 Estiatorio Milos
19 Osteria del Circo
20 Il Gattopardo
21 Beacon
22 Town
23 Fives
24 The Modern
25 Remi
26 Stage Deli
27 Casellula Cheese & Wine Café
28 Vynl
29 Island Burgers
30 René Pujol
31 Tout Va Bien
32 Victor's Café
33 Gallagher's
34 Bar Americain
35 Ben Benson's
35 Delta Grill
36 China Grill
37 Soba Nippon
38 21 Club
39 Anthos
40 Le Bernardin
41 Ruth's Chris Steakhouse
42 Mars 2112
43 Azalea
44 Uncle Nick's
45 Grand Sichuan International

46 La Locanda
47 Pam Real Thai
48 Churrascaria Plataforma
49 Baldoria
50 Ruby Foo's
51 Brasserie Ruhlmann
52 Sea Grill
53 Shaan
54 Pigalle
55 Delta Grill
56 Meskerem
57 Firebird
58 Barbetta
59 Becco
60 Blue Fin
61 Havana Central
62 Le Marais
63 District
64 Via Brasil
65 Planet Hollywood
66 Frankie & Johnnie's
67 Orso
68 Le Rivage
69 Zen Palate
70 Hallo Berlin
71 44 & X Hell's Kitchen
72 Marseille
73 Le Madeleine
74 Esca
75 Chimichurri Grill
76 Carmine's
77 John's Pizzeria
78 Hard Rock Café
79 Virgil's Real BBQ
80 Café Un Deux Trois
81 Triomphe
82 db bistro moderne
83 Chez Josephine
84 Cupcake Cafe
85 Above
86 Bryant Park Grill
87 Market Cafe
88 Uncle Jack's Steakhouse
89 Soul Fixins
90 Nick & Stef's Steakhouse
91 Keen's
92 Tao
93 Dawat
94 Felidia
95 Chola

96 Rosa Mexicano
97 Le Colonial
98 BLT Steak
99 Brasserie 8 1/2
29 Island Burgers
100 Ardour Alain Ducasse
101 Aquavit
102 Shun Lee Palace
103 Tea Box Café
104 San Pietro
105 Oceana
106 Lever House
107 Houston's
108 Vong
109 Le Perigord
110 Peking Duck
111 Solera
112 Nippon
113 Brasserie
114 Four Seasons
115 La Grenouille
116 Tse Yang
117 Maloney & Porcelli
118 Sushiden
119 Barbès
120 Inagiku
121 Peacock Alley
122 Montparnasse
123 Zarela
124 Pampano
125 Chin Chin
126 Smith & Wollensky
127 Heartbeat
128 Avra
129 Hatsuhana
130 Kuruma Zushi
131 Morton's
132 Michael Jordan's
133 Oyster Bar
134 Nanni's
135 Patroon
136 Spark's Steak House
137 Palm
138 Alcalá
139 Sushi Yasuda
140 L'Impero
141 Wu Liang Ye
142 AQ Café
143 Josie's

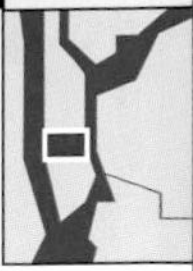

MAP **44**

Listed Alphabetically

Abboccato, 17. 136 W 55th St
☎ 265-4000. Italian. $$$

Above, 85. 234 W 42nd St
☎ 642-2626. American. $$

Adour Alain Ducasse, 100 2 E 55th St
☎ 710-2277. French. $$$$

Alcalá, 138. 342 E 46th St
☎ 370-1866. Spanish. $-$$

Anthos, 39. 36 W 52nd St
☎ 582-6900. Greek. $$-$$$$

AQ Café, 142. 58 Park Ave
☎ 847-9745. Scandinavian. ¢

Aquavit, 101. 65 E 55th St
☎ 307-7311. Scandinavian. $$$$

Asiate, 1. 80 Columbus Circle
☎ 805-8881. Japanese/French. $$$$

Avra, 128. 141 E 48th St ☎ 759-8550.
Greek Seafood. $$-$$$$

Azalea, 43. 224 W 51st St
☎ 262-0105. Italian. $-$$

Baldoria, 49. 249 W 49th St
☎ 582-0460. Italian. $$

Bar Americain, 34. 152 W 52nd St
☎ 265-9700. Brasserie. $$$

Barbès, 119. 21 E 36th St
☎ 684-0215. Moroccan. $-$$

Barbetta, 58. 321 W 46th St
☎ 246-9171. Italian. $$$$

Beacon, 21. 25 W 56th St
☎ 332-0500. American. $$-$$$

Becco, 59. 355 W 46th St
☎ 397-7597. Italian. $$

Ben Benson's, 35. 123 W 52nd St
☎ 581-8888. Steak. $$$$

BLT Steak, 98. 106 E 57th St
☎ 752-7470. Steakhouse. $$$-$$$$

Blue Fin, 60. 1567 Broadway
☎ 918-1400. Seafood. $$-$$$

Blue Ribbon Sushi Bar & Grill, 4.
308 W 58th St ☎ 397-0404.
Sushi/Steak. $$-$$$

Bouchon Bakery, 12. 10 Columbus
Circle ☎ 823-9366. Café. $

Brasserie, 113. 100 E 53rd St
☎ 751-4840. French. $$-$$$

Brasserie 8 1/2, 99. 9 W 57th St
☎ 829-0812. French. $$-$$$

Brasserie Ruhlmann, 51.
45 Rockefeller Pl ☎ 974-2020.
Brasserie. $$-$$$

Burger Joint, 6. 118 W 57th St
☎ 245-5000, Burgers. ¢

Bryant Park Grill, 86. 25 W 40th St
☎ 840-6500. American. $$-$$$

Café Un Deux Trois, 80. 123 W 44th
St ☎ 354-4148. French. $$

Carmine's, 76. 200 W 44th St
☎ 221-3800. Italian. $$

Carnegie Deli, 16. 854 Seventh Ave
☎ 757-2245. Deli. $$

Casellula Chese & Wine Café, 27.
401 W 52nd St ☎ 247-8137.
American. $

Chez Josephine, 83. 414 W 42nd St
☎ 594-1925. International. $$-$$$

Chimichurri Grill, 75. 606 Ninth Ave
☎ 586-8655. Argentine. $-$$

Chin Chin, 125. 216 E 49th St
☎ 888-4555. Chinese. $-$$$

China Grill, 36. 60 W 53rd St
☎ 333-7788. Pan-Asian. $$$-$$$$

Chola, 95. 232 E 58th St
☎ 688-4619. Indian. $-$$

Churrascaria Plataforma, 48.
316 W 49th St ☎ 245-0505.
Brazilian. $$$$

Cupcake Cafe, 84. 545 Ninth Ave
☎ 465-1530. Bakery/Cafe. ¢

Dawat, 93. 210 E 58th St
☎ 355-7555. Indian. $-$$

db bistro moderne, 82. 55 W 44th St
☎ 391-5353. French. $$$

Delta Grill, 55. 700 Ninth Ave
☎ 956-0934. Cajun. $-$$

District, 63. 130 W 46th St
☎ 485-2999. American. $-$$

Esca, 74. 402 W 43rd St ☎ 564-7272.
Italian Seafood. $$-$$$

Estiatorio Milos, 18. 125 W 55th St
☎ 245-7400. Greek Seafood. $$$$

Felidia, 94. 243 E 58th St ☎ 758-1479.
Italian. $-$$$

L'Atelier de Joël Rubuchon, 98.
57 E 57th St ☎ 350-6658. French. $$$$

Firebird, 57. 365 W 46th St
☎ 586-0244. Russian. $$$$

Fives, 23. 700 Fifth Ave
☎ 903-3918. Eclectic. $$$-$$$$

44 & X Hell's Kitchen, 71.
622 Tenth Ave ☎ 977-1170.
American. $-$$$

Four Seasons, 114. 99 E 52nd St
☎ 754-9494. American. $$$$

$$$$ = **over $40** $$$ = **$30-$40** $$ = **$20-$29** $ = **$10-$19**   ¢ = **under $10**
Based on cost per person for an entrée.

MAP 44 **Restaurants/Midtown**

Listed Alphabetically (cont.)

Frankie & Johnnie's, 66.
269 W 45th St ☎ 997-9494.
Steak. $$-$$$

Gallagher's, 33. 228 W 52nd St
☎ 245-5336. Steakhouse. $-$$$$

Grand Sichuan International, 45. 745
Ninth Ave ☎ 582-2288. Chinese. $

Hallo Berlin, 70. 626 Tenth Ave
☎ 977-1944. German. ¢

Hard Rock Cafe, 78. 1501 Broadway
☎ 343-3355. American. $

Hatsuhana, 129. 17 E 48th St
☎ 355-3345. Japanese. $$-$$$$

Havana Central, 61. 151 W 46th St
☎ 398-7440. Cuban. $-$$

Heartbeat, 127. 149 E 49th St ☎ 407-2900.
American. $$-$$$

Houston's, 107. 153 E 53rd St
☎ 888-3828. American. $-$$$

Il Gattopardo, 20. 33 W 54th St
☎ 246-0412. Italian. $$-$$$

Inagiku, 120. 111 E 49th St
☎ 355-0440. Japanese. $$-$$$$

Island Burgers & Shakes, 29.
766 Ninth Ave ☎ 307-7934. ¢

John's Pizzeria, 77. 260 W 44th St
☎ 391-7560. Pizza. ¢-$

Josie's, 143. 565 Third Ave
☎ 490-1558. Healthy. $-$$

Keen's, 91. 72 W 36th St ☎ 947-3636.
Steak. $$-$$$$

Kuruma Zushi, 130. 7 E 47th St
☎ 317-2802. Japanese. $$$-$$$$

La Grenouille, 103. 3 E 52nd St
☎ 752-1495. French. $$$$

La Locanda, 35. 737 Ninth Ave
☎ 258-2900. Italian. $-$$

Landmarc, 2. 10 Columbus Circle
☎ 823-6123. Bistro. $-$$$

Le Bernardin, 46. 155 W 51st St
☎ 489-1515. French Seafood. $$$$

Le Colonial, 99. 149 E 57th St
☎ 752-0808. Vietnamese. $-$$

Le Madeleine, 80. 403 W 43rd St
☎ 246-2993. French. $-$$

Le Marais, 69. 150 W 46th St
☎ 869-0900. French/Kosher. $-$$$

Le Pain Quotidien, 3. 922 Seventh Ave
☎ 757-0775. French Bakery. $

Le Perigord, 109. 405 E 52nd St
☎ 755-6244. French. $$$

Le Rivage, 68. 340 W 46th St
☎ 765-7374. French. $$$

Lever House, 106. 390 Park Ave
☎ 888-2700. Contemporary. $$$-$$$$

L'Impero, 140. 45 Tudor City Pl
☎ 599-5045. Italian. $$-$$$

Maloney & Porcelli, 117. 37 E 50th St
☎ 750-2233. Contemporary. $$-$$$$

Mangia, 9. 50 W 57th St
☎ 582-5882. Italian. ¢-$

Market Cafe, 87. 496 Ninth Ave
☎ 967-3892. American. ¢-$

Mars 2112, 42. 1633 Broadway
☎ 582-2112. Eclectic. $-$$

Marseille, 72. 630 Ninth Ave
☎ 333-3410. French. $$

Masa, 2. 10 Columbus Circle
☎ 823-9800. Japanese. $$$$

Meskerem, 56. 468 W 47th St
☎ 664-0520. Ethiopian. $

**Michael Jordan's The Steak House
NYC, 132.** 23 Vanderbilt Ave
☎ 655-2300. Steak. $$$$

Mickey Mantle's, 7. 42 Central Park S
☎ 688-7777. American. $-$$

The Modern, 24. 9 W 53rd St
☎ 333-1220. French. $$$$

Molyvos, 11. 871 Seventh Ave
☎ 582-7500. Greek. $$-$$$

Montparnasse, 122. 230 E 51st St
☎ 758-6633. French. $$

Morton's, 131. 551 Fifth Ave
☎ 972-3315. Steak. $$$$

Nanni's, 134. 146 E 46th St
☎ 697-4161. Italian. $$-$$$

Nick & Stef's Steakhouse, 90.
9 Penn Plaza ☎ 563-4444.
Steak. $$-$$$$

Nippon, 112. 155 E 52nd St
☎ 758-0226. Japanese. $$-$$$

Nocello, 14. 257 W 55th St
☎ 713-0224. Italian. $-$$

Oceana, 105. 55 E 54th St
☎ 759-5941. Seafood. $$$$

Orso, 67. 322 W 46th St ☎ 489-7212.
Italian. $$

Osteria del Circo, 19. 120 W 55th St
☎ 265-3636. Italian. $$

Oyster Bar Station, 133. Grand Central
Station ☎ 490-6650. Seafood. $$

Palm, 137. 837 Second Ave
☎ 687-2953. Steak. $$$$

Pampano, 124. 209 E 49th St
☎ 751-4545. Mexican. $$-$$$

Pam Real Thai, 47. 404 W 49th St
☎ 333-7500. Thai. ¢-$

MAP 44

Listed Alphabetically (cont.)

Patroon, 135. 160 E 46th St
☎ 883-7373. American. $$–$$$$

Patsy's, 12. 236 W 56th St
☎ 247-3491. Italian. $$–$$$

Peacock Alley, 121. 301 Park Ave
☎ 872-1275. American. $$–$$$

Peking Duck, 110. 236 E 53rd St
☎ 759-8260. Chinese. $–$$$

Per Se, 2. 10 Columbus Circle
☎ 823-9335. French. $$$$

Petrossian, 5. 182 W 58th St
☎ 245-2214. Continental. $$–$$$$

Pigalle, 54. 790 Eighth Ave
☎ 489-2233. French. $–$$

Planet Hollywood, 65.
1540 Broadway ☎ 333-7827.
American. $–$$

Porter House, 2. 10 Columbus Ave
☎ 823-9500. Steakhouse. $$$$

Puttanesca, 13. 859 Ninth Ave
☎ 581-4177. Italian. $

Quality Meats, 8. 57 W 58th St
☎ 371-7777. Steakhouse. $$–$$$$

Remi, 25. 145 W 53rd St ☎ 581-4242.
Italian. $–$$$

René Pujol, 30. 321 W 51st St
☎ 246-3023. French. $$$$

Rosa Mexicano, 96. 1063 First Ave
☎ 753-7407. Mexican. $–$$

Ruby Foo's, 50. 1626 Broadway
☎ 489-5600. Pan-Asian. $–$$

Rue 57, 10. 60 W 57th St
☎ 307-5656. French/Japanese. $$–$$$

Ruth's Chris Steakhouse, 41.
148 W 51st St ☎ 245-9600.
Steak. $$$–$$$$

San Pietro, 104. 18 E 54th St
☎ 753-9015. Italian. $$–$$$$

Sea Grill, 52. 19 W 49th St
☎ 332-7610. Seafood. $$$

Shaan, 53. Rockefeller Ctr, 57 W 48th St
☎ 977-8400. Indian. $–$$

Shun Lee Palace, 102.
155 E 55th St ☎ 371-8844.
Chinese. $$

Smith & Wollensky, 126.
797 Third Ave ☎ 753-1530.
Steak. $–$$$$

Soba Nippon, 37. 19 W 52nd St
☎ 489-2525. Japanese. $–$$

Solera, 111. 216 E 53rd St
☎ 644-1166. Spanish. $$–$$$$

Soul Fixins', 89. 371 W 34th St
☎ 736-1345. Soul. ¢–$

Sparks Steak House, 136.
210 E 46th St ☎ 687-4855. Steak.
$$$$

Stage Deli, 26. 834 Seventh Ave
☎ 245-7850. Deli. $

Sugiyama, 15. 251 W 55th St
☎ 956-0670. Japanese. $$$$

Sushi Yasuda, 139. 204 E 43rd St
☎ 972-1001. Japanese. $$–$$$

Sushiden, 118. 19 E 49th St
☎ 758-2700. Japanese. $$–$$$

Tao, 92. 42 E 58th St ☎ 888-2288.
Pan-Asian. $$–$$$

Tea Box Café, 103. 693 Fifth Ave
(Takashimaya) ☎ 350-0180.
Japanese Café/Bakery. ¢–$

Tout Va Bien, 31. 311 W 51st St
☎ 265-0190. French. $–$$

Town, 22. 15 W 56th St ☎ 582-4445.
Contemporary. $$$$

Triomphe, 81. 49 W 44th St
☎ 453-4233. French. $$–$$$

Tse Yang, 116. 34 E 51st St
☎ 688-5447. Chinese. $–$$$

21 Club, 38. 21 W 52nd St
☎ 582-7200. American. $$$$

Uncle Jack's Steakhouse, 88.
440 Ninth Ave ☎ 244-0005.
Steakhouse. $$$$

Uncle Nick's, 44. 747 Ninth Ave
☎ 245-7992. Greek. $–$$

Via Brasil, 64. 34 W 46th St
☎ 997-1158. Brazilian. $–$$

Victor's Café, 32. 236 W 52nd St
☎ 586-7714. Cuban. $–$$$

Virgil's Real BBQ, 79. 152 W 44th St
☎ 921-9494. Barbecue. $$

Vong, 108. 200 E 54th St ☎ 486-9592.
Pan-Asian. $$–$$$$

Vynl, 28. 759 Ninth Ave ☎ 974-2003.
Eclectic. ¢–$$

Wu Liang Ye, 141. 338 Lexington Ave
☎ 370-9647. Chinese. ¢–$$

Zarela, 123. 953 Second Ave
☎ 644-6740. Mexican. $–$$

Zen Palate, 69. 663 Ninth Ave
☎ 582-1669. Vegetarian. ¢–$

$$$$ = *over $40* $$$ = *$30–$39* $$ = *$20–$29* $ = *$10–$19*   ¢ = *under $10*
Based on cost per person for an entrée.

MAP 45 Restaurants/Upper West Side

Listed by Site Number

1 Charles'
2 Amy Ruth's
3 Miss Mamie's Spoonbread Too
4 Pio Pio
5 Gennaro
6 Saigon Grill
7 Dinosaur Bar-B-Que
8 Alouette
9 Docks
10 Buceo 95
11 Carmine's
12 The Mermaid Inn
13 Barney Greengrass
14 Nonna
15 Celeste
16 Ouest

17 Good Enough to Eat
18 Artie's Delicatessen
19 Fred's
20 Hampton Chutney Co.
21 Flor de Mayo
22 Calle Ocho
23 EJ's Luncheonette
24 Cafe con Leche
25 Sarabeth's
26 Kefi
27 Nice Matin
28 Ruby Foo's
29 Ocean Grill
30 Sushi of Gari
31 Cafe Frida
32 Isabella's
33 Citrus

34 'Cesca
35 Earthen Oven
36 Josie's
37 Shark Bar
38 Penang
39 Pasha
40 Café Luxembourg
41 Café des Artistes
42 Tavern on the Green
43 Telepan
44 Ollie's
45 Shun Lee West
46 Bar Boulud
47 Picholine
48 Jean Georges
49 Gabriel's
50 Rosa Mexicano

MAP 45

Listed Alphabetically

Alouette, 8. 2588 Broadway ☎ 222-6808. French. $-$$

Amy Ruth's, 2. 113 W 116th St ☎ 280-8779. Southern. $

Artie's Delicatessen, 18. 2290 Broadway ☎ 579-5959. Deli. ¢

Bar Boulud, 46. 1900 Broadway ☎ 595-0303. French. $

Barney Greengrass, 13. 541 Amsterdam Ave ☎ 724-4707. Deli. $

Buceo 95, 10. 201 W 95th St ☎ 662-7010. Tapas. $$

Café con Leche, 24. 424 Amsterdam Ave ☎ 595-7000. Latin. ¢-$

Café des Artistes, 41. 1 W 67th St ☎ 877-3500. Continental. $$$-$$$$

Cafe Frida, 31. 368 Columbus Ave ☎ 712-2929. Mexican. $-$$

Café Luxembourg, 40. 200 W 70th St ☎ 873-7411. French. $$

Calle Ocho, 22. 446 Columbus Ave ☎ 873-5025. Latin. $$

Carmine's, 11. 2450 Broadway ☎ 362-2200. Italian. $$

Celeste, 15. 502 Amsterdam Ave ☎ 874-4559. Italian.¢-$

'Cesca, 34. 164 W 75th St ☎ 787-6300. Italian. $$

Charles' Southern Style Kitchen, 1. 2841 Eighth Ave ☎ 926-4313. Soul. ¢

Citrus, 33. 320 Amsterdam Ave ☎ 595-0500. Asian/Latin. $-$$

Dinosaur Bar-B-Que, 7. 646 W 131st St ☎ 694-1777. Barbecue. $

Docks Oyster Bar, 9. 2427 Broadway ☎ 724-5588. Seafood. $$

Earthen Oven, 35. 53 W 72nd St ☎ 579-8888. Indian. $-$$

EJ's Luncheonette, 23. 447 Amsterdam Ave ☎ 873-3444. American. ¢-$

Flor de Mayo, 21. 484 Amsterdam Ave ☎ 787-3388. Latin American/Chinese. ¢-$

Fred's, 19. 476 Amsterdam Ave ☎ 579-3076. American. ¢-$

Gabriel's, 49. 11 W 60th St ☎ 956-4600. Italian. $$-$$$

Gennaro, 5. 665 Amsterdam Ave ☎ 665-5348. Italian. $

Good Enough to Eat, 17. 483 Amsterdam Ave ☎ 496-0163. American. ¢-$

Hampton Chutney Co., 20. 464 Amsterdam Ave ☎ 362-5050. Indian. ¢-$

Isabella's, 32. 359 Columbus Ave ☎ 724-2100. Contemporary $-$$

Jean-Georges, 48. 1 Central Park W ☎ 299-3900. French. $$$$

Josie's, 36. 300 Amsterdam Ave ☎ 769-1212. Healthy American. $

Kefi, 26. 222 W 79th St ☎ 873-0200. Greek. $

Josie's, 36. 300 Amsterdam Ave ☎ 769-1212. Healthy American. $

The Mermaid Inn, 12. 568 Amsterdam Ave ☎ 799-7400. Seafood. $$

Miss Mamie's Spoonbread Too, 3. 366 W 110th St ☎ 865-6744. Southern. $

Nice Matin, 27. 201 W 79th St ☎ 873-6423. French. $-$$

Nonna, 14. 520 Columbus Ave ☎ 579-3194. Italian. $

Ocean Grill, 29. 384 Columbus Ave ☎ 579-2300. Seafood. $$

Ollie's, 44. 1991 Broadway ☎ 595-8181. Chinese. ¢-$

Ouest, 16. 2315 Broadway ☎ 580-8700. Contemporary. $$-$$$$

Pasha, 39. 70 W 71st St ☎ 579-8751. Turkish. $-$$

Penang, 38. 127 W 72nd St ☎ 769-8889. Malaysian. $

Picholine, 47. 35 W 64th St ☎ 724-8585. French. $$$

Pio Pio 4. 702 Amsterdam Ave ☎ 665-3000. Peruvin. $-$$

Rosa Mexicano, 50. 61 Columbus Ave ☎ 977-7700. Mexican. $-$$

Ruby Foo's Dim Sum Palace, 28. 2182 Broadway ☎ 724-6700. Pan-Asian. $$

Saigon Grill, 6. 620 Amsterdam Ave ☎ 875 9072. Vietnamese. $

Sarabeth's, 25. 423 Amsterdam Ave ☎ 496-6280. American. $-$$

Shark Bar, 37. 307 Amsterdam Ave ☎ 874-8500. Southern. $-$$

Shun Lee West, 45. 43 W 65th St ☎ 595-8895. Chinese. $-$$

Sushi of Gari, 30. 370 Columbus Ave ☎ 362-4816. Japanese. $$$-$$$$

Tavern on the Green, 42. Central Park W & 67th St ☎ 873-3200. Contemporary. $$$-$$$$

Telepan, 43. 72 W 69th St ☎ 580-4300. Contemporary. $$-$$$

$$$$ = *over $40* $$$ = *$30-$40* $$ = *$20-$29* $ = *$10-$19*   ¢ = *under $10*
Based on cost per person for an entrée.

MAP 46 Restaurants/Upper East Side

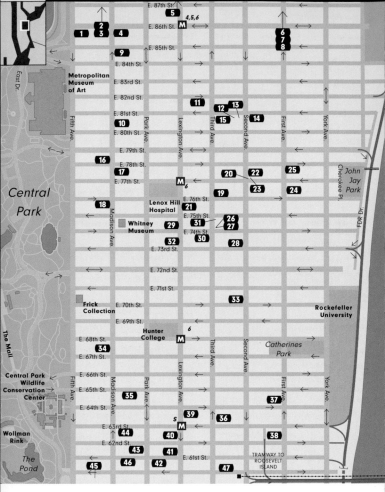

Listed by Site Number

1 Café Sabarsky	17 Viand	34 Kai
2 Table d'Hote	18 Café Boulud	35 Daniel
3 Sarabeth's	19 Atlantic Grill	36 Accademia di Vino
4 Centolire	20 Alforno Pizzeria	37 Maya
5 Sfoglia	21 Orsay	38 Via Oreto
6 Luca	22 Lusardi's	39 JoJo
7 Pio Pio	23 Vermicelli	40 Fig & Olive
8 Café d'Alsace	24 Canyon Road	41 David Burke &
9 Pain Quotidien	25 Sushi of Gari	Donatella
10 E.A.T.	26 JG Melon	42 Circus
11 Zócalo	27 Mezzaluna	43 Park Avenue Café
12 Etats-Unis	28 Persepolis	44 Post House
13 Sistina	29 Payard	45 Nicole's
14 Sandro's	30 Lenox Room	46 Aureole
15 Beyoglu	31 Candle Cafe	47 Serendipity 3
16 Serafina Fabulous Pizza	32 Ikeno Hana	
	33 Trata Estiatorio	

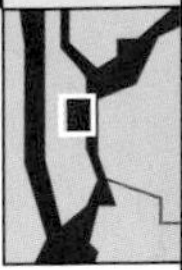

MAP 46

Listed Alphabetically

Accademia di Vino, 36. 1081 Third Ave
☎ 888-6333. Italian. $-$$$

Alforno Pizzeria, 20. 1484 Second Ave
☎ 249-5103. Pizza. ¢-$

Atlantic Grill, 19. 1341 Third Ave
☎ 988-9200. Seafood. $$

Aureole, 46. 34 E 61st St ☎ 319-1660.
Contemporary. $$$$

Beyoglu, 15. 1431 Third Ave
☎ 650-0850. Turkish. $

Café Boulud, 18. 20 E 76th St
☎ 772-2600. French. $$$

Café d'Alsace, 8. 1695 Second Ave
☎ 772-5133. Brasserie. $$$

Café Sabarsky, 1. 1048 Fifth Ave
☎ 288-0665. Austrian. $-$$

Candle Cafe, 31. 1307 Third Ave
☎ 472-0970. Vegetarian/Vegan. $

Canyon Road, 24. 1470 First Ave
☎ 734-1600. Southwestern. $-$$

Centolire, 4. 1167 Madison Ave
☎ 734-7711. Italian. $-$$$$

Circus, 42. 132 E 61st St
☎ 223-2566. Brazilian. $-$$

Daniel, 35. 60 E 65th St ☎ 288-0033.
French. $$$$

David Burke & Donatella, 41.
133 E 61st St ☎ 813-2121.
New American. $$$$

E.A.T., 10. 1064 Madison Ave
☎ 772-0022. American. $ $$

Etats-Unis, 12. 242 E 81st St
☎ 517-8826. Eclectic. $$-$$$

Fig & Olive, 40. 808 Lexington Ave
☎ 207-4555. Mediterranean. $-$$

Ikeno Hana, 32. 1016 Lexington Ave
☎ 737-6639. Japanese. $-$$

JG Melon, 26. 1291 Third Ave
☎ 744-0585. American. ¢-$$

JoJo, 39. 160 E 64th St ☎ 223-5656.
French. $$$

Kai, 34. 822 Madison Ave
☎ 988-7277. Japanese. $$-$$$$

Lenox Room, 30. 1278 Third Ave
☎ 772-0404. American $-$$$

Luca, 6. 1712 First Ave ☎ 987-9260.
Italian. $-$$

Lusardi's, 22. 1494 Second Ave
☎ 249-2020. Italian. $$

Maya, 37. 1191 First Ave
☎ 585-1818. Mexican. $$

Mezzaluna, 27. 1295 Third Ave
☎ 535-9600. Italian. $

Nicole's, 45. 10 E 60th St
☎ 223-2288. Contemporary. $-$$$

Orsay, 21. 1057 Lexington Ave
☎ 517-6400. New American. $$-$$$$

Pain Quotidien, 9. 1131 Madison Ave
☎ 327-4900. Café/Bakery. $

Pamir, 26. 1437 Second Ave
☎ 734-3791. Afghan. $

**Park Avenue Autumn/ Winter/
Summer/Spring, 43.** 100 E 63rd St
☎ 644-1900. American. $$-$$$

Payard Patisserie & Bistro, 29.
1032 Lexington Ave ☎ 717-5252.
French. $$

Persepolis, 27. 1407 Second Ave
☎ 535-1100. Persian. $-$$

Pio Pio, 7. 1746 First Ave ☎ 426-5800.
Peruvian. $-$$

Post House, 44. 28 E 63rd St
☎ 935-2888. Steak. $$-$$$$

Sandro's, 14. 306 E 81st St
☎ 288-7374. Italian. $-$$

Sarabeth's, 3. 1295 Madison Ave
☎ 410-7335. American. $

Serafina Fabulous Pizza, 16.
1022 Madison Ave ☎ 734-2676.
Pizza. $-$$

Serendipity 3, 47. 225 E 60th St
☎ 838-3531. American. $

Sfoglia, 5. 1402 Lexington Ave
☎ 831-1402. Italian. $$

Sistina, 13. 1555 Second Ave
☎ 861-7660. Italian. $$-$$$

Sushi of Gari, 25. 402 E 78th St
☎ 517-5340. Japanese. $$

Table d'Hote, 2. 44 E 92nd St
☎ 348-8125. French. $-$$

Trata Estiatorio, 33. 1331 Second Ave
☎ 535-3800. Greek. $$-$$$$

Vermicelli, 23. 1492 Second Ave
☎ 288-8868. Vietnamese. ¢-$

Via Oreto, 38. 1121 First Ave
☎ 308-0828. Italian. $-$$$

Viand, 17. 1011 Madison Ave
☎ 249-8250. Coffee Shop. ¢-$

Zócalo, 11. 174 E 82nd St ☎ 717-7772.
Mexican. $$

$$$$ = *over $40* $$$ = *$30-$40* $$ = *$20-$29* $ = *$10-$19*   ¢ = *under $10*
Based on cost per person for an entrée.

MAP 47 Restaurants/Chelsea, Flatiron District

Listed by Site Number

1	Gahm Mi Oak	16	I Trulli
2	Kang Suh	17	Blue Smoke
3	Mandoo Bar	18	Dos Caminos
4	HanGawi	19	A Voce
5	Artisanal	20	Bread Bar
6	Wolfgang's Steakhouse	20	Eleven Madison Park
7	Second Avenue Deli	20	Tabla
8	Les Halles	21	Shake Shack
9	Resto	22	Novitá
10	Water Club	23	Beppe
11	Vatan	24	BLT Prime
12	Pongal	25	Tamarind
13	Turkish Kitchen	26	Veritas
14	Curry Leaf	27	Gramercy Tavern
15	Chennai Garden	28	Lunetta
		29	Craftbar

30	Craft
31	Barbounia
31	Le Pain Quotidien
31	Pipa
32	Los Dos Molinos
33	Casa Mono
34	The House
35	Yama
36	Olives NY
37	Lucy of Gramercy
38	Bao Noodles
39	Republic
40	Blue Water Grill
41	Union Square Café
42	15 East
43	Havana Central

E. 36th St.

Herald
Sq.

B,D,F,
N,Q,R,
V,W

E. 35th St.

Fifth Ave.

E. 34th St.

Empire State
Building

1

2   **3**   **4**

E. 33rd St.

6

M

7

5

E. 32nd St.

**Kips
Bay
Plaza**

E. 31st St.

Lexington Ave.

Park Ave. S.

Third Ave.

Second Ave.

First Ave.

Broadway

E. 30th St.

Ave. of the Americas

E. 29th St.

9   **8**

N,R

M

10

E. 28th St.

11

M

12

E. 27th St.

15   **13**

18   **14**

52

E. 26th St.

17 **16**

53

19

E. 25th St.

38

20

Madison
Square
Park

E. 24th St.

21

F,V

N,R

M

E. 23rd St.

54

25   **23**

24

E. 22nd St.

W. 22nd St.

51

22

55

W. 21st St.

Flatiron
Bldg.

E. 21st St.

Gramercy
Park

56   W. 20th St.

28

26

E. 20th St.

50

49

W. 19th St.

29 **27**

E. 19th St.

30

31

47

W. 18th St.

37

32

E. 18th St.

45

48 W. 17th St.

36 **34** **33**

E. 17th St.

43 **39**

35

Stuyvesant
Square

W. 16th St.

41 **40**

E. 16th St.

46 **44**

42

Union
Square
Park

E. 15th St.

F,V

Fifth Ave.

W. 15th St.

W. 14th St.

L,N,Q,R,W,
4,5,6

M

E. 14th St.

M

L

L

M

Listed by Site Number

MAP 47 # Restaurants/Chelsea, Flatiron District

Listed Alphabetically

A Voce, 19. 41 Madison Ave
☎ 545–8555. Italian. $$$

Arezzo, 55. 46 W 22nd St
☎ 206–0555. Italian. $$–$$$

Artisanal, 5. 2 Park Ave ☎ 725–8585.
Brasserie. $$

Bao Noodles, 38. 391 Second Ave
☎ 725–7770. Vietnamese. ¢–$

Barbounia, 31. 250 Park Ave S
☎ 995–0242. Greek. $

Bar Veloce, 63. 176 Seventh Ave
☎ 629–5300. Italian. ¢–$

Beppe, 23. 45 E 22nd St ☎ 982–8422.
Italian. $$–$$$

Bette, 87. 461 W 23rd St ☎ 366–0404.
American. $–$$$

BLT Fish, 48. 21 W 17th St
☎ 691–8888. Seafood. $$$

BLT Prime, 24. 111 E 22nd St
☎ 995–8500. Steakhouse. $$$–$$$$

Blue Smoke, 17. 116 E 27th St
☎ 447–7733. Barbecue. $$

Blue Water Grill, 40. 31 Union Sq W
☎ 675–9500. Seafood. $$–$$$

Bolo, 51. 23 E 22nd St ☎ 228–2200.
Spanish. $$

Boqueria, 49. 53 W 19th St
☎ 255–4160. Tapas. $

Bottino, 83. 246 Tenth Ave
☎ 206–6766. Italian. $–$$

Bread Bar, 19. 11 Madison Ave
☎ 889–0667. Indian. $–$$

Buddakhan, 73. 75 Ninth Ave
☎ 989–6699. Asian. $$$

Cafeteria, 60. 119 Seventh Ave
☎ 414–1717. American. $–$$

Casa Mono, 33. 52 Irving Pl
☎ 253–2773. Tapas. $$

Chennai Garden, 15.
129 E 27th St ☎ 689–1999.
Indian/Vegetarian. ¢–$

City Bakery, 47. 3 W 18th St
☎ 366–1414. Cafe/Bakery. ¢–$

Craft, 30. 43 E 19th St ☎ 780–0880.
New American. $$$

Craftbar, 29. 900 Broadway
☎ 461–4300. New American. $$

Crema, 58. 111 W 17th St ☎ 691–4477.
Mexican. $$

Curry Leaf, 14. 99 Lexington Ave
☎ 725–5558. Indian. $

Da Umberto, 57. 107 W 17th St
☎ 989–0303. Italian. $–$$$

Del Posto, 90. 85 Tenth Ave
☎ 497–8090. Italian. $$$–$$$$

Dévi, 45. 8 E 18th St
☎ 691–1300. Indian. $$

Dos Caminos, 18. 373 Park Ave S
☎ 294–1000. Mexican. $$

Eisenberg's Sandwich Shop, 54.
174 Fifth Ave ☎ 675–5096.
American. ¢

Eleven Madison Park, 20.
11 Madison Ave ☎ 889–0905.
New American. $$$

Elmo, 61. 156 Seventh Ave
☎ 337–8000. American. $–$$

F & B, 67. 269 W 23rd St
☎ 646/486–4441. Hotdogs. ¢

Fifteen East, 42. 15 E 15th St
☎ 647–0015. Japanese. $$–$$$$

Fleur de Sel, 50. 5 E 20th St
☎ 460–9100. French. $$$$

Gahm Mi Oak, 1. 43 W 32nd St
☎ 695–4113. Korean. ¢–$$

Gascogne, 69. 158 Eighth Ave
☎ 675–6564. French. $$

Gramercy Tavern, 27. 42 E 20th St
☎ 477–0777. American. $$$$

Grand Sichuan, 82. 229 Ninth Ave
☎ 620–5200. Chinese. $

Half King, 86. 505 W 23rd St
☎ 462–4300. American. $

HanGawi, 4. 12 E 32nd St
☎ 213–0077. Korean/Vegetarian.
$–$$$

Havana Central, 43. 22 E 17th St
☎ 414–4999. Cuban. $–$$

Hill Country, 52. 30 W 25th St
☎ 255–4544. Barbecue. $–$$

The House, 34. 121 E 17th St
☎ 353–2121. American. $$

I Trulli, 16. 122 E 27th St
☎ 481–7372. Italian. $$–$$$

Kang Suh, 2. 1250 Broadway
☎ 564–6845. Korean. $–$$$

Klee Brasserie, 80. 20 Ninth Ave
☎ 633–8033. Brasserie. $$

La Bergamote, 79. 169 Ninth Ave
☎ 627–9010. Bakery/Cafe. ¢

La Bottega, 75. 88 Ninth Ave
☎ 243–8400. Italian. $–$$

Listed Alphabetically (cont.)

La Lunchonette, 77. 130 Tenth Ave
☎ 675-0342. French. $-$$

La Taza de Oro, 72. 96 Eighth Ave
☎ 243-9946. Puerto Rican. ¢

Le Pain Quotidien, 31. 38 E 19th St
☎ 673-7900. Bakery/Cafe. ¢-$

Les Halles, 8. 411 Park Ave S
☎ 679-4111. Steak. $$

Le Zie, 62. 172 Seventh Ave
☎ 206-8686. Italian. $

Los Dos Molinos, 32. 119 E 18th St
☎ 505-1574. Latin. $

Lucy of Gramercy, 37. 35 E 18th St
☎ 475-5829. Mexican. $$-$$$

Lunetta, 28. 920 Broadway
☎ 533-3663. Italian. $-$$

Mandoo Bar, 3. 2 W 32nd St
☎ 279-3075. Korean. ¢-$

Maroons, 59. 244 W 16th St
☎ 206-8640. Caribbean/Soul. $-$$

Matsuri, 74. 363 W 16th St
☎ 243-6400. Japanese. $$

Mesa Grill, 46. 102 Fifth Ave
☎ 807-7400. Southwestern. $$-$$$

Negril, 81. 362 W 23rd St
☎ 807-6411. Jamaican. ¢-$

Novitá, 22. 102 E 22nd St
☎ 677-2222. Italian. $-$$

Olives NY, 36. 201 Park Ave S
☎ 353-8345. Mediterranean. $$-$$$

O Mai, 78. 158 Ninth Ave
☎ 633-0550. Vietnamese. $

The Park, 89. 118 Tenth Ave
☎ 352-3313. Mediterranean. $-$$

Periyali, 56. 35 W 20th St
☎ 463-7890. Greek. $$

Pipa, 31. 38 E 19th St ☎ 677-2233.
Spanish. ¢-$

Pongal, 12. 110 Lexington Ave
☎ 696-9458. Indian/Vegetarian. ¢-$

Pop Burger, 71. 58-60 Ninth Ave
☎ 414-8686. American. $

The Red Cat, 85. 227 Tenth Ave
☎ 242-1122. American. $$

Republic, 39. 37 Union Sq W
☎ 627-7172. Asian. $

Resto, 9. 111 E 29th St ☎ 685-5585.
Belgian. $-$$

Rocking Horse Cafe, 68.
182 Eighth Ave ☎ 463-9511.
Mexican. $-$$

R.U.B BBQ, 64. 208 W 23rd St
☎ 524-4300. Barbecue. $$

Sapa, 53. 43 W 24th St ☎ 929-1800.
Asian/French. $$

Second Avenue Deli, 7. 162 E 33rd St
☎ 677-0606. Deli. $

Seven, 65. 350 Seventh Ave
☎ 967-1919. American. $-$$

Shake Shack, 21. Madison Square
Park at 23rd St & Madison Ave
☎ 889-6600. Burgers. ¢

Sueños, 76. 311 W 17th St
☎ 243-1333. Mexican. $-$$

Tabla, 20. 11 Madison Ave
☎ 889-0667. Indian Fusion. $$$$

Tamarind, 25. 41-43 E 22nd St
☎ 674-7400. Indian. $$

Tia Pol, 88. 205 Tenth Ave
☎ 675-8805. Tapas. $

Toqueville, 44. 1 E 15th St
☎ 647-1515. New American. $$-$$$$

Trestle on Tenth, 84. 242 Tenth Ave
☎ 645-5659. New American. $-$$

Turkish Kitchen, 13. 386 Third Ave
☎ 679-1810. Turkish. $

Union Square Café, 41. 21 E 16th St
☎ 243-4020. American. $$-$$$

Vatan, 11. 409 Third Ave
☎ 689-5666. Indian/Vegetarian. $$

Veritas, 26. 43 E 20th St ☎ 353-3700.
American. $$$$

Water Club, 10. 500 E 30th St
☎ 683-3333. American. $$-$$$$

Wolfgang's Steakhouse, 6.
4 Park Ave ☎ 889-3369. Steakhouse.
$$-$$$

Yama, 35. 122 E 17th St ☎ 475-0969.
Japanese. $-$$

$$$$ = **over $40** $$$ = **$30-$40** $$ = **$20-$29** $ = **$10-$19**   ¢ = **under $10**
Based on cost per person for an entrée.

MAP 48 # Restaurants/The Village & Downtown

MAP 48 Restaurants/The Village & Downtown

Listed by Site Number

1 Crispo
2 Scarpetta
3 Vento
4 Spice Market
5 Pastis
6 5 Ninth
7 Macelleria
8 Fatty Crab
9 Mi Cocina
10 Café de Bruxelles
11 Benny's Burritos
12 Good
13 Gonzo
14 Café Loup
15 Strip House
16 Gotham Bar & Grill
17 Japonica
18 Piola
19 Cafe Spice
20 Cru
21 Mary's Fish Camp
22 August
23 Barbuto
24 Jarnac
25 Paris Commune
26 Philip Marie
27 Spotted Pig
28 Wallsé
29 Perry Street
30 Mexicana Mama
31 Pink Tea Cup
32 Little Owl
33 One If By Land, Two If By Sea
34 Annisa
35 Las Ramblas
36 Pó
37 Pearl Oyster Bar
38 Babbo
39 Blue Hill
40 Home
41 John's Pizzeria
42 Snack Taverna
43 Do Hwa
44 Blue Ribbon Bakery
45 Deborah
46 'Ino
47 Lupa
48 Tomoe Sushi
49 Arturo's
50 Hundred Acres
51 Jean Claude

52 Raoul's
53 Blue Ribbon
54 Mezzogiorno
55 Aquagrill
56 Fiamma
57 Blue Ribbon Sushi
58 Balthazar
59 Zoë
60 Fanelli's
61 Mercer Kitchen
62 Woo Lae Oak
63 Momofuku Ssäm Bar
64 Una Pizza Napoletana
65 Hearth
66 Angelica Kitchen
67 Danal
68 ChickaLicious
69 Momofuku Noodle Bar
70 Moustache
71 Gnocco
72 Rai Rai Ken
73 Holy Basil
74 Hasaki
75 La Paella
76 Otafuku
77 Veselka
78 La Palapa
79 I Coppi
80 Bao 111
81 Mingala
82 Dok Suni's
83 Jewel Bako
84 Haveli
85 Mermaid Inn
86 Takahachi
87 Le Souk
88 Il Bagatto
89 Prune
90 Great Jones Cafe
91 Chinatown Brasserie
92 Acme Bar & Grill
93 Bond Street
94 Il Buco
95 Five Points
96 Elizabeth
97 Tasting Room
98 Ghenet
99 Savoy
100 Café Habana
101 Public

102 Peasant
103 Eight Mile Creek
104 Spring Street Natural
105 Le Jardin
106 Lombardi's
107 Nyonya
108 Rice
109 XO Kitchen
110 Cendrillon
111 Dylan Prime
112 Bread Tribeca
113 Churrascaria Riodizio Tribeca
114 Arqua
115 Centrico
116 Bubby's
117 Nobu
118 Mai House
119 Tribeca Grill
120 The Harrison
121 Chanterelle
122 Odeon
123 Megu
124 City Hall
125 Blaue Gans
126 Petite Abeille
127 Duane Park
128 Salaam Bombay
129 Danube
130 Kitchenette
131 Nam
132 Ecco
133 Fresh
134 Bouley
135 Nha Trang
136 Jing Fong
137 Great New York Noodletown
138 Joe's Shanghai
139 Ping's Seafood
140 Dim Sum Go Go
141 Bridge Cafe
142 Les Halles
143 2 West
144 Roy's New York
145 Delmonico's
146 Harry's Steak
147 Financier Patisserie

MAP 48

Listed Alphabetically

Acme Bar & Grill, 92. 9 Great Jones St ☎ 420-1934. Southern. ¢-$

Angelica Kitchen, 66. 300 E 12th St ☎ 228-2909. Vegetarian. ¢-$

Annisa, 34. 13 Barrow St ☎ 741-6699. Contemporary. $$

Aquagrill. 55 210 Spring St ☎ 274-0505. Seafood. $$

Arqua, 114. 281 Church St ☎ 334-1888. Italian. $-$$

Arturo's, 49. 106 W Houston St ☎ 677-3820. Pizza. $

August, 22. 359 Bleecker St ☎ 929-4774. Mediterranean. $$

Babbo, 38. 110 Waverly Pl ☎ 777-0303. Italian. $$$

Balthazar, 58. 80 Spring St ☎ 965-1414. Brasserie. $$-$$$

Bao 111, 80. 111 Ave C ☎ 254-7773. Vietnamese. $-$$

Barbuto, 23. 775 Washington St ☎ 924-9700. Italian. $$

Benny's Burritos, 11. 113 Greenwich Ave ☎ 727-0584. Mexican. ¢-$

Blaue Gans, 125. 139 Duane St ☎ 571-8880. Austrian. $$

Blue Hill, 39. 75 Washington Pl ☎ 539-1776. New American. $$$

Blue Ribbon, 53. 97 Sullivan St ☎ 274-0404. Eclectic. $$-$$$

Blue Ribbon Bakery, 44. 35 Downing St ☎ 337-0404. Bistro. $-$$

Blue Ribbon Sushi, 57. 119 Sullivan St ☎ 343-0404. Japanese. $$

Bond Street, 93. 6 Bond St ☎ 777-2500. Japanese. $$-$$$

Bouley, 134. 120 W Broadway ☎ 964-2525. French. $$$$

Bread Tribeca, 112. 301 Church St ☎ 334-0200. Italian. $-$$

Bridge Cafe, 141. 279 Water St ☎ 227-3344. American. $$-$$$

Bubby's, 116. 120 Hudson St ☎ 219-0666. American. $

Café de Bruxelles, 10. 118 Greenwich Ave ☎ 206-1830. Belgian. $-$$

Café Habana, 100. 17 Prince St ☎ 625-2001. Latin. ¢-$

Café Loup, 14. 105 W 13th St ☎ 255-4746. French. $-$$

Cafe Spice, 19. 72 University Pl ☎ 253-6999. Indian. $-$$

Cendrillon, 110. 45 Mercer St ☎ 343-9012. Asian. $-$$

Centrico, 115. 211 W Broadway ☎ 431-0700. Mexican. $-$$

Chanterelle, 121. 2 Harrison St ☎ 966-6960. French. $$$$

ChickaLicious, 68. 203 E Tenth St ☎ 995-9511. Dessert. $

Chinatown Brasserie, 91. 380 Lafayette St ☎ 533-7000. Chinese. $$

Churrascaria Riodizio Tribeca, 113. 221 W Broadway ☎ 212/925-6969. Brazilian.

City Hall, 124. 131 Duane St ☎ 227-7777. American. $$-$$$$

Crispo, 1. 240 W 14th St ☎ 229-1818. Italian. $-$$

Cru, 20. 24 Fifth Ave ☎ 529-1700. New American. $$$$

Danal, 63. 90 E 10th St ☎ 982-6930. French. $-$$

Danube, 129. 30 Hudson St ☎ 791-3771. Austrian/Eclectic. $$$

Deborah, 45. 43 Carmine St ☎ 242-2606. American. $-$$

Delmonico's, 145. 56 Beaver St ☎ 509-1144. Steakhouse. $$$$

Dim Sum Go Go, 140. 5 E Broadway ☎ 732-0797. Chinese. $

Do Hwa, 43. 55 Carmine St ☎ 414-1224. Korean. $-$$

Dok Suni's, 82. 119 First Ave ☎ 477-9506. Korean. $

Duane Park, 127. 157 Duane St ☎ 732-5555. New American. $$

Dylan Prime, 111. 62 Laight St ☎ 334-4783. Steak. $$$$

Ecco, 132. 124 Chambers St ☎ 227-7074. Italian. $$-$$$

Eight Mile Creek, 103. 240 Mulberry St ☎ 431-4635. Australian. $-$$

Elizabeth, 96. 265 Elizabeth St ☎ 334-2426. Eclectic. $-$$

Fanelli's, 60. 94 Prince St ☎ 226-9412. American. $

$$$$ = **over $40** $$$ = **$30-$40** $$ = **$20-$29** $ = **$10-$19**   ¢ = **under $10**
Based on cost per person for an entrée.

MAP 48 **Restaurants/The Village & Downtown**

Listed Alphabetically (cont.)

Fatty Crab, 8. 643 Hudson St
☎ 352–3590. Malaysian. $–$$

Fiamma, 56. 206 Spring St
☎ 653–0100. Italian. $$–$$$

5 Ninth, 6. 5 Ninth Ave
☎ 929–9460. New American. $$$

Financier Patisserie, 147. 62 Stone St
☎ 344–5600. Bakery/Café. ¢

Five Points, 95. 31 Great Jones St
☎ 253–5700. American. $$

Fresh, 133. 105 Reade St
☎ 406–1900. Seafood. $$–$$$$

Ghenet, 98. 284 Mulberry St
☎ 343–1888. Ethiopian. $

Gnocco, 71. 337 E Tenth St
☎ 677–1913. Italian. $$

Gonzo, 13. 140 W 13th St
☎ 645–4606. Italian. $–$$

Good, 12. 89 Greenwich Ave
☎ 691–8080. Eclectic. $–$$

Gotham Bar & Grill, 16. 12 E 12th St
☎ 620–4020. American. $$$

Great Jones Cafe, 90.
54 Great Jones St ☎ 674–9304.
Cajun. ¢–$

Great New York Noodletown, 137.
28 Bowery ☎ 349–0923. Chinese. ¢–$

The Harrison, 120. 355 Greenwich St
☎ 274–9310. American $$

Harry's Steak, 146. 97 Pearl St
☎ 784–9200. Steakhouse. $$$$

Hasaki, 74. 210 E 9th St
☎ 473–3327. Japanese. $–$$$$

Haveli, 84. 100 Second Ave
☎ 982–0533. Indian. $

Hearth, 65. 403 E 12th St
☎ 646/602–1300. Italian. $$–$$$

Holy Basil, 73. 149 Second Ave
☎ 460–5557. Thai. ¢

Home, 40. 20 Cornelia St
☎ 243–9579. American. $$

Hundred Acres, 50. 38 MacDougal St
☎ 475–7500. American. $–$$

I Coppi, 79. 432 E 9th St
☎ 254–2263. Italian. $–$$

Il Bagatto, 88. 192 E 2nd St
☎ 228–0977. Italian. $

Il Buco, 94. 47 Bond St
☎ 533–1932. Italian. $$

'Ino, 46. 21 Bedford St
☎ 989–5769. Italian. ¢–$

Japonica, 17. 100 University Pl
☎ 243–7752. Japanese. $$–$$$

Jarnac, 24. 328 W 12th St
☎ 924–3413. French. $–$$

Jean Claude, 51. 137 Sullivan St
☎ 475–9232. French. $–$$

Jewel Bako, 83. 239 E Fifth St
☎ 979–1012. Japanese. $$$

Jing Fong, 136. 20 Elizabeth St
☎ 964–5256. Chinese. $

Joe's Shanghai, 138. 9 Pell St.
☎ 233–8888. Chinese. $

John's Pizzeria, 41. 278 Bleecker St
☎ 243–1680. Pizza. ¢–$

Kitchenette, 130. 156 Chambers St
☎ 267–6740. American. $

La Paella, 75. 214 E 9th St
☎ 598–4321. Spanish. $

La Palapa, 78. 77 St Mark's Pl
☎ 777–2537. Mexican. $

Las Ramblas, 35. 170 W Fourth St
☎ 415–7924. Tapas. ¢–$

Le Jardin, 105. 25 Cleveland Pl
☎ 343–9599. Bistro. $–$$

Les Halles, 142. 15 John St
☎ 285–8585. French. $–$$

Le Souk, 87. 47 Avenue B
☎ 777–5454. Moroccan. $–$$

Little Owl, 32. 90 Bedford St
☎ 741–4695. New American. $$

Lombardi's, 106. 32 Spring St
☎ 941–7994. Pizza. $

Lupa, 47. 170 Thompson St
☎ 982–5089. Italian. $–$$

Macelleria, 7. 48 Gansevoort St
☎ 741–2555. Italian/Steakhouse.
$–$$$$

Mai House, 118. 186 Franklin St
☎ 431–0606. Vietnamese. $$

Mary's Fish Camp, 21. 64 Charles St
☎ 646/486–2185. Seafood. $–$$

Megu, 123. 62 Thomas St
☎ 964–7777. Japanese. $$–$$$$

Mercer Kitchen, 61. 99 Prince St
☎ 966–5454. New American. $–$$$

Mermaid Inn, 85. 96 Second Ave
☎ 674–5870. Seafood. $–$$

Mexican Mama, 30. 525 Hudson St
☎ 924–4119. Mexican $

Mezzogiorno, 54. 195 Spring St
☎ 334–2112. Italian. $–$$

Mi Cocina, 9. 57 Jane St
☎ 627–8273. Mexican. $–$$

Mingala, 81. 213 E 7th St
☎ 529–3656. Burmese. ¢–$

MAP 48

Listed Alphabetically (cont.)

Momofuku Noodle Bar, 69.
171 First Ave ☎ 777-7773. Asian. $

Momofuku Ssäm Bar, 63.
207 Second Ave ☎ 254-3500.
Asian. $-$$

Moustache, 70. 265 E Tenth St
☎ 228-2022. Middle Eastern. ¢-$

Nam, 131. 110 Reade St
☎ 267-1777. Vietnamese. $

Nha Trang, 135. 87 Baxter St
☎ 941-9292. Vietnamese. ¢-$

Nobu, 117. 105 Hudson St
☎ 219-0500. Japanese. $$$

Nyonya, 107. 194 Grand St
☎ 334-3669. Malaysian. ¢-$

Odeon, 122. 145 W Broadway
☎ 233-0507. Bistro. $$-$$$

One If By Land, Two If By Sea, 33.
17 Barrow St ☎ 255-8649. Continental. $$$$

Otafuku, 76. 236 E 9th St
☎ 353-8503. Japanese. ¢

Paris Commune, 25. 99 Bank St
☎ 929-0509. French. $-$$

Pastis, 5. 9 Ninth Ave ☎ 929-4844.
Brasserie. $$

Pearl Oyster Bar, 37. 18 Cornelia St
☎ 691-8211. Seafood. $

Peasant, 102. 194 Elizabeth St
☎ 965-9511. Italian. $$

Petite Abeille, 126. 134 W Broadway
☎ 727-2989. Belgian. $-$$

Perry Street, 29. 176 Perry St
☎ 352-1900. New American.
$$$-$$$$

Philip Marie, 26. 569 Hudson St
☎ 242-6200. New American. $-$$

Ping's Seafood, 139. 22 Mott St
☎ 602-9988. Chinese. $$

Pink Tea Cup, 31. 42 Grove St
☎ 807-6755. Soul. $

Piola, 18. 48 E 12th St ☎ 777-7781.
Pizza. $

Pó, 36. 31 Cornelia St
☎ 645-2189. Italian. $-$$

Prune, 89. 54 E 1st St
☎ 677-6221. American. $$

Public, 101. 210 Elizabeth St
☎ 343-7011. Eclectic. $$

Rai Rai Ken, 72. 214 E 10th St
☎ 477-7030. Japanese. ¢

Raoul's, 52. 180 Prince St
☎ 966-3518. French. $-$$$

Rice, 108. 292 Elizabeth St
☎ 226-5775. Eclectic. ¢-$

Roy's New York, 144.
130 Washington St ☎ 266-6262.
Hawaiian Fusion. $$-$$$

Salaam Bombay, 128.
319 Greenwich St ☎ 226-9400.
Indian. $-$$

Savoy, 99. 70 Prince St
☎ 219-8570. American. $$$

Scarpetta, 2. 355 W 14th St
☎ 691-0955. Italian. $$-$$$

Snack Taverna, 42. 63 Bedford St
☎ 929-3499. Greek. $-$$

Spice Market, 4. 403 W 13th St
☎ 675-2322. Asian. $$

Spotted Pig, 27. 314 W 11th St
☎ 620-0393. American. $$

Spring Street Natural, 104.
62 Spring St ☎ 966-0290.
Healthy American. $-$$

Strip House, 15. 13 E 12th St
☎ 328-0000. Steak. $$$$

Takahachi, 86. 85 Ave A
☎ 505-6524. Japanese. $

Tasting Room, 97. 264 Elizabeth St
☎ 358-7831. New American. $$

Tomoe Sushi, 48. 172 Thompson St
☎ 777-9346. Japanese. $-$$$

Tribeca Grill, 119. 375 Greenwich St
☎ 941-3900. Contemporary. $$-$$$

2 West, 143. 2 West St (Ritz Carlton)
☎ 344-0800. Steakhouse. $$-$$$$

Una Pizza Napoletana, 64.
349 E 12th St ☎ 477-9950. Pizza. $$

Vento, 3. 675 Hudson St ☎ 699-2400.
Italian. $$

Veselka, 77. 144 Second Ave
☎ 228-9682. East European. ¢-$

Wallsé, 28. 344 W 11th St
☎ 352-2300. Austrian. $$$

Woo Lae Oak, 62. 148 Mercer St
☎ 925-8200. Korean. $$

XO Kitchen, 109. 148 Hester St
☎ 965-8645. Chinese. ¢-$

Zoë, 59. 90 Prince St
☎ 966-6722. American. $-$$$$

$$$$ = *over $40* $$$ = *$30-$40* $$ = *$20-$29* $ = *$10-$19* ¢ = *under $10*
Based on cost per person for an entrée.

MAP 49 Restaurants/Lower East Side

Listed by Site Number

1 Pala	**15** Rayuela	**30** Orchard
2 Katz's	**16** Le Lupanar	**31** Kuma Inn
3 Yozakura Kushiyaki Bar	**17** Festival Mexicano	**32** Spitzer's Corner
4 Frankies Spuntino	**18** Falai	**33** Thor
5 Clinton Street Baking Co.	**19** Alias	**34** Essex
6 Thai on Clinton	**20** Falai Panetteria	**35** Tides Seafood
7 Sachiko's	**21** Bondi Road	**36** Suba
8 Tapéo 29	**22** wd-50	**37** Allan & Delancey
9 Azul	**23** Schiller's Liquor Bar	**38** Sammy's Roumanian Steak House
10 El Sombrero	**24** Tiny's Giant Sandwich Shop	**39** Little Giant
11 Paladar	**25** 'inoteca	**40** Bacaro
12 Stanton Social	**26** Teany	
13 Epicerie Café Charbon	**27** Kampuchea Noodle Bar	
14 Ápizz	**28** Kuta Satay House	
	29 Loreley	

Listed Alphabetically

Alias, 19. 76 Clinton St ☎ 505-5011. New American. $-$$

Allen & Delancey, 37. 115 Allen St ☎ 253-5400. New American. $$

Ápizz, 14. 217 Eldridge St ☎ 253-9199. Italian. $-$$

Azul, 9. 152 Stanton St ☎ 602-2004. Argentine. $-$$

Bacaro, 40. 136 Division St ☎ 941-5060. Italian. ¢-$

Bondi Road, 21. 153 Rivington St ☎ 253-5311. Australian. ¢-$

Clinton St. Baking Company, 5. 4 Clinton St ☎ 646/602-6263. American. $-$$

El Sombrero, 10. 108 Stanton St ☎ 254-4188. Mexican. ¢-$

Epicerie Café Charbon, 13. 168-170 Orchard St ☎ 420-7520. Bistro. $

Essex, 34. 120 Essex St ☎ 533-9616. American. $-$$

Falai, 18. 68 Clinton St ☎ 253-1960. Italian. $-$$$

Falai Panetteria, 20. 79 Clinton St ☎ 777-8956. Café/Bakery. ¢

Festival Mexicano, 17. 120 Rivington St ☎ 995-0154. Mexican. $

Frankies Spuntino, 4. 17 Clinton St ☎ 253-2303. Italian. ¢-$

'inoteca, 25 98 Rivington St ☎ 614-0473. Italian. $$

Kampuchea Noodle Bar, 27. 78 Rivington St ☎ 529-3901. Cambodian. $

Katz's Delicatessen, 2. 205 E Houston St ☎ 254-2246. Deli. $

Kuma Inn, 31. 113 Ludlow St ☎ 353-8866. Asian Tapas. ¢-$

Kuta Satay House, 28. 65 Rivington St ☎ 777-5882. Indonesian. ¢-$$

Le Lupanar, 16. 103 Essex St ☎ 260-2036. French. $$

Little Giant, 39. 85 Orchard St ☎ 226-5047. New American. $$

Loreley, 29. 7 Rivington St ☎ 253-7077. German. $-$$

Orchard, 30. 162 Orchard St ☎ 353-3570. Mediterranean. $$-$$$

Pala, 1. 198 Allen St ☎ 614-7252. Pizza. $-$$

Paladar, 11. 161 Ludlow St ☎ 473-3535. Pan-Latin. $

Rayuela, 15. 165 Allen St ☎ 253-8840. Pan-Latin. $$-$$$

Sachiko's on Clinton, 7. 25 Clinton St ☎ 253-2900. Japanese. $-$$

Sammy's Roumanian Steak House, 38. 157 Chrystie St ☎ 673-0330. Jewish. $-$$$

Schiller's Liquor Bar, 23. 131 Rivington St ☎ 260-4555. Bistro. $

Spitzer's Corner, 32. 101 Rivington St ☎ 228-0027. Gastropub. $

Stanton Social Club, 12. 99 Stanton St ☎ 995-0099. New American. ¢-$$

Suba, 36. 109 Ludlow St ☎ 982-5714. Spanish. $-$$$

Tapéo, 29. 29 Clinton St ☎ 979-0002. Tapas. ¢-$

Teany, 26. 90 Rivington St ☎ 475-9190. Vegetarian/Vegan. ¢-$

Thai on Clinton, 6. 6 Clinton St ☎ 228-9388. Thai. $

Thor, 33. 107 Rivington St ☎ 796-8040. New American. $-$$$

Tides Seafood, 35. 102 Norfolk St ☎ 254-8855. Seafood. $$

Tiny's Giant Sandwich Shop, 24. 129 Rivington St ☎ 982-1690. Sandwiches. ¢

wd-50, 22. 50 Clinton St ☎ 477-2900. New American. $$$

Yozakura Kushiyaki Bar, 3. 168 Stanton St ☎ 260-2066. Japanese. ¢-$

$$$$ = *over $40* $$$ = *$30-$40* $$ = *$20-$29* $ = *$10-$19*   ¢ = *under $10*
Based on cost per person for an entrée.

MAP **50** Hotels/Midtown & Uptown

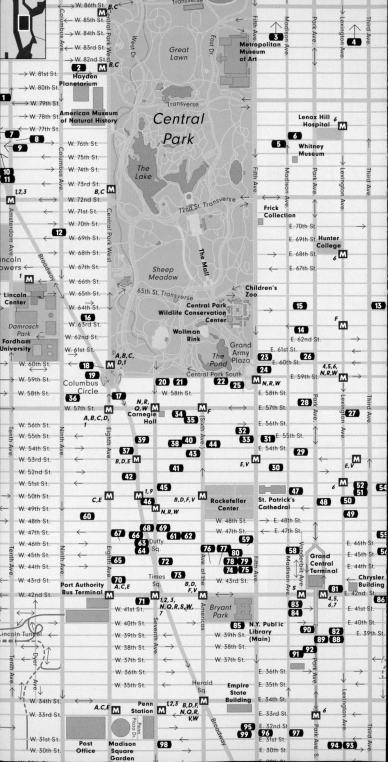

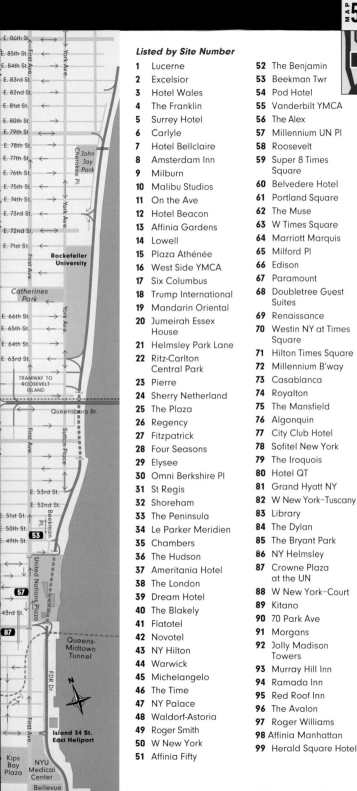

MAP 50

Listed by Site Number

MAP **50** Hotels/Midtown & Uptown

Listed Alphabetically

Affinia Fifty, 51. 155 E 50th St
☎ 751-5710. 📠 753-1468. $$

Affinia Gardens, 13.
215 E 64th St ☎ 355-1230.
📠 758-7858. $-$$

Affinia Manhattan, 98.
371 Seventh Ave ☎ 563-1800.
📠 643-8028. $$

The Alex, 56. 205 E 45th St
☎ 867-5100. 📠 867-7878. $$

Algonquin, 76. 59 W 44th St
☎ 840-6800. 📠 944-1419. $-$$$

Ameritania Hotel, 37. 230 W 54th St
☎ 247-5000. 📠 247-3316. $

Amsterdam Inn, 8.
340 Amsterdam Ave ☎ 579-7500.
📠 579-6127. ¢

The Avalon, 96. 16 E 32nd St
☎ 299-7000. 📠 299-7001. $$

Beekman Tower, 53. 3 Mitchell Pl
☎ 320-8018. 📠 465-3697. $-$$$$

Belvedere Hotel, 60. 319 W 48th St
☎ 245-7000. 📠 245-4455. $

The Benjamin, 52. 125 E 50th St
☎ 715-2500. 📠 715-2525. $-$$$$

The Blakely, 40. 136 W 55th St
☎ 245-1800. 📠 582-8332. $$

Bryant Park, 85. 40 W 40th St
☎ 869-0100. 📠 869-4446. $$$-$$$$

Carlyle, 6. 35 E 76th St
☎ 744-1600. 📠 717-4682. $$$$

Casablanca, 73. 147 W 43rd St
☎ 869-1212. 📠 391-7585. $$

Chambers, 35. 15 W 56th St
☎ 974-5656. 📠 974-5657. $$-$$$

City Club Hotel, 77. 55 W 44th St
☎ 921-5500. 📠 944-5544. $$

Crowne Plaza at the UN, 87.
304 E 42nd St ☎ 968-8800.
📠 297-3440. $$

Doubletree Guest Suites, 68.
1568 Broadway ☎ 719-1600.
📠 921-5212. $$-$$$

Dream Hotel, 39. 210 W 55th St
☎ 247-2000. 📠 646-756-2088. $$

The Dylan, 84. 52 E 41st St
☎ 338-0500. 📠 338-0569. $$-$$$

Edison, 66. 228 W 47th St
☎ 840-5000. 📠 596-6850. $

Elysee, 29. 60 E 54th St
☎ 753-1066. 📠 980-9278. $-$$

Excelsior, 2. 45 W 81st St
☎ 362-9200. 📠 721-2994. $

Fitzpatrick, 27. 687 Lexington Ave
☎ 355-0100. 📠 355-1371. $-$$

Flatotel, 41. 135 W 52nd St
☎ 887-9400. 📠 887-9442. $-$$

Four Seasons, 28. 57 E 57th St
☎ 758-5700. 📠 758-5711. $$$$

The Franklin, 4. 164 E 87th St
☎ 369-1000. 📠 894-5220. $

Grand Hyatt NY, 81. Park Ave & 42nd
St ☎ 883-1234. 📠 697-3772. $-$$

Helmsley Park Lane, 21.
36 Central Park S ☎ 371-4000.
📠 750-7279. $$-$$$

Herald Square Hotel, 99. 19 W 31st St
☎ 279-4017. 📠 643-9208. $

Hilton Times Square, 71.
234 W 42nd St ☎ 642-2500.
📠 840-5516. $

Hotel Beacon, 12. 2130 B'way
☎ 787-1100. 📠 724-0839. $$

Hotel Belleclaire, 7. 250 W 77th St
☎ 362-7700. 📠 362-1004. $-$$

Hotel QT, 80. 125 W 45th St
☎ 354-2323. 📠 302-8585. $-$$

Hotel Wales, 3. 1295 Madison Ave
☎ 876-6000. 📠 860-7000. $$$

The Hudson, 36. 356 W 58th St
☎ 554-6000. 📠 554-6001. $-$$$

The Iroquois, 79. 49 W 44th St
☎ 840-3080. 📠 398-1754. $$-$$$

Jumeirah Essex House, 20.
160 Central Park S
☎ 247-0300. 📠 315-1839. $$$

Jolly Madison Towers, 92.
22 E 38th St ☎ 802-0600.
📠 447-0747. $-$$

Kitano, 89. 66 Park Ave
☎ 885-7000. 📠 885-7100. $-$$

Le Parker Meridien, 34. 118 W 57th St
☎ 245-5000. 📠 307-1776. $$$-$$$$

Library Hotel, 83. 299 Madison Ave
☎ 983-4500. 📠 499-9099. $$-$$$

The London NYC, 38. 151 W 54th St
☎ 866/690-2029. 📠 468-8747. $$$

Loew's Regency, 26. 540 Park Ave
☎ 759-4100. 📠 826-5674. $$$-$$$$

Lowell, 14. 28 E 63rd St
☎ 838-1400. 📠 319-4230. $$$

Lucerne, 1. 201 W 79th St
☎ 875-1000. 📠 721-1179. $

Malibu Studios, 10. 2688 Broadway
☎ 222-2954. 📠 678-6842. $

Mandarin Oriental, 19.
80 Columbus Circle ☎ 805-8800.
📠 805-8888. $$$$

The Mansfield, 75. 12 W 44th St
☎ 944-6050. 📠 764-4477. $$$

Marriott Marquis, 64. 1535 B'way
☎ 398-1900. 📠 704-8930. $-$$$

Michelangelo, 45. 152 W 51st St
☎ 765-1900. 📠 541-7618. $-$$$

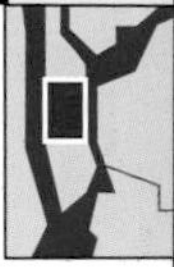

MAP 50

Listed Alphabetically (cont.)

Milburn, 9. 242 W 76th St
☎ 362-1006. 🖷 721-5476. $

Milford Plaza, 65. 700 8th Ave
☎ 869-3600 🖷 944-8357. $

Millennium Broadway, 72.
145 W 44th St ☎ 768-4400.
🖷 788-0847. $-$$

Millennium Hotel UN Plaza, 57.
1 UN Plaza ☎ 758-1234. 🖷 702-5051.
$-$$

Morgans, 91. 237 Madison Ave
☎ 686-0300. 🖷 779-8352. $$

Murray Hill Inn, 93. 143 E 30th St
☎ 683-6900. 🖷 545-0103. $

The Muse, 62. 130 W 46th St
☎ 485-2400. 🖷 485-2789. $$-$$$$

NY Helmsley, 86. 212 E 42nd St
☎ 490-8900. 🖷 986-4792. $$

NY Hilton, 43. 1335 Sixth Ave
☎ 586-7000. 🖷 315-1374. $-$$

NY Palace, 47. 455 Madison Ave
☎ 888-7000. 🖷 303-6000. $$$-$$$$

Novotel, 42. 226 W 52nd St
☎ 315-0100. 🖷 765-5365. $$-$$$

Omni Berkshire Place, 30. 21 E 52nd St
☎ 753-5800. 🖷 754-5020. $$-$$$

On The Ave, 11. 2177 Broadway
☎ 362-1100. 🖷 787-9521. $-$$

Paramount, 67. 235 W 46th St
☎ 764-5500. 🖷 354-5237. $-$$

The Peninsula, 33. 700 Fifth Ave
☎ 956-2888. 🖷 903-3949. $$$$

Pierre, 23. 2 E 61st St
☎ 838-8000. 🖷 758-1615. $$$$

The Plaza, 25. Fifth Ave & W 59th St
☎ 759-3000. 🖷 759-3001. $$$$

Plaza Athénée, 15. 37 E 64th St
☎ 734-9100. 🖷 772-0958. $$$$

Pod Hotel, 54. 230 E 51st St
☎ 355-0300. 🖷 755-5029. ¢-$

Portland Square Hotel, 61. 132 W 47th
St ☎ 382-0600. 🖷 382-0684. $

Ramada Inn, 94. 161 Lexington Ave
☎ 545-1800. 🖷 790-2760. ¢-$

Red Roof Inn, 95. 6 W 32nd St
☎ 643-7100. 🖷 643-7101. $

Renaissance, 69. 714 7th Ave
☎ 765-7676. 🖷 765-1962. $-$$$

Ritz-Carlton Central Park, 22.
50 Central Park S ☎ 308-9100.
🖷 207-8831. $$$$

Roger Smith, 49. 501 Lexington Ave
☎ 755-1400. 🖷 758-4061. $-$$

Roger Williams, 97.
131 Madison Ave ☎ 448-7000.
🖷 448-7007. $-$$$

Roosevelt, 58. 45 E 45th St
☎ 888-TEDDY-NY. 🖷 885-6161. $-$$

Royalton, 74. 44 W 44th St
☎ 869-4400. 🖷 575-0012. $$$

St Regis, 31. 2 E 55th St
☎ 753-4500. 🖷 787-3447. $$$$

70 Park Ave, 90. 70 Park Ave
☎ 687-7050. 🖷 973-2401. $$$

Sherry-Netherland, 24. 781 Fifth Ave
☎ 355-2800. 🖷 319-4306. $$-$$$

Shoreham, 32. 33 W 55th St
☎ 247-6700. 🖷 765-9741. $$

Six Columbus, 17. 6 Columbus Circle
☎ 204-3000. 🖷 204-3030. $$-$$$

Sofitel New York, 78. 45 W 44th St
☎ 354-8844. 🖷 782-3002. $$

Super 8 Times Square, 59.
59 W 46th St ☎ 719-2300.
🖷 768-3477. ¢-$

Surrey Hotel, 5. 20 E 76th St
☎ 288-3700. 🖷 628-1549. $$

The Time, 46. 224 W 49th St
☎ 320-2900. 🖷 245-2305. $-$$$

Trump International Hotel & Towers, 18. 1 Central Park West
☎ 299-1000. 🖷 299-1150. $$$$

Vanderbilt YMCA, 55. 224 E 47th St
☎ 756-9600. 🖷 752-0210. ¢

W New York, 50. 541 Lexington Ave
☎ 755-1200. 🖷 319-8344. $$$

W New York—The Court, 88.
130 E 39th St ☎ 685-1100.
🖷 889-0287. $$$$

W New York—Tuscany, 82.
120 E 39th St ☎ 779-7822.
🖷 696-2095. $$$$

W Times Square, 63. 1567 Broadway
☎ 930-7400. 🖷 930-7500. $$$$

Waldorf-Astoria, 48. 301 Park Ave
☎ 355-3000. 🖷 872-7272. $$-$$$

Warwick, 44. 65 W 54th St
☎ 247-2700. 🖷 713-1751. $-$$$$

Westin NY at Times Square, 70.
270 W 43rd St ☎ 201-2700.
🖷 201-2701. $

West Side YMCA, 16. 5 W 63rd St
☎ 875-4100. 🖷 875-4291. $

$$$$ = over $600 $$$ = $450-$599 $$ = $300-$449 $ = $150-$299   ¢ = under $150
All prices are for a standard double room, excluding 13.625% city and state sales tax and $2 occupancy tax.

MAP 51 Hotels/Downtown

Listed by Site Number

1 Chelsea Star Hotel
2 Hotel Wolcott
3 Thirty Thirty Hotel
4 Ramada Inn
5 The Gershwin
6 Hotel Giraffe
7 Park South Hotel
8 Carlton Arms
9 Le Semana Hotel
10 Inn on 23rd
11 Chelsea Savoy
12 Colonial House Inn
13 Chelsea Lodge
14 Maritime Hotel
15 Hotel Gansevoort

16 Chelsea Inn
17 Gramercy Park
18 Inn at Irving Place
19 W - Union Square
20 Hotel 17
21 Second Home on Second Ave
22 Larchmont Hotel
23 Washington Sq Hotel
24 St. Mark's Hotel
25 The Bowery Hotel
26 Howard Johnson Express Inn
27 Hotel on Rivington
28 Mercer Hotel

29 60 Thompson
30 SoHo Grand
31 Holiday Inn Dtn
32 Tribeca Grand
33 Cosmopolitan
34 Embassy Suites Hotel
35 Millennium Hilton
36 Best Western Seaport
37 Holiday Inn Wall St
38 Wall Street Inn
39 Ritz-Carlton Battery Park
40 NY Marriott Brooklyn

Hotels/Downtown

Listed Alphabetically

Best Western Seaport Inn, 36.
33 Peck Slip ☎ 766–6600.
☏ 766–6615. $

The Bowery Hotel, 25. 335 Bowery
☎ 505–9100. ☏ 505–9700. $$$

Carlton Arms, 8. 160 E 25th St
☎ 684–8337. ¢

Chelsea Inn, 16. 46 W 17th St
☎ 645–8989. ☏ 645–1903. ¢

Chelsea Lodge, 13. 318 W 20th St
☎ 243–4499. ☏ 243–7852. ¢

Chelsea Savoy, 11. 204 W 23rd St
☎ 929–9353. ☏ 741–6309. ¢–$

Chelsea Star Hotel, 1. 300 W 30th St
☎ 244–7827. ☏ 279–9018. ¢–$

Colonial House Inn, 12.
318 W 22nd St ☎ 243–9669.
☏ 633–1612. ¢–$

Cosmopolitan, 32. 95 W Broadway
☎ 566–1900. ☏ 566–6909. $

Embassy Suites Hotel, 34.
102 North End Ave ☎ 945–0100.
☏ 945–3012. $–$$$

The Gershwin, 5. 7 E 27th St
☎ 545–8000. ☏ 684–5546. ¢–$

Gramercy Park Hotel, 17.
2 Lexington Ave ☎ 920–3300.
☏ 673–5890. $$$

Holiday Inn Downtown, 31.
138 Lafayette St ☎ 966–8898.
☏ 966–3933. $–$$$

Holiday Inn Wall Street, 37.
15 Gold St ☎ 232–7700. ☏ 425–0330.
$–$$

Hotel Gansevoort, 15. 18 Ninth Ave
☎ 206–6700. ☏ 255–5858. $$$

Hotel Giraffe, 6. 365 Park Ave S
☎ 685–7700. ☏ 685–7771. $$–$$$

Hotel on Rivington, 27. 107 Rivington
☎ 475–2600. ☏ 479–5959. $$–$$$

Hotel 17, 20. 225 E 17th St ☎ 475–2845.
☏ 677–8178. ¢–$

Hotel Wolcott, 2. 4 W 31st St
☎ 268–2900. ☏ 563–0096. $

Howard Johnson Express Inn, 26.
135 E Houston St ☎ 358–8844.
☏ 473–3500. $

Inn at Irving Place, 18. 56 Irving Pl
☎ 533–4600. ☏ 533–4611. $$–$$$

Inn on 23rd, 10. 131 W 23rd St
☎ 463–0330. ☏ 463–0302. $–$$

La Semana Hotel, 9.
25 W 24th St ☎ 255–5944.
☏ 646/638–4604. $

Larchmont Hotel, 22. 27 W 11th St
☎ 989–9333. ☏ 989–9496. ¢

Maritime Hotel, 14. 363 W 16th St
☎ 242–4300. ☏ 242–1188. $$

Mercer Hotel, 28. 147 Mercer St
☎ 966–6060. ☏ 965–3838. $$$

Millennium Hilton, 35. 55 Church St
☎ 693–2001. ☏ 571–2316. $$$

NY Marriott Brooklyn, 40.
333 Adams St ☎ 718/246–7000.
☏ 718/246–0563. $

Park South Hotel, 7. 122 E 28th St
☎ 448–0888. ☏ 448–0811. $

Ramada Inn, 4. 161 Lexington Ave
☎ 545–1800. ☏ 790–2760. $

Ritz-Carlton Battery Park, 39.
2 West St ☎ 344–0800. ☏ 344–3801.
$$–$$$

St Mark's Hotel, 24. 2 St Marks Pl
☎ 674–2192. ☏ 420–0854. ¢

Second Home on Second Avenue, 21.
221 Second Ave ☎ 677–3161. ¢–$

60 Thompson, 29. 60 Thompson St
☎ 877/431–0400. ☏ 431–0200. $$$

SoHo Grand, 30. 310 W Broadway
☎ 965–3000 ☏ 965–3244. $$

Thirty Thirty Hotel, 3. 30 E 30th St
☎ 689–1900. $

Tribeca Grand, 32. 2 Sixth Ave
☎ 519–6600. ☏ 519–6700. $$

W–Union Square, 19. 201 Park Ave S
☎ 253–9119. ☏ 253–9229. $$–$$$

Wall Street Inn, 38. 9 S William St
☎ 747–1500. ☏ 747–1900. $

Washington Square Hotel, 23.
103 Waverly Pl ☎ 777–9515.
☏ 979–8373. $

$$$$ = *over $600* $$$ = *$450–$599* $$ = *$300–$449* $ = *$150–$299*   ¢ = *under $150*
All prices are for a standard double room, excluding 13.625% city and state sales tax and $2 occupancy tax.

MAP 52 **Performing Arts**

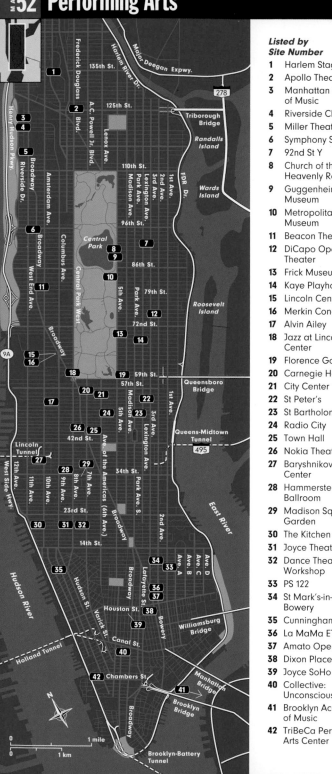

Listed by Site Number

1 Harlem Stage
2 Apollo Theater
3 Manhattan School of Music
4 Riverside Church
5 Miller Theater
6 Symphony Space
7 92nd St Y
8 Church of the Heavenly Rest
9 Guggenheim Museum
10 Metropolitan Museum
11 Beacon Theater
12 DiCapo Opera Theater
13 Frick Museum
14 Kaye Playhouse
15 Lincoln Center
16 Merkin Concert Hall
17 Alvin Ailey
18 Jazz at Lincoln Center
19 Florence Gould Hall
20 Carnegie Hall
21 City Center
22 St Peter's
23 St Bartholomew's
24 Radio City
25 Town Hall
26 Nokia Theatre
27 Baryshnikov Arts Center
28 Hammerstein Ballroom
29 Madison Square Garden
30 The Kitchen
31 Joyce Theater
32 Dance Theatre Workshop
33 PS 122
34 St Mark's-in-the-Bowery
35 Cunningham Studio
36 La MaMa ETC
37 Amato Opera
38 Dixon Place
39 Joyce SoHo
40 Collective: Unconscious
41 Brooklyn Academy of Music
42 TriBeCa Performing Arts Center

MAP 52

Listed Alphabetically

Alvin Ailey American Dance Theater, 17. 405 W 55th St ☎ 405-9000

Amato Opera, 37.
319 Bowery ☎ 228-8200

Apollo Theater, 2.
253 W 125th St ☎ 531-5305

Baryshnikov Arts, 27. 450 W 37th St
www.baryshnikovfoundation.org

Beacon Theater, 11.
2124 Broadway ☎ 465-6500

Brooklyn Academy of Music, 41.
30 Lafayette Ave ☎ 718/636-4100

Carnegie Hall, 20.
154 W 57th St ☎ 247-7800

Church of the Heavenly Rest, 8.
2 E 90th St ☎ 289-3400

City Center, 21.
131 W 55th St ☎ 581-1212

Collective: Unconscious, 40.
279 Church St ☎ 254-5277

Cunningham Studio, 35.
55 Bethune St www.merce.org

Dance Theatre Workshop, 30.
219 W 19th St ☎ 924-0077

DiCapo Opera Theater, 12.
184 E 76th St ☎ 288-9438

Dixon Place, 38.
258 Bowery ☎ 219-0736

Florence Gould Hall, 19.
55 E 59th St ☎ 355-6160

Frick Museum, 13.
1 E 70th St ☎ 288-0700

Guggenheim Museum, 9.
1071 Fifth Ave ☎ 423-3500

Hammerstein Ballroom, 28.
311 W 34th St ☎ 307-7171

Harlem Stage, 1.
150 Convent Ave at W 135th St
☎ 281-9240

Jazz at Lincoln Center, 18.
Broadway & 60th St ☎ 721-6500

Joyce SoHo, 39.
155 Mercer St ☎ 334-7479

Joyce Theater, 31.
175 Eighth Ave ☎ 242-0800

Kaye Playhouse, 14.
695 Park Ave ☎ 772-4448

The Kitchen, 30.
512 W 19th St ☎ 255-5793

La MaMa ETC, 36.
74A E 4th St ☎ 475-7710

Lincoln Center, 15.

Broadway & 64th St
☎ 875-5000
·Alice Tully Hall ☎ 721-6500
·Avery Fisher Hall ☎ 875-5030
·Juilliard Theatre ☎ 769-7406
·Metropolitan Opera ☎ 362-6000
·Mitzi E Newhouse Theater
☎ 239-6200
·NY State Theater ☎ 870-5570
·Vivian Beaumont Theater
☎ 239-6200

Madison Square Garden, 29.
Seventh Ave & 32nd St ☎ 465-6741

Manhattan School of Music, 3.
120 Claremont Ave ☎ 749-2802

Merkin Concert Hall, 16.
129 W 67th St ☎ 501-3330

Metropolitan Museum, 10.
1000 Fifth Ave ☎ 570-3949

Miller Theater, 5. Columbia Univ,
Broadway & W 116th St ☎ 854-7799

92nd St Y, 7.
1395 Lexington Ave ☎ 415-5500

Nokia Theatre, 26.
1515 Broadway ☎ 930-1950

PS 122, 33.
150 First Ave ☎ 352-3101

Radio City Music Hall, 24.
1260 Sixth Ave ☎ 247-4777

Riverside Church, 4.
120th St & Riverside Dr ☎ 870-6784

St Bartholomew's Church, 23.
109 E 50th St ☎ 378-0248

St Mark's-in-the-Bowery, 34.
Second Ave & 10th St ☎ 674-8194

St Peter's Church, 22.
619 Lexington Ave ☎
www.saintpeters.org

Symphony Space, 6.
2537 Broadway ☎ 864-5400

Town Hall, 25.
123 W 43rd St ☎ 840-2824

**TriBeCa Performing Arts
Center, 42.** 199 Chambers St
☎ 220-1460

MAP 53 Theaters/Broadway

W. 57th St.

A,B,C,D

N,R,Q,W

F

Carnegie Hall

W. 56th St.

W. 55th St.

Tenth Ave.

1

Ninth Ave.

Eighth Ave.

Broadway

W. 54th St.

2

Seventh Ave.

(Sixth)

B,D,E

5

W. 53rd St.

3

4

W. 52nd St.

6

N

8

W. 51st St.

7

9

C,E

10

B,D,F,V

W. 50th St.

W. 49th St.

11

N,R,W

12

13

14

20

W. 48th St.

15

W. 47th St.

17

16

19

Ave. of the Americas

21

W. 46th St.

18

24

25 26

23

Duffy Square

22

W. 45th St.

27

28 29 30 31 32

33 34 35

36

W. 44th St.

Ninth Ave.

38 39

Tenth Ave.

46

40

Times Square

W. 43rd St.

Eighth Ave.

41

37

47

A,C,E

42 44

B,D,F,V

W. 42nd St.

48

49

Port Authority Bus Terminal

45 43

1,2,3,7,
N,Q,R,S,W

W. 41st St.

50

Seventh Ave.

Broadway

Bryant Park

W. 40th St.

Dyer Ave.

W. 39th St.

0   900 feet

W. 38th St.

0   300 meters

W. 37th St.

MAP 53

Listed Alphabetically

Al Hirschfeld, 27. 302 W 45th St
☎ 239-6200

Ambassador, 10. 219 W 49th St
☎ 239-6200

American Airlines, 42. 227 W 42nd St
☎ 719-1300

American Theatre of Actors, 2.
314 W 54th St ☎ 581-3044

August Wilson, 4. 245 W 52nd St
☎ 239-6200

Belasco, 36. 111 W 44th St
☎ 239-6200

Bernard B. Jacobs, 29. 242 W 45th St
☎ 239-6200

Biltmore/Manhattan Theatre Club, 15.
261 W 47th St ☎ 239-6200

Booth, 31. 222 W 45th St ☎ 239-6200

Broadhurst, 34. 235 W 44th St
☎ 239-6200

Broadway, 3. 1681 Broadway
☎ 239-6200

Brooks Atkinson, 16. 256 W 47th St
☎ 307-4100

Circle in the Square, 9.
1633 Broadway ☎ 239-6200

Cort, 20. 138 W 48th St ☎ 239-6200

Douglas Fairbanks, 48.
432 W 42nd St ☎ 239-6200

The Duke, 45. 229 W 42nd St
☎ 239-6200

Ensemble Studio Theatre, 5.
549 W 52nd St ☎ 247-4982

Ethel Barrymore, 14. 243 W 47th St
☎ 239-6200

Eugene O'Neill, 11. 230 W 49th St
☎ 239-6200

Gershwin, 7. 222 W 51st St
☎ 307-4100

Golden, 28. 252 W 45th St
☎ 239-6200

Helen Hayes, 39. 240 W 44th St
☎ 239-6200

Henry Miller, 37. 124 W 43rd St
☎ 239-6200

Hilton Theatre, 41. 213 W 43rd St
☎ 307-4100

Imperial, 25. 249 W 45th St
☎ 239-6200

Julia Miles, 1. 424 W 55th St
☎ 239-6200

Laura Pels, 21. 111 W 46th St
☎ 719-1300

Longacre, 13. 220 W 48th St
☎ 239-6200

Lunt-Fontanne, 18. 205 W 46th St
☎ 307-4747

Lyceum, 22. 149 W 45th St
☎ 239-6200

Majestic, 33. 247 W 44th St
☎ 239-6200

Marquis, 23. 1535 Broadway
☎ 307-4100

Minskoff, 32. 200 W 45th St
☎ 307-4747

Music Box, 26. 239 W 45th St
☎ 239-6200

Nederlander, 50. 208 W 41st St
☎ 307-4100

Neil Simon, 6. 250 W 52nd St
☎ 307-4100

New Amsterdam, 43. 214 W 42nd St
☎ 307-4747

New Victory, 44. 209 W 42nd St
☎ 239-6200

Palace, 19. 1554 Broadway
☎ 307-4100

Playwrights Horizons, 49.
416 W 42nd St ☎ 279-4200

Puerto Ricon Travelling Theatre, 17.
304 W 47th St ☎ 354-1293

Richard Rogers, 24. 226 W 46th St
☎ 239-6200

St James, 38. 246 W 44th St
☎ 239-6200

Schoenfeld, 30. 236 W 45th St
☎ 239-6200

Second Stage, 40. 307 W 43rd St
☎ 246-4422

Shubert, 35. 225 W 44th St
☎ 239-6200

Signature Theater, 47.
555 W 42nd St ☎ 244-7529

Walter Kerr, 12. 219 W 48th St
☎ 239-6200

Westside Theatre, 46.
407 W 43rd St ☎ 239-6200

Winter Garden, 8.
1634 Broadway ☎ 563-5544

MAP 54 **Theaters/Off Broadway**

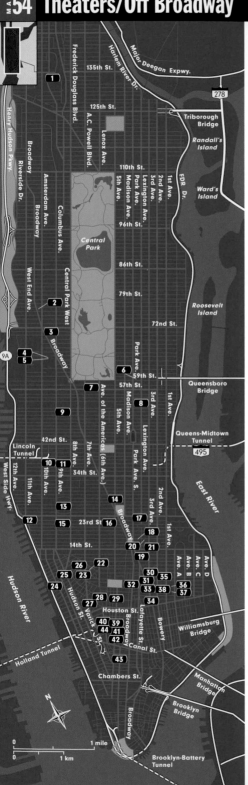

**Listed by
Site Number**

1 Harlem Stage
2 McGinn Cazale
2 Promenade
3 Triad
4 Mitzi Newhouse
5 Vivian Beaumont
6 59E59
6 Primary Stages
7 Manhattan Theatre Club
8 York
9 New World Stages
10 37 Arts
11 The Zipper Factory
12 Sanford Meisner
13 Upright Citizens Brigade
14 TADA!
15 Atlantic Theater Company
16 Irish Rep
17 Gramercy Theatre
18 Union Square
19 Classic Stage Co
20 Daryl Roth Theatre
21 Vineyard Theatre
22 Barrow Street Theater
23 Actor's Playhouse
24 Wings
25 Lucille Lortel
26 Rattlestick Theatre
27 Cherry Lane
28 Minetta Lane
29 The Village Theater
30 Pearl Theatre Co
31 The Public
32 Astor Place
33 New York Theatre Workshop
34 45 Bleecker
35 Orpheum
36 La MaMa ETC
37 Horse Trade Theater Group
38 Jean Cocteau Rep
39 Ohio
40 Soho Playhouse
41 Culture Project
42 Performing Garage
43 Flea
44 HERE

MAP 54

Listed Alphabetically

Actor's Playhouse, 23.
100 Seventh Ave S ☎ 239-6200

Astor Place, 32.
434 Lafayette St ☎ 254-4370

Atlantic Theater Company, 15.
336 W 20th St ☎ 279-4200

Barrow Street Theater, 22.
27 Barrow St ☎ 239-4200

Cherry Lane, 27.
38 Commerce St ☎ 989-2020

Classic Stage Company, 19.
136 E 13th St ☎ 677-4210

Culture Project, 41.
55 Mercer St ☎ 925-1900

Daryl Roth Theatre, 20.
20 Union Sq E ☎ 239-6200

59E59, 6.
59 E 59th St ☎ 279-4200

Flea Theatre, 43.
41 White St ☎ 226-0051

45 Bleecker, 34.
45 Bleecker St ☎ 307 4100

Gramercy Theatre, 17.
127 E 23rd St ☎ 307-4100

HERE, 44. 145 Sixth Ave ☎ 352-3101

Irish Repertory Theatre, 16.
132 W 22nd St ☎ 727-2737

Jean Cocteau Rep, 38.
330 Bowery ☎ 677-0060

Harlem Stage, 1. 150 Convent Ave
☎ 281-9240

Horse Trade Theater Group, 37.
85 E 4th St ☎ 777-6088

La MaMa ETC, 36.
74A E 4th St ☎ 475-7710

Lucille Lortel, 25.
121 Christopher St ☎ 279-4200

Manhattan Theatre Club, 7.
131 W 55th St ☎ 581-1212

McGinn Cazale, 2.
2162 Broadway ☎ 352-3101

Minetta Lane, 28.
18 Minetta La ☎ 420-8000

Mitzi Newhouse, 4.
Lincoln Center, 150 W 65th St
☎ 239-6200

New World Stages, 9. 340 W 50th St
☎ 239-6200

New York Theatre Workshop, 33.
79 E 4th St ☎ 239-6200

Ohio, 39. 66 Wooster St ☎ 352-3101

Orpheum, 35.
126 Second Ave ☎ 477-2477

Pearl Theatre Co, 30.
80 St Marks Pl ☎ 598-9802

Performing Garage, 42.
33 Wooster St ☎ 966-3651

Primary Stages, 6.
59 E 59th St ☎ 279-4200

Promenade, 2.
2162 Broadway ☎ 239-6200

The Public, 31.
425 Lafayette St ☎ 967-7555

Rattlestick Theatre, 26.
224 Waverly Pl ☎ 868-4444

Sanford Meisner, 12
164 Eleventh Ave ☎ 352-3101

SoHo Playhouse, 40.
15 Vandam St ☎ 691-1555

TADA! Youth Theater, 14.
15 W 28th St ☎ 252-1619

37 Arts, 10. 450 W 37th St ☎ 560-8912

Triad, 3. 158 W 72nd St ☎ 362-2590

Union Square Theatre, 18.
100 E 17th St ☎ 505-0700

Upright Citizens Brigade Theatre, 13.
307 W 26th St ☎ 366-9176

The Village Theater, 29.
158 Bleecker St ☎ 307-4100

Vineyard Theatre, 21.
108 E 15th St ☎ 353-0303

Vivian Beaumont, 5.
Lincoln Center, Broadway
& W 64th St ☎ 239-6200

Wings Theater, 24.
154 Christopher St ☎ 627-2961

York, 8.
619 Lexington Ave ☎ 935 5820

The Zipper Factory, 11.
336 W 37th St ☎ 352-3101

MAP **55** **Movies/Midtown & Uptown**

MAP
55

Listed by Site Number

1 Coliseum Theater
2 AMC Magic Johnson's Harlem USA
3 Symphony Space
4 AMC Loew's 84th St
5 Guggenheim Museum
6 AMC Loews Orpheum VIII
7 City Cinemas E 86th St
8 United Artist East
9 Metropolitan Museum
10 Naturemax
11 Loews Lincoln Square
12 Asia Society
13 Loews 72nd St East
14 Clearview's Beekman One & Two
15 United Artist 64th & Second
16 Walter Reade
17 Lincoln Plaza Cinemas
18 62nd & Broadway

19 French Institute
20 Paris
21 City Cinemas 1,2,3
22 Clearview's First & 62nd
23 ImaginAsian
24 Clearview's Ziegfeld Theatre
25 Museum of Modern Art
26 Museum of Television and Radio
27 Instituto Cervantes
28 Japan Society
29 AMC Kips Bay Loews
30 Scandinavia House
31 Regal Stadium E Walk
32 AMC Empire 25
33 AMC Loews 34th Street
34 Clearview's Chelsea West
35 Clearview's Chelsea

Listed Alphabetically

AMC Empire 25, 32.
234 W 42nd St ☎ 398-3939

AMC Loews 34th St, 33.
312 W 34th St ☎ 244-8850

AMC Loews 72nd St East, 13.
1230 Third Ave ☎ 50L-OEWS #704

AMC Loews 84th St, 4.
2310 Broadway ☎ 50L-OEWS #701

AMC Loews Kips Bay, 29.
570 Second Ave ☎ 50L-OEWS #558

AMC Loews Lincoln Square (1-13), 11.
1998 Broadway ☎ 50L-OEWS #638

AMC Loews Orpheum VIII, 6.
1538 Third Ave
☎ 50L-OEWS #964

AMC Magic Johnson's Harlem USA, 2.
124th St & Frederick Douglass Blvd
☎ 665-8742

Asia Society, 12.
725 Park Ave ☎ 288-6400

City Cinemas 1, 2, 3, 21.
Third Ave & 60th St ☎ 777-FILM #635

City Cinemas East 86th St, 7.
210 E 86th St ☎ 734-4427 #753

Clearview's Beekman One & Two, 14.
1271 Second Ave ☎ 249-4200

Clearview's Chelsea (1-9), 35.
260 W 23rd St ☎ 777-FILM #597

Clearview's Chelsea West, 34.
333 W 23rd St ☎ 777-FILM #614

**Clearview's First & 62nd Cinemas
(1-6), 22.** 400 E 62nd St
☎ 777-FILM #957

Clearview's 62nd & Broadway, 18.
Broadway & 62nd St ☎ 777-FILM #864

Clearview's Ziegfield Theatre, 26.
141 W 54th St ☎ 765-7600

Coliseum Theater, 1.
703 W 181st St ☎ 740-1545

Crown NY Twin, 14.
1271 Second Ave ☎ 249-4200

French Institute, 19.
55 E 59th St ☎ 355-6100

Guggenheim Museum, 5.
1071 Fifth Ave ☎ 423-3500

ImaginAsian, 23.
239 E 59th St ☎ 371-6682

Instituo Cervantes, 27.
211-215 E 49th St ☎ 308-7720

Japan Society, 28.
333 E 47th St ☎ 832-1155

Lincoln Plaza Cinemas (1-6), 17.
B'way & 63rd St ☎ 757-2280

Regal E Walk Stadium, 31.
8th Ave & 42nd St ☎ 840-7761

Metropolitan Museum of Art, 9.
1000 Fifth Ave ☎ 535-7710

Museum of Modern Art, 25.
11 W 53rd St ☎ 708-9400

Museum of Television and Radio, 26.
25 W 52nd St ☎ 621-6800

Naturemax, 10.
American Museum of Natural History,
Central Park W & 79th St ☎ 769-5200

Paris, 20. 4 W 58th St ☎ 688-3800

Scandinavia House, 30.
58 Park Ave ☎ 879-9779

Symphony Space, 3.
Broadway & 95th St ☎ 864-5400

United Artist East, 8.
First Ave & 85th St
☎ 800/FANDANGO #627

United Artist 64th & Second, 15.
Second Ave & 64th St
☎ 800/FANDANGO #626

Walter Reade Theater, 16.
165 W 65th St ☎ 875-5600

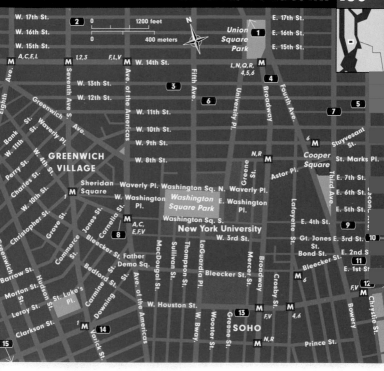

Movies/Downtown

MAP **56**

Listed by Site Number

1 Loews 19th St East
2 Rubin Museum of Art
3 Quad Cinema
4 Regal Union Square
5 Village East Cinemas
6 Cinema Village

7 Village Theatre VII
8 Independent Film Center
9 Millennium Film Workshop
10 Pioneer

11 Anthology Film Archives
12 Landmark Sunshine
13 Angelika Film Center
14 Film Forum
15 Regal Battery Park 11

Listed Alphabetically

AMC Loews 19th St East (1–6), 1.
Broadway & E 19th St
☎ 50L-OEWS #858

**AMC Loews Village Theatre VII
(1–7), 7.** Third Ave & 11th St
☎ 50L-OEWS #952

Angelika Film Center (1–6), 13.
18 W Houston St ☎ 995–2000

Anthology Film Archives, 11.
32 Second Ave ☎ 505–5181

Cinema Village, 6. 22 E 12th St
☎ 924–3363

**City Cinema Village East Cinemas
(1–7), 5.** Second Ave & 12th St
☎ 50L-OEWS #922

Film Forum (1–3), 14.
209 W Houston St ☎ 727–8110

Independent Film Center, 8.
323 Sixth Ave ☎ 924–7771

Landmark Sunshine, 12.
143 E Houston St ☎ 330–8182

Millennium Film Workshop, 9.
66 E 4th St ☎ 673–0090

Pioneer Theater, 10.
155 E 3rd St ☎ 591–0434

Quad Cinema (1–4), 3. 34 W 13th St
☎ 255–8800

Regal Battery Park, 15.
102 North End Ave
☎ 800/FANDANGO #629

Regal Union Square 14, 4.
13th St & Broadway
☎ 800/FANDANGO #628

Rubin Museum of Art, 2.
150 W 17th St ☎ 620–5000

MAP **57** **Nightlife/Above 42nd Street**

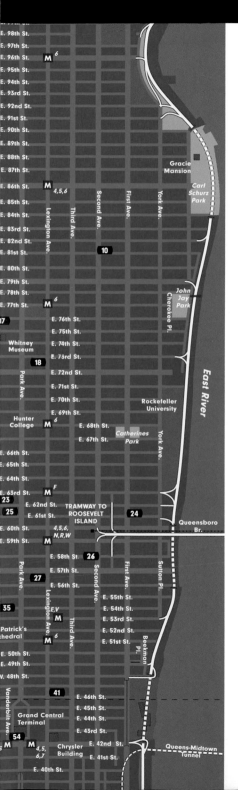

MAP 57

E. 98th St.
E. 97th St.
E. 96th St.
E. 95th St.
E. 94th St.
E. 93rd St.
E. 92nd St.
E. 91st St.
E. 90th St.
E. 89th St.
E. 88th St.
E. 87th St.
E. 86th St.
E. 85th St.
E. 84th St.
E. 83rd St.
E. 82nd St.
E. 81st St.
E. 80th St.
E. 79th St.
E. 78th St.
E. 77th St.
E. 76th St.
E. 75th St.
E. 74th St.
E. 73rd St.
E. 72nd St.
E. 71st St.
E. 70th St.
E. 69th St.
E. 68th St.
E. 67th St.
E. 66th St.
E. 65th St.
E. 64th St.
E. 63rd St.
E. 62nd St.
E. 61st St.
E. 60th St.
E. 59th St.
E. 58th St.
E. 57th St.
E. 56th St.
E. 55th St.
E. 54th St.
E. 53rd St.
E. 52nd St.
E. 51st St.
E. 50th St.
E. 49th St.
W. 48th St.
E. 46th St.
E. 45th St.
E. 44th St.
E. 43rd St.
E. 42nd St.
E. 41st St.
E. 40th St.

Lexington Ave.
Third Ave.
Second Ave.
First Ave.
York Ave.
Park Ave.
Vanderbilt Ave.

Gracie Mansion
Carl Schurz Park
John Jay Park
Cherokee Pl.
East River
Rockefeller University
Catherines Park
York Ave.
Sutton Pl.
Beekman Pl.
Whitney Museum
Hunter College
TRAMWAY TO ROOSEVELT ISLAND
Queensboro Br.
Patrick's Cathedral
Grand Central Terminal
Chrysler Building
Queens-Midtown Tunnel

4,5,6
6
F
4,5,6, N,R,W
E,V
6
4,5, 6,7

MAP 57 **Nightlife/Below 42nd Street**

MAP **57**

Listed by Site Number

MAP 57 Nightlife

Listed Alphabetically

Algonquin, 50. 59 W 44th St
☎ 840-6800. Cabaret

APT, 79. 419 W 13th St
☎ 414-4245. Dance Club

Arlene's Grocery, 129. 95 Stanton St
☎ 995-1652. Rock

Back Fence, 124. 155 Bleecker St
☎ 475-9221. Rock/Folk

Baggot Inn, 123. 82 W 3rd St
☎ 477-0622. Eclectic Live Music

Bar 13, 87. 281 E 13th St
☎ 979-6677. Bar/Lounge/Club

Barracuda, 70. 35 13th St
☎ 645-8613. Gay

Barrage, 43. 401 W 47th St
☎ 586-9390. Gay

B. B. King Blues Club, 55.
237 W 42nd St ☎ 997-4144. Blues/Soul

Beauty Bar, 86. 231 E 14th St
☎ 539-1389. Bar/Club

Bemelmans Bar, 17.
35 E 76th St ☎ 744-1600. Bar/Cabaret

Birdland, 45. 315 W 44th St
☎ 581-3080. Jazz

Bitter End, 122. 147 Bleecker St
☎ 673-7030. Jazz/Blues/R&B

Blind Tiger Ale House, 112.
281 Bleecker St ☎ 462-4682. Bar

Blondies Sports, 12. 212 W 79th St
☎ 362-4360. Sports Bar

Blue Note, 116. 131 W 3rd St
☎ 462-46822. Bar

The Boiler Room, 103. 86 E 4th St
☎ 254-7536. Gay

Bowery Ballroom, 140. 6 Delancey St
☎ 533-2111. Rock

Bowlmor Lanes, 94. 110 University Pl
☎ 255-8188. Bowling

Boxcar Lounge, 97. 168 Ave B
☎ 473-2830. Lounge

Bubble Lounge, 154. 228 W Broadway
☎ 431-3433. Champagne Bar

Bungalow 8, 61. 515 W 27th St
☎ 629-3333. Lounge

Cafe Carlyle, 17. 35 E 76th St
☎ 744-1600. Cabaret

Café des Artistes, 22. 1 W 67th St
☎ 877-3500. Bar

Cafe Wha, 118. 115 MacDougal St
☎ 254-3706. Brazilian/Funk

Cain, 60. 544 W 27th St
☎ 947-8000. DJ/Club

Cake Shop, 136. 152 Ludlow St
☎ 253-0036. Live Music

Campbell Apartment, 54.
15 Vanderbilt Ave ☎ 953-0409. Bar

Canal Room, 151. 285 W Broadway
☎ 941-8100. Rock/Dance

Candle Bar, 15. 309 Amsterdam Ave
☎ 874-9155. Gay

Carnegie Club, 32.
156 W 56th St ☎ 957-9676. Jazz

Caroline's, 38. 1626 Broadway
☎ 757-4100. Comedy

Cellar Bar, 56. 40 W 40th St
☎ 642-2260. Bar

Chicago City Limits, 33.
318 W 53rd St ☎ 888-5233. Comedy

China Club, 48. 268 W 47th St
☎ 398-3800. Nightclub

Cielo, 88. 18 Little West 12th St
☎ 645-5700. Dance Club

Circa Tabac, 149. 32 Watts St
☎ 941-1781. Cigar Bar/Lounge

Cleopatra's Needle, 5.
2485 Broadway ☎ 769-6969. Jazz

Club Macanudo, 23. 26 E 63rd St
☎ 752-8200. Cigar Bar

Club Shelter, 145. 150 Varick St
☎ 862-6117. Dance Club

Comedy Cellar, 117.
117 MacDougal St ☎ 254-3480.
Comedy

Comic Strip, 10. 1568 Second Ave
☎ 861-9386. Comedy

Comix, 77. 353 W 14th St
☎ 524-2500. Comedy

Connolly's, 44. 121 W 45th St
☎ 597-5126. Irish Music

Continental, 105. 25 Third Ave
☎ 529-6924. Bar

Copacabana, 58. 560 W 34th St
☎ 239-2672. Latin Dance

Cornelia Street Café, 113.
29 Cornelia St ☎ 989-9319. Jazz

Corner Bar, 90. 331 W 4th St
☎ 242-9502. Bar

Cotton Club, 1.
125th St & West Side Hwy
☎ 663-7980. Swing/Jazz

Crocodile Lounge, 85. 325 E 14th St
☎ 477-7747. Bar

Cub Room, 144. 131 Sullivan St
☎ 677-4100. Bar/Lounge

Cubby Hole, 93. 281 W 12th St
☎ 243-9041. Lesbian

Cutting Room, 67.
19 W 24th St ☎ 691-1900. Live Music

Dangerfield's, 24. 1118 First Ave
☎ 593-1650. Comedy

The Dead Poet, 8. 450 Amsterdam
Ave ☎ 595-5670. Bar

Death & Co., 99. 433 E 6th St
☎ 388-0882. Bar

The Delancey, 138. 168 Delancey St
☎ 254-9920. Bar/DJ

MAP 57

Listed Alphabetically (cont.)

Dizzy's Club Coca-Cola, 30. Broadway at 60th St ☎ 258-9595. Jazz

Doc Holiday's, 98. 141 Ave A ☎ 979-0312. Bar

Don Hill's, 148. 511 Greenwich St ☎ 219-2850. Dance Club

Don't Tell Mama, 47. 343 W 46th St ☎ 757-0788. Cabaret/Comedy

Duplex, 108. 61 Christopher St ☎ 255-5438. Cabaret/Comedy

Ear Inn, 146. 326 Spring St ☎ 226-9060. Eclectic Live Music

Eastern Bloc 101. 505 E 6th St ☎ 777-2555. Gay

ESPN Zone, 52. 1472 Broadway ☎ 921-ESPN. Sports Bar

Evelyn Lounge, 11. 380 Columbus Ave ☎ 724-2363. Lounge/Bar

Feinstein's at the Regency, 25. 540 Park Ave ☎ 339-4095. Cabaret

Fillmore NY at Irving Plaza, 83. 17 Irving Place ☎ 777-6800. Rock

40/40, 66. 6 W 25th St ☎ 832-4040. Sports Bar/Lounge

420 Bar & Lounge, 9. 420 Amsterdam Ave ☎ 579-8450. Bar

Gotham Comedy Club, 69. 208 W 23rd St ☎ 367-9000. Comedy

Gym, 73. 167 Eighth Ave ☎ 337-2439. Gay/Sports

Henrietta Hudson, 114. 438 Hudson St ☎ 924-3347. Lesbian

Highline Ballroom, 76. 431 W 16th St ☎ 414-8994. Live Music

Hill Country, 68. 30 W 26th St ☎ 255-4544. Country Music

Hiro Ballroom, 75. 371 W 16th St ☎ 307-7171. Live Music/DJ

Home, 59. 532 W 27th St ☎ 273-3700. Bar/Lounge

Hudson Bar, 31. 356 W 58th St ☎ 554-6217. Bar/Lounge

Iridium, 37. 1650 Broadway ☎ 582-2121. Jazz

Jazz Gallery, 147. 290 Hudson St ☎ 242-1063. Jazz

The Jazz Standard, 65. 116 E 27th St ☎ 576-2232. Jazz

Joe's Pub, 107. 425 Lafayette St ☎ 539-8777. Nightclub/Cabaret

Kava Lounge, 89. 605 Hudson St ☎ 989-7504. Bar/Lounge

Kenny's Castaways, 121. 157 Bleecker St ☎ 979-9762. Rock

KGB Bar, 102. 85 E 4th St ☎ 505-3360. Bar/Spoken Word

King Cole Bar, 34. St Regis Hotel, 2 E 55th St ☎ 753-4500. Bar

Knitting Factory, 155. 74 Leonard St ☎ 219-3132. Rock/Jazz

Laugh Factory, 51. 303 W 42nd St ☎ 586-7829. Comedy

Lenox Lounge, 3. 288 Lenox Ave ☎ 427-0253. Jazz

Lexington Bar and Books, 18. 1020 Lexington Ave ☎ 717-3902. Cigar Bar

Living Room, 134. 154 Ludlow St ☎ 533-7235. Rock

Little Branch, 115. 20 Seventh Ave S ☎ 929-4360. Bar

Lotus, 78. 409 W 14th St ☎ 243-4420. Nightclub

LQ, 41. 511 Lexington Ave ☎ 593-7575. Club/Lounge

Maker's Bar, 62. 405 Third Ave ☎ 779-0306. Bar

Marion's Continental, 104. 354 Bowery ☎ 475-7621. Bar

Marquee, 71. 289 10th Ave ☎ 646/473-0202. Nightclub

McSorley's, 106. 15 E 7th St ☎ 473-9148. Bar

Merc Bar, 142. 151 Mercer St ☎ 966-2727. Bar/Lounge

Mercury Lounge, 130. 217 E Houston St ☎ 260-4700. Rock

Metropolitan Room, 72. 34 W 22nd St ☎ 206-0440. Cabaret

Minton's Playhouse, 2. 208 W 118th St ☎ 864-8346. Jazz

Monkey Bar, 35. 60 E 54th St ☎ 838-2600. Bar

The Monster, 110. 80 Grove St ☎ 924-3558. Gay/Disco

Morgan's Bar, 57. 237 Madison Ave ☎ 726-7755. Bar/Lounge

Morrell Wine Bar, 40. 1 Rockefeller Plz ☎ 262-7700. Wine Bar

Motor City Bar, 137. 127 Ludlow St ☎ 358-1595. Bar

Naked Lunch, 153. 17 Thompson St ☎ 343-0828. Bar/Lounge

New York Comedy Club, 64. 241 E 24th St ☎ 696-5233. Comedy

Old Town Bar, 81. 45 E 18th St ☎ 529-6732. Bar

169 Bar, 156. 169 E Broadway ☎ 473-8866. Bar

Opia, 27. 130 E 57th St ☎ 688-3939. Bar/Lounge

Pacha NYC, 42. 618 W 46th St ☎ 209-7500. Dance Club

MAP **57** **Nightlife**

Listed Alphabetically (cont.)

The Park, 74. 118 Tenth Ave
☎ 352-3313. Bar/Lounge

The Parlour, 6. 250 W 86th St
☎ 580-8923. Bar

Pegu Club, 126. 77 W Houston St
☎ 473-7348. Cocktail Lounge

Pete's Tavern, 84. 129 E 18th St
☎ 473-7676. Bar

Pianos, 135. 158 Ludlow St
☎ 505-3733. Rock

Plumm, 80. 246 W 14th St
☎ 675-1567. Night Club

Pravda, 141. 281 Lafayette St
☎ 226-4696. Bar

Prohibition, 8. 503 Columbus Ave
☎ 579-3100. Eclectic Live Music

Pyramid Club, 100. 101 Avenue A
☎ 228-4888. Dance Club

Rififi, 96. 332 E 11th St ☎ 677-1027.
DJ/Burlesque

Rockwood Music Hall, 127.
196 Allen St ☎ 477-4155.

Rise, 157. 2 West St
☎ 344-0800. Rooftop Bar

Rodeo Bar, 63. 375 Third Ave
☎ 683-6500.
Country/Rockabilly/Blues

Roseland, 36. 239 W 52nd St
☎ 777-6800. Live Music

Royalton Bar, 53. 44 W 44th St
☎ 869-4400. Bar

Salt Bar, 133. 29A Clinton St
☎ 979-8471. Bar

Sapphire Lounge, 128.
249 Eldridge St ☎ 777-5153.
DJ/Dance Club

Shalel Lounge, 21. 65 W 70th St
☎ 799-9030. Lounge

Shark Bar, 16. 307 Amsterdam Ave
☎ 874-8500. Bar

The Slipper Room, 131.
167 Orchard St ☎ 253-7246.
Bar/Lounge/Burlesque

Smalls, 92. 183 W 10th St ☎ 252-5091.
Jazz

Smoke, 4. 2751 Broadway
☎ 864-6662. Jazz

SOB's, 150. 204 Varick St
☎ 243-4940. Brazilian/Reggae/Jazz

Splash, 82. 50 W 17th St
☎ 691-0073. Gay

Stand Up NY, 9. 236 W 78th St
☎ 595-0850. Comedy

The Stone, 132. 2nd St at Avenue C
www.thestonenyc.com

Stone Rose, 30. 10 Columbus Cir
☎ 823-9769. Bar

Sweet Rhythm, 111. 88 Seventh Ave S
☎ 255-3626. Jazz

Swing 46, 46. 349 W 46th St
☎ 262-9554. Swing/Jazz

Temple Bar, 120. 332 Lafayette St
☎ 925-4242. Bar

Terminal 5, 39. 610 W 56th St
☎ 260-4700. Rock

Terra Blues, 125. 149 Bleecker St
☎ 777-7776. Blues

Time Out, 14. 349 Amsterdam Ave
☎ 362-5400. Sports Bar

Townhouse, 26. 236 E 58th St
☎ 754-4649. Gay

Triad, 20. 158 W 72nd St
☎ 362-2590. Cabaret/Live Music

Village Underground, 124.
130 W 3rd St ☎ 777-7745. Rock

Village Vanguard, 91.
178 Seventh Ave S ☎ 255-4037.
Jazz/Blues

Walker's 152. 16 N Moore St
☎ 941-0142. Bar

Webster Hall, 95. 125 E 11th St
☎ 353-1600. Rock, etc.

Westside Brewery, 13.
340 Amsterdam Ave ☎ 721-2161. Bar

Whiskey Bar, 49. 1567 Broadway
☎ 930-7444. Bar

Whiskey Park, 28. 100 Central Park S
☎ 307-9222. Bar/Lounge

White Horse Tavern, 109.
567 Hudson St ☎ 243-9260. Bar

Wine & Roses, 19. 286 Columbus Ave
☎ 579-WINE. Wine Bar

Zinc Bar, 145. 90 W Houston St
☎ 477-8337. Jazz